FATHERS

*A celebration in prose, poetry,
and photography
of fathers and fatherhood—
fathers loved and fathers feared,
famous fathers and fathers obscure,
real-life fathers and fathers from fiction.
A varied and wonderfully human portrait
of the men who are at the heart
of that special relationship that so shapes
our lives forever: father and child.*

Edited by
ALEXANDRA TOWLE

SIMON AND SCHUSTER • NEW YORK

Copyright © 1986 by The Watermark Press
All rights reserved
including the right of reproduction
in whole or in part in any form
Published by Simon and Schuster
A Division of Simon & Schuster, Inc.
Simon & Schuster Building
Rockefeller Center
1230 Avenue of the Americas
New York, New York 10020
Originally published in 1986
in Australia by The Watermark Press.
SIMON AND SCHUSTER and colophon are
registered trademarks of Simon & Schuster, Inc.
Designed by Edith Fowler
Manufactured in the United States of America

10   9   8   7   6   5   4   3   2   1

Library of Congress Cataloging in Publication Data

Fathers

   Includes index.
   1. Fathers — Miscellanea.   2. Father and
child — Miscellanea.   3. Fathers — Literary
collections.   I. Towle, Alexandra, date.
HQ756.F383 1986   306.8'742   86-29753
ISBN 0-671-63859-9

Dedicated to the memory of
FREDERIC TOWLE, 1910–1975

CONTENTS

FATHERHOOD

There are to us no ties at all just in being a father.
A son is distinctly an acquired taste. It's the practice
of parenthood that makes you feel that, after all,
there may be something in it.

—HEYWOOD BROUN

Jeremy Taylor

TWENTY-FIVE SERMONS (1653)

No man can tell but he that loves his children, how many delicious accents make a man's heart dance in the pretty conversation of those dear pledges: their childishness, their stammering, their little angers, their innocence, their imperfections, their necessities are so many little emanations of joy and comfort to him that delights in their persons and society; but he that loves not his wife and children, feeds a lioness at home, and broods a nest of sorrow.

Frederick Exley

A FAN'S NOTES

By one o'clock, after helping Freddy move the tables and get the bar ready, I was sitting on a stool sipping my second or third brandy and coffee and recalling the Counselor's melancholy departure some weeks before, when Freddy suddenly pointed at my wallet, which lay open before me on the bar, and said, "Who're the little guys?"

I told him they were my sons.

"Your sons?" he said. He was surprised, very surprised. His dark eyes widened exposing the whites, and his mouth went lax, forming a cavern of disbelief. "I didn't know you were married."

I told him my problem was that I hadn't known it either.

He thought this witty and began to laugh. He was engaged in washing a great mass of dirty glasses from the night before. As his hand pumped up and down in the soapy water, he kept looking at me and smiling idiotically, waiting for me to tell him that it wasn't true. I smiled, too. He had only known me as a drinker — practically a solitary one — with no life apart from booze and football. He was trying to get used to that part of me which existed away from The Parrot. Drying his hands, he walked down the bar to me and picked up the wallet again. He stared at the picture, then at me, then at the picture again, shaking his head in good-natured disbelief. Laying it down, he said, "Healthy little bastards, aren't they?" I proudly agreed. He looked at me as though to say, "C'mon who are they? Your nephews or who?" He seemed incredulous about this discovery. I just kept smiling. Then he began doing an imitation of me, one with which he often got laughs from the regulars in the place. I didn't recognize it as resembling me. Dropping his eyelids to half-mast, and weaving slightly but steadily, he began talking in a dull monotone, slurring his words terribly and demanding from some imaginary bartender what time the Giants game went on. Then he began improvising. "I can see you ten years from now," he said, "in some saloon waiting for the game to go on." Now he picked up the wallet and went on with the imitation. Staggering down the bar, he pretended to be showing the picture to imaginary customers. "Dese here's my sons," he kept saying with pathetic insistence, pretending that the customers were intractable and finding this aspect of my life as hard to believe as he did. "Dey are," he repeated to these phantom skeptics. "Dey are! Dey are! I ain't lyin' to yuh!" Abruptly Freddy fell to one side. Apparently one of those phantoms had brushed him rudely away, not really caring whether he had sons or not. We were alone in the bar, Freddy and I, and we laughed like hell, laughed and laughed and laughed.

But then, quite suddenly, quite frightfully, my laughter went cold in my stomach, and my joy and my exhilaration curdled to the point where I thought I might vomit. With a kind of omniscient clarity I suddenly recognized the truth of this vision. I saw myself some years hence, drunk, waiting "for the game," without self-denial, without perseverance, without hope. In this vision there was nothing but dark rooms from which love and grace and charm were fled, and indeed — how very acute Freddy was! — all I had to cling to, yellowing now with age, was this fading photo of my twin sons, my only and final link with humanity, and one, at that, which people neither believed in nor really cared about.

William Feather

Setting a good example for your children takes all the fun out of middle age.

John Nicholson

MEN & WOMEN— HOW DIFFERENT ARE THEY?

FATHERS AND THEIR CHILDREN

The fact that it is usually the mother who plays the major role in bringing up a child seems to be the result of economic rather than biological necessity. Someone has to go out and earn the money, and since most husbands earn more than their wives, partly because they tend to be older, it usually makes economic sense for them to sacrifice her salary rather than his. But very few husbands today follow Oscar Wilde's prescription for fatherhood ("Fathers should be neither seen nor heard; that is the only proper basis for family life"). In fact, we know that men can rear children, in a slightly different way from mothers but—so far as we can tell—no less effectively.

A recent series of experiments shows that even the male rhesus monkey, who is usually an aggressive and inflexible creature not given to nurturant behaviour, is capable of rearing a child when encouraged to do so in the laboratory. In these experiments, a baby monkey was taken away from his mother a month after being born and placed first in the cage next door to an adult male, and then — for a very short time — in a small protective cage inside the adult's. This was a necessary precautionary measure, in view of the fact that male monkeys normally have little to do with the young, and sometimes attack or even kill them. Once the adult had stopped making threatening gestures, the baby monkey was released from the small cage and soon approached the adult and tried to cling to him. At first he was repulsed angrily, but after a while the adult began to groom him — an important ice-breaker in the social life of rhesus monkeys — and from then on the two became steadily more attached to each other. In fact they became closer than most rhesus mothers and their children, and remained so long after the time when young monkeys usually break with their mothers and start to lead an independent life. Their relationship was not the same as that of the typical rhesus mother and child — they went in for more rough-and-tumble play than female monkeys will tolerate — but the younger monkey developed into a perfectly normal adult male and remained on excellent terms with his foster-father.

. . . It is [dangerous] to assume that what holds for other animals must hold for humans too. But the fact that a male rhesus monkey, who would normally be indifferent or hostile towards his offspring, can find within himself the ability to rear a baby gives us a powerful incentive to look at the results of studies in human infants, in order to investigate the role which human fathers play in child-rearing and to see what happens when the father replaces the mother as the principal caretaker of a young child.

This is an area of great rhetorical interest to psychologists, but also a matter of considerable practical importance. There are already couples where the man assumes the major responsibility for bringing up the children, usually because the woman earns a higher salary than he does and they are not prepared to entrust the task to a hired help. The arrangement is probably most common in Sweden, where either parent is entitled to seven months off work after the birth of a child at 95 percent of their full salary.

I doubt whether this complete reversal of roles will ever appeal to more than a small minority of couples, though more than half of the women and 43 per cent of the men in the survey of readers of *Cosmo-politan* . . . said that they would like the Swedish system to be introduced in this country. But the rapidly increasing number of women who want to share responsibility for child-rearing with their husbands or professional child-minders in order to pursue their careers would obviously feel better about doing so if they knew that mothers do not occupy a uniquely important position in their children's lives.

Fortunately for their peace of mind, this is exactly what the evidence suggests. The most striking finding to emerge from the scientific analysis of a baby's world is that mothers are less important figures than we thought, and that fathers play a vital role — particularly when they are at hand all the time, but even when they are not. Careful observation of couples who both participate in looking after their children reveals that when both parents are present during the first three days of life, it is fathers who spend more time stimulating their babies by holding and rocking them, though mothers smile more at their babies. The father may be the main source of stimulation, but it is the mother who assumes the bulk of the caretaking duties such as cleaning and feeding, even though most babies feed just as well when their father is holding the bottle, and fathers are just as good as mothers at interpreting a child's distress signals. By the time a baby is three months old, its parents have often swapped duties: when both parents are present, he now does more of the caretaking while she provides more stimulation, by playing with the child. A year later, the mother still tends to be the child's main playmate, though this changes later: at eighteen months, both parents share the privilege, while by the age of three, most children prefer to play with their father.

When both parents are involved in child-rearing, their roles are not interchangeable . . . fathers tend to be more physical when they play with children, while mothers favour conventional games like peek-a-boo, and also provide them with more intellectual stimulation by reading to them or encouraging them to manipulate objects. During the first year of their lives, children tend to laugh and smile more at their fathers, but are more likely to turn to their mothers for reassurance when threatened or in distress.

The quality of a child's relationship with his or her father seems to be the most important factor in deciding how he or she will react to the rest of the world. For example, an experiment carried out on six-month-old boys found that those who had most contact with their fathers were least disturbed when a stranger of either sex picked them up. Similarly, a recent American study shows that the less frequently babies of both sexes are dressed and bathed by their fathers, the longer they cry when they are left alone with an adult they don't know.

Nor is social development the only area in which fathers make a significant contribution. The rocking, talking and touching that fathers provide in response to their children's signals teaches a baby that it can affect other people by its actions, and encourages its intellectual curiosity. As a result, research shows that the more contact a child has with its father, the more advanced it is likely to be. This effect is more marked for boys, though other aspects of a father's behaviour can also have a direct effect on a daughter's intellectual development: more specifically, it seems that fathers who are imaginative at playing have the most advanced sons, while those who are generous with their praise and good at responding to a child's initiatives do most to accelerate their daughters' development.

Children seem to seek different things from their parents: security from their mother, friendship and stimulation from their father. But they do not show a consistent preference for either until they are about a year old. By the time they are one, however, most children have become more attached to one parent than to the other, though they have usually formed an important relationship with both, and perhaps with other adults as well. Roughly a half of children show a marked preference for their mother over their father; they are more distressed when she leaves the room, and they spend more time with her when both parents are present. But about a quarter of children (mainly, though not exclusively, boys) show a marked preference for their father, while the remaining quarter seem equally attached to both parents.

The picture is more complicated than I have painted it here: for example, the sex of a child is significant, as is the amount of time an individual father spends with his children. But the fact that only one child in two would rather be with its mother than its father makes it very difficult to maintain the view that biology dictates that mothers must occupy a unique position in the life of their children. Where once it seemed that babies must form a unique bond with their mothers to have any chance of developing normally, psychologists now believe that what matters is that they should form at least one close relationship with someone.

It actually seems to be beneficial for young children to spend time with and become attached to more than one person, because this makes them less concerned about being left with a stranger. If more than one person is responsible for looking after them, they get used to adults coming and going. As long as there are not so many caretakers that the child is unable to form a close relationship with any of them—four is acceptable, but a dozen too many—the chances are that he or she will be less affected by separation trauma and spend less time in the "clinging" phase. In societies where fathers have virtually no contact with their children when they are young, babies start to show distress at being separated from their mothers at a younger age and in a more extreme form than in a society such as ours, where most fathers participate to some extent in the task of looking after their children. It is also of course extremely useful for a child to be attached to more than one person if its "favourite" has to go away or if the child has to go into hospital and be looked after by unfamiliar people. In these circumstances, the child who is used to being looked after by more than one person—whether it is its father, granny or a regular baby-sitter—has a distinct advantage over a child looked after solely by its mother.

We have seen how important a father can be to a young baby when he is prepared to play his part to the full. But how much time does the average father actually spend with his children when they are young? Estimates vary enormously, but even progressive, middle-class American fathers spend no more than an average of eight hours a week with their children, according to the results of a survey carried out in Boston in the early 1970s: three-quarters of the fathers in this sample, whose children were about nine months old, said that they did no regular caretaking, and only half of them had ever changed a nappy! There were large individual differences between the men—one spent an average of seven minutes a day with his child, another as much as four hours—but their involvement was surprisingly modest, in view of the importance which babies seem to attach to them. Research carried out on first-time fathers in London ten years later suggests that little has changed, despite the fact that so many more women are now at work: it was found that only one father in twenty made a convincing claim to share child-rearing duties equally with his wife, while two-thirds had never bathed their babies.

Some researchers have come round to the view that paternal deprivation is just as serious a threat to children's welfare as maternal deprivation, a suggestion which must be taken seriously, since we know that children—especially boys—who are brought up in the total absence of a father are more likely to become delinquent and tend to do less well at school (interestingly, it is their visual-spatial ability which is particularly affected).

Since children obviously enjoy and benefit from the company of their fathers, it is important to establish why most fathers spend so little time with them. The answer to this question is vital for women too. If it is really true that nurturance is a quality which has been selectively bred out of men . . . then the outlook is bleak for women who hope to solve the problem of combining motherhood with a career by asking the father of their children to make a greater contribution towards bringing them up. Fortunately for them, the evidence is overwhelmingly against the proposition that men simply cannot rear children. We have already seen that a male monkey can do it, and we know that a man who is present at the birth of his child will hold, look at, talk to, kiss and imitate the baby as much as — if not more than — the child's mother. And although it is girls who are brought up to expect that they will become mothers and have to look after babies, most boys, even when they are in the roughest stage of their development, enjoy holding and playing with their baby brothers and sisters.

The most likely reason why men spend so little time with their children has nothing to do with biology. It is simply a matter of the way in which our society is organized, as we can see by looking at what happens when the rules are changed, or by examining other societies which have different traditions of child-rearing from our own. It is still too early to assess properly the success of the Swedish experiment with paternity leave mentioned earlier, although we do know that five years after it was introduced approximately one couple in eight was taking advantage of the scheme, though this figure was much higher among professional public-sector workers. (Another provision of the Swedish legislation was that both sexes should have an equal right to take time off to look after sick children: within two years of its inception, almost two-thirds of Swedish men were taking more than seven working days off each year for this reason, which was only slightly lower than the figure for Swedish women.) There are however enough instances of children in Europe and America being brought up primarily by their fathers for us to be fairly certain that it is no more damaging for a child to be raised in this than in the more traditional manner.

Where the children of single-parent families are concerned, we know that they run a greater risk of getting into trouble than other children. But the dangers do not seem to be greater when the single parent is a father rather than a mother. Compared with single mothers who do not go out to work, single fathers are found to be much less anxious about making alternative caretaker arrangements, and less bothered by the possibility that their children will be distressed at being left. They are also less likely than single mothers to blame themselves for any unhappiness their children may experience, and they give a greater priority to their own personal needs. When the comparison is made between single fathers and working single mothers, all these differences are much less marked (interestingly, it seems that single mothers are less likely to take a job if they have a boy to look after). Nevertheless, it sounds as though children looked after by a single father should be more at risk. But this does not seem to be the case. Generally speaking, the finding is that children in one-parent families appear to suffer least by living with a parent of their own sex. Boys living with their fathers tend to be more mature and sociable, and to be higher on self-esteem than those reared by their mothers; for girls, the opposite seems to be true.

The fact that children brought up by only one parent are more at risk than those from homes where both parents are present of course reinforces the point that it is not just mothers who benefit when fathers are willing to make a contribution to bringing up children. But perhaps the most convincing evidence that men could play a much greater role in child-rearing comes from observations made by anthropologists. Although women are responsible for child-rearing in most societies, there are a few in which men play a much greater role. Western societies place a uniquely heavy burden on the shoulders of the mother: for example, in most primitive societies all the villagers feel responsible for any child they see playing, whereas in our society mothers cannot rely on this kind of help. In at least one language the word meaning "to give birth" applies to both sexes, and in many societies the custom known as the Couvade operates: when a mother becomes pregnant both she and her husband jointly observe certain rituals, such as avoiding some types of food, and when she goes into labour he may take to his bed too. If you are tempted to dismiss this as no more than a quaint primitive custom, bear in mind that more than half of the husbands in a survey carried out in Britain had experienced mysterious symptoms when their wives were pregnant. They defied rational explanation, but cleared up as soon as their wives gave birth!

Richard Harding-Davis

to his nine-month-old daughter

October 24

My Dear Daughter:

So many weeks have passed since I saw you that by now you are able to read this without your mother looking over your shoulder and helping you with the big words. I have six sets of pictures of you. Every day I take them down and change them. Those your dear mother put in glass frames I do not change. Also, I have all the sweet fruits and chocolates and red bananas. How good of you to think of just the things your father likes. Some of them I gave to a little boy and girl. I play with them because soon my daughter will be as big. They have no mother like you, *of course*; they have no mother like *yours*—for except my mother there never was a mother like yours; so loving, so tender, so unselfish and thoughtful. If she is reading this, kiss her for me. These little children have a father. He dresses them and bathes them himself. He is afraid of the cold; and sits in the sun; and coughs and shivers. His children and I play hide-and-seek, and, as you will know some day, for that game there is no such place as a steamer, with boats and ventilators and masts and alleyways. Some day we will play the game hiding behind the rocks and trees and rose bushes. Every day I watch the sun set, and know that you and your pretty mother are watching it, too. And all day I think of you both.

Be very good. Do not bump yourself. Do not eat matches. Do not play with scissors or cats. Do not forget your dad. Sleep when your mother wishes it. Love us both. Try to know how we love you. *That* you will never learn. Good-night and God keep you, and bless you.

Your Dad

Myron Brenton

To be sure, working — that is, earning a living — is one aspect of fathering. It's one means that the father has of extending protection to his family. But it's *just* one. If he concentrates on this to the exclusion of other aspects, it becomes not a form of fathering, but an escape.

Thomas Hardy

THE MAYOR OF CASTERBRIDGE

Henchard and Elizabeth sat conversing by the fire. It was three weeks after Mrs. Henchard's funeral; the candles were not lighted, and a restless, acrobatic flame, poised on a coal, called from the shady walls the smiles of all shapes that could respond — the old pier-glass, with gilt columns and huge entablature, the picture-frames, sundry knobs and handles, and the brass rosette at the bottom of each riband bell-pull on either side of the chimney-piece.

"Elizabeth, do you think much of old times?" said Henchard.

"Yes, sir; often," said she.

"Who do you put in your pictures of 'em?"

"Mother and father — nobody else hardly."

Henchard always looked like one bent on resisting pain when Elizabeth-Jane spoke of Richard Newson as "father." "Ah! I am out of all that, am I not?" he said . . . "Was Newson a kind father?"

"Yes, sir; very."

Henchard's face settled into an expression of stolid loneliness which gradually modulated into something softer. "Suppose I had been your real father?" he said. "Would you have cared for me as much as you cared for Richard Newson?"

"I can't think it," she said quickly. "I can think of no other as my father, except my father."

Henchard's wife was dissevered from him by death; his friend and helper Farfrae by estrangement; Elizabeth-Jane by ignorance. It seemed to him that only one of them could possibly be recalled, and that was the girl. His mind began vibrating between the wish to reveal himself to her and the policy of leaving well alone, till he could no longer sit still. He walked up and down, and then he came and stood behind her chair, looking down upon the top of her head. He could no longer restrain his impulse. "What did your mother tell you about me — my history?" he asked.

"That you were related by marriage."

"She should have told more — before you knew me! Then my task would not have been such a hard one . . . Elizabeth, it is I who am your father, and not Richard Newson. Shame alone prevented your wretched parents from owning this to you while both of 'em were alive."

The back of Elizabeth's head remained still, and her shoulders did not denote even the movements of breathing. Henchard went on: "I'd rather have your scorn, your fear, anything than your ignorance; 'tis this that I hate. Your mother and I were man and wife when we were young. What you saw was our second marriage. Your mother was too honest. We had thought each other dead — and — Newson became her husband."

This was the nearest approach Henchard could make to the full truth. As far as he personally was concerned he would have screened nothing; but he showed a respect for the young girl's sex and years worthy of a better man.

When he had gone on to give details which a whole series of slight unregarded incidents in her past life strangely corroborated; when, in short, she believed his story to be true, she became greatly agitated, and turning round to the table flung her face upon it weeping.

"Don't cry — don't cry!" said Henchard, with vehement pathos, "I can't bear it, I won't bear it. I am your father; why should you cry? Am I so dreadful, so hateful to 'ee? Don't take against me, Elizabeth-Jane!" he cried, grasping her wet hand. "Don't take against me — though I was a drinking man once and used your mother roughly — I'll be kinder to you than *he* was! I'll do anything, if you will only look upon me as your father!"

She tried to stand up and confront him trustfully; but she could not;

she was troubled at his presence, like the brethren at the avowal of Joseph.

"I don't want you to come to me all of a sudden," said Henchard in jerks, and moving like a great tree in a wind. "No, Elizabeth, I don't. I'll go away and not see you till tomorrow, or when you like; and then I'll show 'ee papers to prove my words. There, I am gone, and won't disturb you any more . . . Twas I that chose your name, my daughter; your mother wanted it Susan. There, don't forget 'twas I gave you your name!" He went out at the door and shut her softly in, and she heard him go away into the garden. But he had not done. Before she had moved, or in any way recovered from the effect of his disclosure, he reappeared.

"One word more, Elizabeth," he said. "You'll take my surname now—hey? Your mother was against it; but it will be much more pleasant to me. 'Tis legally yours, you know. But nobody need know that. You shall take it as if by choice. I'll talk to my lawyer—I don't know the law of it exactly; but will you do this—let me put a few lines into the newspaper that such is to be your name?"

"If it is my name I must have it, mustn't I?" she asked.

"Well, well; usage is everything in these matters."

"I wonder why mother didn't wish it?"

"Oh, some whim of the poor soul's. Now get a bit of paper and draw up a paragraph as I shall tell you. But let's have a light."

"I can see by the firelight," she answered. "Yes—I'd rather."

"Very well."

She got a piece of paper, and bending over the fender wrote at his dictation words which he had evidently got by heart from some advertisement or other—words to the effect that she, the writer, hitherto known as Elizabeth-Jane Newson, was going to call herself Elizabeth-Jane Henchard forthwith. It was done, and fastened up and directed to the office of the *Casterbridge Chronicle*.

"Now," said Henchard, with the blaze of satisfaction that he always emitted when he had carried his point—though tenderness softened it this time—"I'll go upstairs and hunt for some documents that will prove it all to you. But I won't trouble you with them till tomorrow. Goodnight, my Elizabeth-Jane!"

He was gone before the bewildered girl could realize what it all meant, or adjust her filial sense to the new centre of gravity. She was thankful that he had left her to herself for the evening, and sat down over the fire. Here she remained in silence, and wept—not for her mother now, but for the genial sailor Richard Newson, to whom she seemed doing a wrong.

Henchard in the meantime had gone upstairs. Papers of a domestic nature he kept in a drawer in his bedroom, and this he unlocked. Before turning them over he leant back and indulged in reposeful thought. Elizabeth was his at last and she was a girl of such good sense and kind heart that she would be sure to like him. He was the kind of man whom some human object for pouring out his heat upon — were it emotive or were it choleric — was almost a necessity. The craving of his heart for the reestablishment of this tenderest human tie had been great during his wife's lifetime, and now he had submitted to its mastery without reluctance and without fear. He bent over the drawer again, and proceeded in his search.

Among the other papers had been placed the contents of his wife's little desk, the keys of which had been handed to him at her request. Here was the letter addressed to him with the restriction. *Not to be opened till Elizabeth-Jane's wedding-day*.

Mrs. Henchard, though more patient than her husband, had been no practical hand at anything. In sealing up the sheet, which was folded and tucked in without an envelope, in the old-fashioned way, she had overlaid the junction with a large mass of wax without the requisite under-touch of the same. The seal had cracked, and the letter was open. Henchard had no reason to suppose the restriction one of serious weight, and his feeling for his late wife had not been of the nature of deep respect. "Some trifling fancy or other of poor Susan's, I suppose," he said; and without curiosity he allowed his eyes to scan the letter:

My dear Michael — For the good of all of us I have kept one thing a secret from you till now. I hope you will understand why; I think you will; though perhaps you may not forgive me. But, dear Michael, I have done it for the best. I shall be in my grave when you read this, and Elizabeth-Jane will have a home. Don't curse me. Mike — think of how I was situated. I can hardly write it, but here it is. Elizabeth-Jane is not your Elizabeth-Jane — the child who was in my arms when you sold me. No; she died three months after that, and this living one is my other husband's. I christened her by the same name we had given to the first, and she filled up the ache I felt at the other's loss. Michael, I am dying, and I might have held my tongue; but I could not. Tell her husband of this or not, as you may judge; and forgive, if you can, a woman you once deeply wronged, as she forgives you.

Susan Henchard

Her husband regarded the paper as if it were a windowpane through which he saw for miles. His lips twitched, and he seemed to compress his frame, as if to bear it better. His usual habit was not to consider whether destiny were hard upon him or not—the shape of his ideas in cases of affliction being simply a moody "I am to suffer, I perceive." "This much scourging, then, is it for me?" But now through his passionate head there stormed this thought—that the blasting disclosure was what he had deserved.

His wife's extreme reluctance to have the girl's name altered from Newson to Henchard was now accounted for fully. It furnished another illustration of that honesty in dishonesty which had characterized her in other things.

He remained unnerved and purposeless for near a couple of hours; till he suddenly said, "Ah—I wonder if it is true!"

He jumped up in an impulse, kicked off his slippers, and went with a candle to the door of Elizabeth-Jane's room, where he put his ear to the keyhole and listened. She was breathing profoundly. Henchard softly turned the handle, entered, and shading the light, approached the bedside. Gradually bringing the light from behind a screening curtain he held it in such manner that it fell slantwise on her face without shining on her eyes. He steadfastly regarded her features.

They were fair; his were dark. But this was an unimportant preliminary. In sleep there come to the surface buried genealogical facts, ancestral curves, dead men's traits, which the mobility of daytime animation screens and overwhelms. In the present statuesque repose of the young girl's countenance Richard Newson's was unmistakably reflected. He could not endure the sight of her, and hastened away.

Misery taught him nothing more than defiant endurance of it. His wife was dead, and the first impulse for revenge died with the thought that she was beyond him. He looked out at the night as at a fiend. Henchard, like all his kind, was superstitious, and he could not help thinking that the concatenation of events this evening had produced was the scheme of some sinister intelligence bent on punishing him. Yet they had developed naturally. If he had not revealed his past history to Elizabeth he would not have searched the drawer for papers, and so on. The mockery was, that he should have no sooner taught a girl to claim the shelter of his paternity than he discovered her to have no kinship with him.

This ironical sequence of things angered him like an impish trick from a fellow-creature. Like Prester John's, his table had been spread, and infernal harpies had snatched up the food. He went out of the house, and moved sullenly onward down the pavement till he came to the bridge at the bottom of the High Street. Here he turned in upon a bypath on the river bank, skirting the north-east limits of the town.

These precincts embodied the mournful phases of Casterbridge life, as the south avenues embodied its cheerful moods. The whole way along here was sunless, even in summer time; in spring, white frosts lingered here when other places were steaming with warmth; while in winter it was the seed-field of all aches, rheumatisms, and torturing cramps of the year. The Casterbridge doctors must have pined away for want of sufficient nourishment but for the configuration of the landscape on the north-eastern side.

The river — slow, noiseless, and dark — the Schwarzwasser of Casterbridge — ran beneath a low cliff, the two together forming a defence which had rendered walls and artificial earthworks on this side unnecessary. Here were ruins of a Franciscan priory, and a mill attached to the same, the water of which roared down a back-hatch like the voice of desolation. Above the cliff, and behind the river, rose a pile of buildings, and in the front of the pile a square mass cut into the sky. It was like a pedestal lacking its statue. This missing feature, without which the design remained incomplete, was, in truth, the corpse of a man; for the square mass formed the base of the gallows, the extensive buildings at the back being the county gaol. In the meadow where Henchard now walked the mob were wont to gather whenever an execution took place, and there to the tune of the roaring weir they stood and watched the spectacle.

The exaggeration which darkness imparted to the glooms of this region impressed Henchard more than he had expected. The lugubrious harmony of the spot with his domestic situation was too perfect for him, impatient of effects, scenes and adumbrations. It reduced his heartburning to melancholy, and he exclaimed, "Why the deuce did I come here!" He went on past the cottage in which the old local hangman had lived and died, in times before that calling was monopolized over all England by a single gentleman; and climbed up by a steep back lane into the town.

For the sufferings of that night, engendered by his bitter disappointment, he might well have been pitied. He was like one who had half fainted, and could neither recover nor complete the swoon. In words he could blame his wife, but not in his heart; and had he obeyed the wise directions outside her letter this pain would have been spared him for long — possibly for ever, Elizabeth-Jane seeming to show no ambition to quit her safe and secluded maiden courses for the speculative path of matrimony.

The morning came after this night of unrest, and with it the necessity for a plan. He was far too self-willed to recede from a position, especially as it would involve humiliation. His daughter he had asserted her to be, and his daughter she should always think herself, no matter what hypocrisy it involved.

But he was ill-prepared for the first step in this new situation. The moment he came into the breakfast-room Elizabeth advanced with open confidence to him and took him by the arm.

"I have thought and thought all night of it," she said frankly. "And I see that everything must be as you say. And I am going to look upon you as the father that you are, and not to call you Mr. Henchard any more. It is so plain to me now. Indeed, father, it is. For, of course, you would not have done half the things you have done for me, and let me have my own way so entirely, and bought me presents, if I had only been your stepdaughter! He — Mr. Newson — whom my poor mother married by such a strange mistake" (Henchard was glad that he had disguised matters here), "was very kind — O so kind!" (she spoke with tears in her eyes); "but that is not the same thing as being one's real father after all. Now, father, breakfast is ready!" said she cheerfully.

Henchard bent and kissed her cheek. The moment and the act he had prefigured for weeks with a thrill of pleasure; yet it was no less than a miserable insipidity to him now that it had come. His reinstation of her mother had been chiefly for the girl's sake, and the fruition of the whole scheme was such dust and ashes as this.

Dr. Benjamin Spock

Boys and girls need chances to be around their father, to be enjoyed by him and if possible to do things with him. Better to play 15 minutes enjoyably and then say, "Now I'm going to read my paper" than to spend all day at the zoo crossly.

Alan Brien

BULLY FOR WHO?

Wandering around London last week, during the half-term holiday, with my ten-year-old son, I realised what adults secretly know but conveniently suppress — that a child's world is much more extreme, emotional, erratic and baffling than ours . . .

Children exist in an enclave of barbarism, a society with rituals and initiations and dictatorships and tortures and taboos and totems, which exists just a few feet away from our own civilised, domesticated domain. We push them towards each other while we have our drinks, lock them up in schools while we go to work, drop them off at summer camps, leave them alone all night in dormitories, as if they possessed instincts for democracy, freedom and justice which three-quarters of our grown-up world has not yet evolved.

The years rush by for us, while the days crawl for them, forgetting that no child can grasp the concept of a fortnight. We assume that all members of their age group are more or less interchangeable without considering how choosy we are about our friends and colleagues. We deny them the right to have moods, obsessions, inexplicable likes and dislikes, fads and fancies, which make us so interesting and complex personalities.

We deprive them of the solace of sex and drink, money and responsibility. We sort through their possessions, throwing out what we regard as broken or useless. We dress them to suit our tastes and illustrate our style. We betray them in public by reproving them for behaviour we practise in private.

And yet we are surprised when, at adolescence, we discover that, after a lifetime of waiting, they seem to want all our pleasures and privileges and vices now.

Our mistake is not that we fail to treat children as adults, but that we fail to realise how childish adults are. They feel everything we feel and we should not be surprised or shocked to learn that our cowardice, greed, vanity, envy and ambition is already there among them. If it were not, where did it spring from? The best I can do for my offspring is to assume that they are as fallible and vulnerable as I am.

When I discuss bullying with my son, I should not try to travel backwards in time and imagine what I would have done in his place. I have to ask myself what I would do here and now. The exercise may not help him but it teaches me a few truths.

You've got to face such people, son, take a risk, hit back. Should I speak to the boy from my immense superior strength and size? What's that, speak to his father? His father's a boxer? Well now, let's not be hasty. We don't want to descend to his level, do we?

Guinness Book of Records

The last Sharifian Emperor of Morocco, Moulay Ismail (1627—1727), known as "The Bloodthirsty," was reputed to have fathered a total of 548 sons and 340 daughters.

Diane Johnson

THE LIFE OF DASHIELL HAMMETT

He . . . wrote to Jo [his younger daughter] on her eighteenth birthday:

So now you're eighteen and I'm all out of child daughters. My family is cluttered up with grown women. There's nobody who has to say "Sir," to me anymore and there are no more noses to wipe. I feel old and caught-up with. But there's no use sulking about it, I guess, and I might as well try to make the best of it and welcome you into the ranks of the adult. I'm sure you'll like our little club.

As you've probably found out by now, this world of grown-ups into which you have been admitted is a very, very superior world indeed, inhabited only by people of sound, mature and mellow mentality — all of which they can of course prove simply by showing the dates on their birth certificates.

But what you may not yet have noticed is that all these people stand on their own feet as independently as all get-out, being beholden to their fellows only for food, shelter, clothing, safety, happiness, love, life and picture post cards.

Another thing you'll discover is that one of the chief differences — some cynics say it's the only difference — between a child and an adult is a child is under some sort of obligation to grow, while an adult doesn't have to if he doesn't want to. Isn't he already grown up? What do you want 'im to do? Try to make himself into God or something?

You'll *love* our little club . . .

He wrote letters signed Love, Love and kisses, Kisses and hugs, Many kisses, Lots of love. But it was real love that he could never speak of, except when drinking; a drink enabled him sometimes, to call a man a liar or a fool, or to speak of love. Once, about now, drinking, he wrote a letter to Jo in which he said:

I don't suppose it's been a secret that I've loved you since I first saw you half-an-hour fresh from the womb and looking very much like my father whom I don't love; but now you've grown into the kind of woman I'd always hoped you'd grow up into—only better, of course. Once, while I was in California, I said fumblingly that I was proud of you, which sounded a little like a parent taking some sort of credit. I didn't mean that, honey: I meant I was proud of being your father, which, if you understand me, is a bit different . . . The other things I said—that you're not only lovely to look at, but also lovely—I stand by; and when your face lights up with laughter you are to me the loveliest thing I've ever seen; but if on that account, you go round lighting your face like a Cheshire Cat all the time I can see how people are going to think you're a gibbering idiot . . . I love you, darling, deeply and completely . . .

Ian Hoare

THE SOUL BOOK

In 1972, Norman Whitfield and Barrett Strong wrote a song which, for the first time in a pop/soul context, spoke frankly and explicitly about a key black male stereotype: the Temptations' *Papa Was a Rollin' Stone*. The song opens with various sons asking their mama whether the stories they hear about their father are true: that he did no work, had three outside children and another wife, used to steal in the name of the Lord, was "never much on thinking" and "spent all his money chasing women and drinking." Mama does not deny it. She just hangs her head and delivers a tautly ambiguous piece of reflection, one of the greatest choruses in soul:

> Papa was a rolling stone
> Wherever he laid his hat was his home
> And when he died
> All he left us was alone.

Soul songs usually depict a state of affairs where it is mama — rather than an authoritarian father who is "head of the household" — through whom notions about the need to accept responsibility most commonly reach the family, and through whom the sex battle is resolved. They strongly suggest that the black culture is far more mother-centred than the western mainstream. *My Daddy Knows Best* is an obvious exception in early soul; and two seventies hits the Chi-Lites' *Let Me Be the Man My Daddy Was* and the Winstons' *Colour Him Father*, depict an ideal male parent, steady, protective, kind and willing to struggle against adversity for the sake of the family — an attitude which is very much in tune with the recent trend towards social self-consciousness and black pride, of course. But even here it's notable that the Winstons sing "I got to color him father": the real father is absent, killed in the war, apparently. The general rule remains clear enough: mother passes on the worldly wisdom and the sense of what's right and wrong.

James Douglas

We think of a father as an old, or at least a middle-aged man. The astounding truth is that most fathers are young men, and that they make their greatest sacrifices in their youth. I never meet a young man in a public park on Sunday morning wheeling his first baby in a perambulator without feeling an ache of reverence.

Bronson Alcott

to his daughters

For Louisa May Alcott
Elizabeth Sewell Alcott
and
Abba May Alcott

Concordia Cottage — from their father
15 July 1842

My dear Girls:
I think of you all every day and desire to see you all again: Abba with her beauty-loving eyes and sweet visions of graceful motions, of golden hues and all fair and mystic shows and shapes — Louisa with her quick and ready services, her agile limbs and boundless curiosity, her penetrating mind and tear-shedding heart, alive to all moving, breathing things — Elizabeth with her quiet-loving disposition and serene thoughts, her happy gentleness, deep sentiment, self-centred in the depths of her affections — and last, but yet dearest too in her joys and impetuous griefs, the little Abba with her fast falling footsteps, her sagacious eye and auburn locks . . . and mother too, whose unsleeping love and painstaking hands provide for your comforts and pleasant things and is your hope and stay and now more near and important to you while I am taken from your eyes. All and each of you I have in my mind: daily I see you in my thoughts and as I lay my head on my pillow at night or wake from sleep in the morning . . . nor can the tumbling waters hide my group of loves from my eyes: the little cottage there behind the Elm, the garden round, strawberry red or coloured vines . . . or corn barn play house, or street or bridge or winding stream, or Anna or Louisa, their lessons loved (and learned by heart, not rote) and Lizzie too with little Ab in parlor, study, chamber, lawn, with needle, book or pen . . . and so you see, my gentle girls, I cannot leave you quite: though my body is far away my mind is near and all the while, I hear and see and touch and think and feel your very selves — the life that lives in all you are and say and do, the mind,

the Heart, the Soul—the God that dwells in you. And now be loving little girls and grow far more fair with every day and when I come to see my garden plot then shall my flowers scent the fields and I shall joy in every scent they lend, in every tint and form they wear. So now, my dears, adieu.

Let mother read this with you and talk long and sweetly with her about what is in it and then kiss her all and each other and then her all again for Father's sake.

King George VI

to Princess Elizabeth

I was so proud of you and thrilled at having you so close to me on our long walk in Westminster Abbey, but when I handed your hand to the Archbishop I felt I had lost something very precious. You were so calm and composed during the Service and said your words with such conviction, that I knew everything was all right.

I am so glad you wrote and told Mummy that you think the long wait before your engagement and the long time before the wedding was for the best. I was rather afraid that you had thought I was being hard-hearted about it. I was so anxious for you to come to South Africa as you know. Our family, us four, the "Royal Family" must remain together with additions of course at suitable moments!! I have watched you grow up all these years with pride under the skilful direction of Mummy, who as you know is the most marvellous person in the World in my eyes, and I can, I know, always count on you, and now Philip, to help us in our work. Your leaving us has left a great blank in our lives but do remember that your old home is still yours and do come back to it as much and as often as possible. I can see that you are sublimely happy with Philip which is right but don't forget us is the wish of

Your ever loving & devoted
Papa

William Wharton

DAD

At home we sit around the living room. There are some times when I'm sure Dad has left us. I'm itching to ask but I'm embarrassed. It's like asking a woman if she's having her period because she's acting differently. There's no real justification except simple curiosity and it's an invasion.

Mom's tough to be with. Luckily, Billy's gone back up on the forty acres. Mother, wandering around, the Lady Macbeth of Colby Lane, bugs Billy beyond endurance. I can't blame him. Mom's impossible when she's scared; she's striking out in all directions, trying to give some substance to things. Nobody's safe near her.

We're sitting there in the living room and she starts off. Dad's in his rocking chair, Mom's on one of the dining chairs turned half around from the table and I'm sitting in an upholstered chair by the door. We're all within a few feet of each other.

She begins talking to me about how crazy Dad is. She's pulling out all her memorized litany of Tremont variations from the norm through four generations. She's tolling them off like a rosary, the infamous mysteries; I listen and fume. Dad's between pretending it isn't happening, and listening. He's like a very genteel woman who's forced by circumstances to hear barroom language.

It goes on and on; nothing's enough. I know she's wanting me to argue and I don't want to. But then I can't help myself. You only kid yourself into thinking you've grown out of it, that you can respond as an adult logically, sensibly, to parents. I turn to Dad.

"Dad, why do you let her talk like this? Why do you put up with it? It's not good for either of you to have her spout all this rot. She's the one who's acting crazy."

Mother keeps talking over my first sentence, but then shuts up. If I'd talked to her directly she'd have kept on only louder. Using a carom shot, talking to Dad, has her buffaloed.

"We all know she does this because she's scared, but backbiting at everybody doesn't help. You've got to help her stop."

I turn toward Mom.

"And, Mom, you should know better. You don't really believe this nonsense; you're only saying it to make yourself feel like a big shot and three-star martyr. Dad's doing his best. We have an expert working with him. This doctor says Dad's not crazy. In fact, he's impressed with how Dad's survived the past thirty or so years without going crazy.

"If you're so convinced Dad's crazy, tell me in private and we'll work things out. We can put Dad in a home, or you in a home, or something. But for god's sake don't sit there talking in front of him as if he's a dog who doesn't understand!"

Dad's turned white. He leans forward and lurches out of his platform rocker. Instinctively I stand with him. I've no idea what he's going to do. Maybe take a punch at me or maybe Mom. It could be anything.

He leaves his cane and shuffles towards us. Mother's up, too; looking even more scared than I feel. Dad spreads his thin arms and we go toward him. He pulls us close to his breast and holds us tight. His whole body is shaking. Nobody says anything. It's as if we're in a two-hand-touch huddle, except we're not leaning over, our faces are straight up, pushed next to each other at different heights.

Dad kisses us both several times; it's the first time I can remember his kissing me since the day I was sent off to first grade. He begins talking and his voice is low, cracked.

"Don't do it, Johnny. Please don't say those things to your mother; you're too clever, you know too much. We're family, that's all that counts. Let's love each other and forget. Loving more than anything means letting people do the things they have to do. Mother here has to do some things too; so do I. It's the way it is. Please don't fight; it kills me hearing you talk this way."

Then he starts crying hard and Mother breaks into sobs. I'm crying, too. Now we're the Burghers of Calais standing in our own rain. Maybe it's time to break the huddle, call the signals and snap the ball. These kinds of stupid thoughts are tramping through my mind. Real emotion is tough for me to handle; I've got about twenty lines of defense to keep from feeling.

Finally we sit again. Dad sighs and begins talking. I can't get my mind around it; who the hell is this guy?

"There are some things maybe you don't know Johnny. When I met Bess she was only fifteen. She was just recovering from a bad nervous breakdown. She could never even go back to school again. I was eighteen and working at Hog Island as a carpenter. I wasn't happy; in fact, I was miserable. I didn't like living in the city and I was missing the farm. I felt everybody could see I was only a farm boy and was laughing at me.

"It was a big change, John. You know, winter and summer, none of us kids wore shoes regularly on the farm. We walked to school with shoes tied around our necks and put them on when we went inside. I never owned a pair of shoes till we got to Philadelphia. I'd get Orin's. Those shoes never wore out; we only put them on for school and church.

"You can't know what a change it was coming from Wisconsin where I knew maybe twenty people all together and half of them were my brothers and sisters. There I was in Philadelphia, talking funny with a farm-boy Wisconsin hick accent; I was afraid to open my mouth. I'd be jammed in trolley cars with people who didn't know anything about me and didn't care. Everybody seemed to know what to do and where they were going. People would bump into me because I couldn't get out of the way. I didn't know how to flush a toilet, use a telephone or dance.

"I met Mother on a rainy day in a doorway near John Wanamaker's. She came into the doorway crying her eyes out. She was crying because she'd borrowed her older sister Maggie's fancy hat without asking and now it was getting ruined in the rain.

"I had a big old-time umbrella my mother made me carry and I opened it over her. Gosh, I guess if Mom hadn't made me carry that umbrella I'd never even 've gotten to know you, Bess, think of that.

"Well, Bess was pretty, and scared. She was the scaredest person I'd ever met. It wasn't just the hat; she was scared about the thunder and lightning, she was scared the trolley wasn't going to come; she was scared about what time it was, and she was scared of me. Something inside me wanted to help her not be so scared.

"And, Johnny, Mother's always been that way. Sometimes she acts strong and likes to be bossy, but inside she's scared. It's something you've got to remember.

"That day she finally let me go along with her in the trolley, and when she got out I followed her, keeping my umbrella over the hat. She led me to a big stone house and said this was where she lived, and goodbye. I stood across the street waiting to see her safe inside but two big dogs came barking at the door. She ran away and down the street in the rain; it wasn't where she lived at all.

"That's the kind of thing she does, Johnny, because she's so scared. I chased her, laughing, but she was mad and I thought she might be crazy but I loved her already."

I looked at Mom. Her eyes are blank, her face a mask; she's stunned.

"And you're not much different, Johnny. You were the scrawniest baby I've ever seen in my life. For the first three months you cried without stopping. It's a wonder that didn't drive your poor mother absolutely crazy. Then, you grew up to be the scaredy-cattest kid in the neighborhood. I used to think sometimes you caught it from your mother.

"You were afraid of the dark. You were afraid of loud noises; you used to hold your fingers in your ears at a baseball game and you'd stuff cotton in them on the Fourth of July. You were afraid to ride a bike, to roller-skate, even to swim. I don't think you learned swimming till you were over thirteen years old.

"And you were afraid of all the other kids on the block. You'd come running home with some little kid half your size chasing you. That's how you learned to run, running away from everybody.

"I was sure you'd never learn to take care of yourself; that you'd live with us all your life. I remember being so embarrassed because you were one of the world's worst baseball players.

"And you grew so fast, early. For a while, when you were about ten or twelve, you were a head taller than anybody in your class. This made it worse. Little kids would take turns beating up on you so they could say they licked the big sissy down the block. Summers, you spent your time hiding in the cellar, on the porch reading or later fooling around with your birds.

"Sometimes I look at you now and I can't believe it's the same person.

"What I want to say is, you're a lot like your mother, John. You're fighting all the time but in your own way. Maybe that's why you live in France instead of America. You don't want to compete, you want to stay apart.

"But, in another way, you're different from Bess. You get that part from me. There's something in me that's wild, wild like a wild animal. It was in my father, it's in my brothers and two of my sisters; we aren't quite human, quite civilized. There's some animal quality and it can come out anytime. I'm surprised we've gotten as far as we have without having a murder in the family.

"I don't know what brings it on; could be all those years living in the woods, or it could be the Indian blood.

"You know, Johnny, your great-grandfather was a trapper. He never lived in a house from the time he was thirteen; he married a full-blooded

Oneida Indian. Your great-grandmother, my father's mother, was over six feet tall. She was stronger than any man, and could talk only Indian and French.

"I never heard her speak one word. That grandfather and grand-mother of mine lived practically like prehistoric people. They didn't homestead and settle till my dad was seven years old. They lived with the Indians and had no real religion; so far as I know they never got married — at least, not in a church.

"Dad used to tell stories about how they'd drift along, tending the traps, buying furs, catching, then packing them all out in canoes. They were animals, Johnny, and it's still there. It's in me, it's in you, too, and we always have to fight it."

Mother's nodding her head now; this is something she can live with. Jack the Ripper, North American version of Tarzan the apeman.

"One reason I married Bess was she liked beautiful things. She'd always lived in cities and all her family'd lived in cities as far back as anybody could remember. She likes nice furniture, she keeps a clean house and we live like decent human beings.

"You can see I'm not like my brothers or even my father; I'm civilized. I don't drink much and I don't run around. My brothers are all dangerous men, except Ed. Ed was lucky like me and married a good woman. Aunt Mary trained him just fine. You could never predict my father or my brothers; never tell what they were thinking or what they were going to do. None of them ever held full-time jobs in their lives. Pete and Orin and Caleb were always drinking or running back into the woods to hunt. Winters they'd curl up and hibernate like bears.

"Now, my mom did a good job with Dad. At least she got him into church and he took care of us kids. But he didn't dress like a normal person or do things like other people. You know, Johnny, he never paid a dime to Social Security or paid any income tax in his life? He lived on the outside of everything. He lived down there in southwest Philadelphia as if he was living on a farm or in the woods. All those buildings, cars and everything didn't mean a thing to him.

"I didn't want to live that way. Look, I'm a civilized man; look at these hands, they're clean, I've got all my fingers. Look at this house we've got here, with this beautiful furniture, rugs and all. We live like real city people and that's all your mother's doing. Don't forget that."

What can I say? I know he's serious; he wants me to understand. I'm wishing Delibro could hear this. Mother's sitting there, still crying. She's sniffing and peering at me, eye-talk, See what I mean, Jacky, see what I mean? And Dad's making such sense. I feel awful, like a child. He's been seeing through it all these years and saying nothing, letting it happen because he respected us.

"John, I know sometimes you must worry about Billy and little Jacky.

"It's hard for fathers to wait, but you have to give boys time, they're slow. Sons are what worry a man because most men are scared, so they're scared for their sons.

"Johnny, I'm not worrying about you anymore and I don't want you worrying about me or Mother. Let's enjoy our own lives. We're all fine.

"I'll keep going to that psychiatrist doctor till I get myself straightened out. Johnny, you go home to Veronica and Jacky. Mother and I will be OK; we all just have to stop worrying so much."

After this long speech, he leans back, rocking, smiling from one to the other of us, smiling as if all the rules of the family haven't been broken into a thousand pieces. The odd thing is Dad doesn't act as if all this talking is out of the ordinary. Here he's talked more in fifteen minutes, said more than he has in the past fifteen years; and he's just rocking and smiling.

Gerard Manley Hopkins

TRIOLET

"The child is father to the man."
How can he be? The words are wild.
Suck any sense from that who can:
"The child is father to the man."
No; what the poet did write ran,
"The man is father to the child."
"The child is father to the man!"
How *can* he be? The words are wild.

P. G. Wodehouse

FAIR PLAY FOR FATHERS

The advent of Father's Day in America has inspired the advertisement pages of the magazines to suggestions for brightening the life of this poor underprivileged peon. "Buy him an outboard runabout speedboat 14 foot long with a 62 foot beam," say the magazines. "Buy him a synchromatic wrist watch, water and shock resistant. Buy him a fishing-rod 7 foot long with reinforced ferrules and large-capacity spinning Beachcomber reel," say the magazines, knowing perfectly well that if he gets anything, it will be a tie with pink horseshoes on a blue background.

What he really wants, of course, is a square deal from the hellhounds of Television.

It is difficult to say when the thing started, but little by little the American Father has become established on the Television screen as Nature's last word in saps, boobs and total losses, the man with two left feet who can't make a move in any direction without falling over himself. Picture a rather exceptionally I Q-less village idiot and you will have the idea. Father, as he appears in what is known in Television circles as heartwarming domestic comedy, is a bohunkus who could walk straight into any establishment for the care of the feeble-minded and no questions asked.

There are two sorts of heart-warming domestic comedy on American Television. One deals with the daily doing of the young husband and the young wife who converse for thirty minutes without exchanging a civil word. The other features Father, showing him, to quote a recent writer, as "a miserable chinless half wit with barely enough mechanical skill to tie his own shoes." Almost any domestic crisis will do to make him a mockery and a scorn to twenty million viewers. The one the writer selects is Operation Refrigerator. Mom finds that the refrigerator won't work, and Pop says leave it to him, he'll fix it.

Now Pop, says the writer, may be a mechanic during his working hours — he may even be a refrigerator repair man — but in the home he reverts to the Stone Age. He strews the floor with more parts than there are in six refrigerators and a cyclotron. Then, baffled, he (a) goes berserk, (b) collapses or (c) so assembles the parts that the refrigerator spouts boiling water.

It is at this point that Junior steps forward. Junior is an insufferably bumptious stripling of ten or eleven with a freckled face and a voice like a cement-mixer. He straightens everything out with effortless efficiency, speaking patronizing words to Pop over his shoulder. It is obvious that he regards the author of his being as something that ought not lightly to be allowed at large.

I suppose the dim-witted American Father will some day go into the discard like the comic Frenchman with the beard and top-hat and the comic Englishman with the front teeth and whiskers, but it is going to be a grim struggle to get him out of Television. Those Television boys don't often get an idea, but when they do they cling to it. But where they got this idea of the American Child as a mechanical genius it is hard to say.

In the village to which I retire in the summer months the trouble shooters who come round to me when anything goes wrong are grave elderly men in overalls who are obviously experts at their job. I cannot believe that in their homes they have to rely on a freckled child to fix the leaking washer in the scullery tap. I have never come across any mechanically-minded children. Fred Garcia, one of our younger set, has "souped up" his car so that it will do a hundred and thirty m.p.h. and recently covered the fourteen hundred miles between Miami, Fla, and New York, NY, in thirty hours, which is unquestionably good going; but Fred is eighteen and training to be a jet pilot. Junior in those heart-warming domestic comedies is never more than twelve at the outside. Often he is nearer six, with curls and an all-day sucker.

What the American child *is* good at is dialogue. There he definitely shines. One specimen of the breed in knickerbockers and a Brigade of Guards tie (to which I am almost sure he was not entitled) looked in on me the other day as I worked in the garden and fixed me with an un-winking stare.

"Hi!" he said.

"Hi to you," I responded civilly.

A pause.

"Wotcher doin'?"

"Gardening."

"Oops."

Another pause.

"Have you got a father?" he said.

I said I had not.

"Have you got a mother?"

"No."

"Have you got a sister?"

"No."

"Have you got a brother?"

"No."

"Have you got any candy?"

Crisp. That is the word I was trying to think of. The American child's dialogue is crisp.

Coming back to the American Father, there was the other day just a gleam of light in his darkness. On the Kraft Theatre programme a family was shown having all sorts of family problems, and who should the wise, kindly person who solved them be but Father. It seems incredible, and several people have told me that I must have imagined it or that I switched the thing off before the big scene at the end showing Father trying to fix the electric light. It may be so.

Meanwhile, I think it only right to warn the Television authorities that if they allow things to continue as they are, they are in grave peril. There has been a good deal of angry muttering of late in the Amalgamated Union of American Fathers, and if you ask me, I think the men are about ready to march.

I am watching the situation very closely.

Euripides

To an old father, nothing is more sweet
Than a daughter.
Boys are more spirited, but their ways
Are not so tender.

Carey Winfrey

FATHERHOOD POSTPONED

My first wife and I were out of synch when it came to children. When I wanted them, she didn't, and vice versa. Perhaps that should have told us something, though even now I'm not sure quite what. In any case, the marriage was over before I knew it — literally — and once we were separated, people kept saying wasn't it fortunate there hadn't been any children. I couldn't argue with that.

For a while, after my divorce, I didn't give the idea of kids a lot of thought, though somewhere at the back of my mind lay the assumption that I would someday have them. If pressed, I would have said that being a father was not something I wanted to miss out on but that I was in no rush. There were still things I wanted to do before I got tied down.

By the time I got married again, at the age of 40, three-and-a-half years ago, I was more than ready to be a daddy. It was as if some slow-release time capsule had suddenly gone off in my psyche, unleashing a pool of paternal yearnings. And when Jane and I had twin sons, most of our close friends our age were having babies, too. As much as I hate to think of myself as a part of any trend, it seems undeniable that Jane and I have become soldiers in the growing army of late-blooming urban parents.

The thing I was always warned against about waiting a long time to have children was that I wouldn't be able to throw a ball with them. Well, I'm here to say that I don't think it's going to be a problem. Either I'll throw balls with the best of them and that'll be that, or I won't and it won't matter a damn. Two-plus years into this fatherhood business, I know at least that what kids require of their fathers is a lot of attention, a lot of love and, I suspect, if mine ever reach the age of understanding, a lot of that, too. They can find other people to throw balls at them.

I like being a father. I *love* being a father. And I think I'm a better one for having waited. Though no number of years can ever adequately prepare one for the enormous delights and anxieties of fatherhood —

worry and fear for his child's well-being will never be far from any father's consciousness—I also believe that coming late to it has some real pluses. One of them is the rejuvenating way kids force you to experience the world anew, a world filled with Dr. Seuss and showing off any funny animals and marching bands. Maybe some younger fathers get just as big a kick as I do vicariously viewing the world this way, but I wouldn't be surprised if it takes a bit of mileage on the old odometer fully to appreciate what Wordsworth was getting at with his line about the child's being father of the man.

I know I resent the dramatic way my kids have circumscribed my life less than I would have a decade or more ago. I can hardly say I did it all, but I did enough—read enough books, saw enough movies, went to enough parties—not to mind much the degree to which those activities have been curtailed. I'm often even grateful to my children for providing the excuse, as well as the reason, to stay home. I don't want to make too much of this because certainly there are times my wife and I would (and do) pay any price to escape "the boys" for a little while (and then, inevitably, we spend most of our precious time alone talking about them). But nine nights out of 10—O.K., four out of five—our sons (and whatever happens to be on the tube in the hour left to us after getting them to bed) provide sufficient diversion.

Of course, truth also compels me to confess that, lacking the energy I once had, my tyros can grind me exceedingly fine, particularly when they have a full day to do so. Many Saturday and Sunday nights find me close to tears from exhaustion. (Around *our* house, it's TGIM— "Thank God It's Monday.") But when morning comes around, assuming the boys have not awakened too many times in the wee small hours to wail for "appa juice," or "Mommy," or both, I'm again ready to give them as much of me as they want.

Then there's the money part. Admittedly, twins cost more than single babies (about double, roughly), but even one child these days creates financial burdens better borne by mature than by starting salaries. Though the financial plateau I've reached after 20 years of for-the-most-part-gainful employment remains modest by almost any objective standard, it is nonetheless proportionally higher than it was a decade or so ago. It is not hyperbole but fact that the woman who takes care of our children while Jane and I cavort at work makes as much money as I did not many years ago, even when the dollars are adjusted for inflation. But even if she didn't, children would have taken a much greater share of my expendable income just a few short years ago. More important, I almost certainly begrudge them the financial drain less today than I would have in all my yesterdays.

Recently, for example, my wife and I took out an amount of life insurance that makes each of us far more valuable as a dear departed than in the here and now. In my salad years, that money might have gone quite effortlessly into travel or clothes or cameras. I signed the insurance checks, if not joyously, with a satisfied sense that few expenditures could ever feel as warranted. It's hard to think of a better use for money than my sons' welfare.

Once insurance was taken care of, Jane and I made out new wills. Since embarking on my fifth decade, I've given what she considers an indecent amount of thought to my own mortality; still, nothing so focuses the mind on the subject as the making out of a will. Sitting in the lawyer's office, listening to the stream of whereases and parties-of-the-first-parts, it occurred to me with the force of revelation that the expectation of being survived by one's children is yet another unanticipated pleasure of parenthood postponed. The thought of my sons carrying on after I'm gone is probably about as close to a belief in an afterlife as an aging pagan like myself is likely to get. But curiously, it's close enough for comfort.

Claude Debussy

to his eight-year-old daughter

Saint-Petersbourg, Grand Hotel de l'Europe
11 December 1913

My dear little Chouchou,
Your poor papa is late in answering your lovely little letter. You should not hold it against him . . . It is sad to be deprived for so many days of

the pretty little face of Chouchou, to hear no more of your songs, your bursts of laughter, of all the noise, in fact, that makes you sometimes an insupportable little person, but most often a charming one.

What has become of M. Czerny, who has so much genius? . . . And old Xantho? Is he still as good? Does he still ruin the garden? I authorize you to scold him in a loud voice.

At the Koussevitskys in Moscow there are two charming bulldogs who have eyes like the frog that is in the salon (we are very good friends; I think that they would please you much), and a bird that sings almost as well as Miss Teyte.

All of this is indeed nice, but do not think that it is possible for me to be able to forget you for a second. On the contrary I think only of the day when I shall be with you again. In the meantime, think with tenderness of your old papa who embraces you a thousand times.

Claude Debussy

Be very nice to your poor little mama; do all you can not to annoy her too much.

Richard Yallop

FATHER'S DAY 1984

Ray, who is 41, says he prefers being a full-time father to working, despite some male disapproval. "You get frowned upon. My brother condemned me. He thought I should be working to support the child. He doesn't see the significance of staying home and giving the child guidance." Most of his married friends have drifted away, and his best friends are now two other single fathers.

"I want to work, but I want to see Mark off to school and be home when he gets home. He's 13 now and I think the next two years are the most vital of his life." So Ray has opted for a daily routine of getting up at six, cutting the sandwiches for Mark's lunch, waking him up in time for a 7 o'clock breakfast, doing the washing, making the beds, and shopping . . .

Father and son sleep in adjacent single beds and Mark used to go to sleep holding Ray's hand.

Mark's move to his father was to have been a six-month trial, but it has worked so well he is staying . . .

"Every dog has its day, and I feel mine is now," Ray said. "Life restarted when Mark came back."

Charles Peguy

Any father whose son raises his hand against him is guilty of having produced a son who raised his hand against him.

Svetlana Aliluyeva (Stalin)

TWENTY LETTERS TO A FRIEND

With her children my mother was firm and aloof. It wasn't unkindness or lack of love, but the fact that she expected a great deal of both herself and us . . .

My father, on the other hand, was always carrying me in his arms, giving me loud, moist kisses and calling me pet names like "little sparrow" and "little fly." Once I ruined a new tablecloth with a pair of scissors.

My mother spanked me across the hands until it hurt. I cried so loud that my father came and took me by the hand. He kissed me and comforted me and quieted me down. He couldn't stand the sound of a child crying or screaming and there were times when he saved me from cupping and mustard plasters. My mother, on the other hand, never gave in to me and scolded him for spoiling me . . .

But he was a bad and neglectful . . . father and husband. He devoted his whole being to something else, to politics and struggle. And so people who weren't personally close were always more important to him than those who were.

As a rule my father didn't nag or find fault with me. His guidance as a parent was of the most general sort—that I should study hard, be out in the fresh air as much as possible, and that I ought not to be given in to or spoiled . . .

Once the war started, even our infrequent meetings came to an end and he and I drifted apart. After the war we were never really close again. I had grown up. My childish games and amusements which had been a diversion to him once were now a thing of the far-off past.

Blanche d'Alpuget

ROBERT J. HAWKE

It was in church that parishioners first noticed how he was being reared. "The trouble was," a Bordertown man complained, "his mother wouldn't smack him. He'd be up there in the front, wriggling and throwing things on the floor, or yelling. He was completely undisciplined. It wasn't fair to Clem, trying to give the sermon, when there was a baby disrupting things. I used to want to knock his block off." In the twenty-five years Hawke lived with his parents he was never once struck by either of them. "I was," he said, "dreadfully spoiled." The spoiling came from both parents, especially from Hawke's father.

Clem adored his second son. He said,

"From early on I felt a special affinity, a drawing towards Bobbie. It's a mysterious thing—Ellie had it with Neil. It's something that just happens sometimes in families—you remember Joseph and the coat of many colours? His father felt it. You can't say it's right or wrong to have a favourite child . . . Bobbie had an outflowing magic about him."

He bathed and dressed this baby, things he had not done for Neil, and Hawke's earliest memories were all of love—an overwhelming love. "I can't describe how passionately my father loved me; I was just dad's boy."

The relationship between father and son, which was so intense that Ellie worried about their dependence upon each other, equipped Hawke for life with the capacity to feel and, without embarrassment, to express love for his own sex . . .

Throughout Hawke's life men have been drawn by "the outflowing magic" that Clem felt—and encouraged—and have responded to it by behaving like fathers or doting uncles . . .

It seems as if, in his earliest years, an emotional stage were set and roles allotted to actors, and that the play was performed again and again. While this welded psychological bonds of great strength between Hawke and his friends the son-parent configuration of relationships became, with Hawke's increasing age, inappropriate—even undesirable—for it was holding part of his personality in limbo. Men and women only a few years older than Hawke called him "The Boy" when he was in his late forties; he was treated, by intimates, as a boy who needed adult care and guidance. The role began to exasperate Hawke, and his friends.

Clem's special son, however, was also Ellie's special baby, a gift to her from God. But the intensity of affection between father and son tended to challenge her status with the child, and later events in the family were to cause whatever incipient competition there may have been between the parents to develop into rivalry for the boy. A relation recalled, "Bob could play his family off against each other: he was the centre of attention and the adults competed for him." . . .

Certainly the difference in parental treatment of the Hawke boys was profound: Neil had few of the indulgences allowed to Bobbie. Before he was a teenager Neil was punished for misdemeanours "with a hiding from me once a fortnight—and that's when he was good," Ellie said; sometimes Clem gave him the strap. In his teenage years, in school holidays, Neil worked as a farmhand. Hawke took his first holiday job when he was at university.

Bordertown parishioners remembered Neil as a quiet, well-mannered boy yet Clem and Ellie both fondly described him as a young firebrand, physically reckless and deaf to caution, while Hawke, they said, was a quiet, angelic child with whom they could reason. Perhaps both accounts are accurate, from different perspectives. But as Hawke grew older he developed some of the characteristics that his parents attributed to their elder son. Most people want their children to live for them the lives they cannot: it may be that at an unspoken level the Hawkes encouraged their sons to break free of the extreme decorousness of genteel, *petit bourgeois* parish life, while insisting that they maintain the essence of Christian values . . .

At the beginning of 1933 the family made an important decision. Neil, who was eleven, was sent to boarding school. Ellie was determined that he should have the best possible opportunities so he was enrolled at King's College, a Baptist and Congregational school in Adelaide. Neil's departure from home turned Hawke, in effect, into an only child. His "spoiling" increased.

In 1935 Clem was called to his next post in the Yorke Peninsula town of Maitland. The congregation there knew nothing about their new minister and his wife, with the exception of a detail that had drifted across hundreds of miles of pasture, bush and desert: "The Hawkes have a terrible kid."

Theodore Zeldin

THE FRENCH

Having a baby is still seen, except in the most "advanced" manuals, as involving the father only in a minor capacity. Laurence Pernoud says firmly: "The paternal instinct does not exist—at least before birth. When a man learns that he is to become a father, this news has no emotional effect on him and no reality." The child needs a mother in its first year: "it will not really suffer if it does not know its father." The father is seen as useful to console and encourage the mother: "Be the guardian of her nerves." Changing nappies is something that men are instinctively nauseated by, and it is natural to leave that to the mothers, says Dr. Cohen-Salal, the very latest expert on *Having a Child*. The man's main role starts at around seven or eight months when he begins playing with the baby for "a few privileged moments": he is the sugar daddy . . .

The husband takes little interest in the children's education: he might argue with them for five minutes, but once he gets himself in front of the television, no one is allowed to move. He takes them fishing, because he wants them to enjoy that as he does, but, "to play with them, do things with them, all that, no." From time to time he gives them a spanking . . .

The eldest boy is now married, and he behaves exactly like his father: when he gets home, he flops into his armchair, and leaves the housework to his wife. He regrets that he was never able to have any real communication with his father, and hopes to do better with his own child. Though his parents give the impression of having been lenient to their children, he thinks they were severe with him. This is a very frequent tale. The traditional father sets things up so that he is left in peace, which means things are done to suit him. He feels he is liberal because he does not bother with what does not affect him.

PROVERB

Children suck the mother when they are young, and the father when they are old.

Stanley Reynolds

SPEAK ROUGHLY
TO YOUR LITTLE BOY
OR TRY IGNORING HIM

I have often woken in a sweat, frightened by a nightmare in which my old father had been a pal to me, had prodded me in the chest with his cigar butt and had carried out long man-to-man chats like Mickey Rooney's dad in the *Andy Hardy* movies. Worse still are the night dreads when my sons in my dreams seek my advice. Often nowadays I touch them for money, even when I don't need it, just to keep them away.

Luckily enough when I was a boy most fathers were away at the war or, being too old for service, came from a generation that believed a good clout on the ear was parental guidance . . .

I am sure my father must have spoken directly to me but I cannot remember anything he ever said to me about any particular subject. As for my mother, I can only remember her saying, "Wait until your father comes home."

When my father did come home he'd ask me about my day. I did not say, "I have been standing on top of Tuck Brook's garage roof with a wire in between my front teeth trying to get WHYN." Instead he would say, "Where have you been?" "Out." "And what did you do?" "Nothing."

You were either "in" or "out" or "at school" and that took care of everything . . . I certainly have followed the same lines with my own sons, although often when I am lounging in the grass wondering just why you cannot turn the human body into a radio receiver—I mean, we've got all this electricity inside us—and I see the boys in their tree house trying to entice wasps into an empty Tizer bottle, I wonder what little problems may be on their little minds that Dad could perhaps set right. Actually I know what is on the eldest one's little mind because I've just seen a flash of young blonde legs climbing up the holly tree and disappearing inside the tree house. No need to worry about the kids of today . . . you can rest assured they will be the fathers of tomorrow.

Charles Dickens

LITTLE DORRIT

Gentlemen, God bless you!

Such was the homily with which he improved and pointed the occasion to the company in the Lodge, before turning into the sallow yard again, and going with his own poor shabby dignity past the Collegian in the dressing-gown who had no coat, and past the Collegian in the sea-side slippers who had no shoes, and past the stout greengrocer Collegian in the corduroy knee-breeches who had no cares, and past the lean clerk Collegian in buttonless black who had no hopes, up his own poor shabby staircase, to his own shabby room.

There, the table was laid for his supper, and his old grey gown was ready for him on his chair-back at the fire. His daughter put her little prayer-book in her pocket — had she been praying for pity on all prisoners and captives? — and rose to welcome him.

Uncle had gone home, then? she asked him, as she changed his coat and gave him his black velvet cap. Yes, uncle had gone home. Had her father enjoyed his walk? Why, not much, Amy; not much. No? Did he not feel quite well?

As she stood behind him, leaning over his chair so lovingly, he looked with downcast eyes at the fire. An uneasiness stole over him that was like a touch of shame; and when he spoke, as he presently did, it was in an unconnected and embarrassed manner.

"Something, I — hem! — I don't know what, has gone wrong with Chivery. He is not — ha! — not nearly so obliging and attentive as usual to-night. It — hem! — it's a little thing, but it puts me out, my love. It's impossible to forget," turning his hands over and over, and looking closely at them, "that—hem!—that in such a life as mine, I am unfortunately dependent on these men for something, every hour in the day."

Her arm was on his shoulder, but she did not look in his face while he spoke. Bending her head, she looked another way.

"I—hem!—I can't think, Amy, what has given Chivery offence. He is generally so—so very attentive and respectful. And to-night he was quite—quite short with me. Other people there too! Why, good Heaven! if I was to lose the support and recognition of Chivery and his brother-officers, I might starve to death here."

While he spoke, he was opening and shutting his hands like valves; so conscious all the time of that touch of shame, that he shrunk before his own knowledge of his meaning.

"I—ha!—I can't think what it's owing to. I am sure I cannot imagine what the cause of it is. There was a certain Jackson here once, a turnkey of the name of Jackson (I don't think you can remember him, my dear, you were very young), and—hem!—and he had a—brother, and this—young brother paid his address to—at least, did not go so far as to pay his addresses to—but admired—respectfully admired—the —not the daughter, the sister—of one of us; a rather distinguished Collegian; I may say, very much so. His name was Captain Martin; and he consulted me on the question whether it was necessary that his daughter—sister—should hazard offending the turnkey brother by being too—ha!—too plain with the other brother. Captain Martin was a gentleman and a man of honour, and I put it to him first to give me his—his own opinion. Captain Martin (highly respected in the army) then unhesitatingly said, that it appeared to him that his—hem!—sister was not called upon to understand the young man too distinctly, and that she might lead him on—I am doubtful whether lead him on was Captain Martin's exact expression; indeed I think he said tolerate him— on her father's—I should say, brother's—account. I hardly know how I have strayed into this story. I suppose it has been through being unable to account for Chivery; but as to the connexion between the two, I don't see—"

His voice died away, as if she could not bear the pain of hearing him, and her hand gradually crept to his lips. For a little while, there was a dead silence and stillness; and he remained shrunk in his chair, and she remained with her arm round his neck, and her head bowed down upon his shoulder.

His supper was cooking in a saucepan on the fire, and, when she moved, it was to make it ready for him on the table. He took his usual seat, she took hers, and he began his meal. They did not, as yet, look at one another. By little and little he began; laying down his knife and fork with a noise, taking things up sharply, biting at his bread as if he were offended with it, and in other similar ways showing that he was out of sorts. At length he pushed his plate from him, and spoke aloud. With the strangest inconsistency.

"What does it matter whether I eat or starve? What does it matter whether such a blighted life as mine comes to an end, now, next week, or next year? What am I worth to any one? A poor prisoner, fed on alms and broken victuals; a squalid, disgraced wretch!"

"Father, father!" As he rose, she went on her knees to him, and held up her hands to him.

"Amy," he went on in a suppressed voice, trembling violently, and looking at her as wildly as if he had gone mad. "I tell you, if you could see me as your mother saw me, you wouldn't believe it to be the creature you have only looked at through the bars of this cage. I was young, I was accomplished, I was good-looking. I was independent—by God I was, child!—and people sought me out, and envied me. Envied me!"

"Dear father!" She tried to take down the shaking arm that he flourished in the air, but he resisted, and put her hand away.

"If I had but a picture of myself in those days, though it was ever so ill done, you would be proud of it, you would be proud of it. But I have no such thing. Now, let me be a warning! Let no man," he cried, looking haggardly about, "fail to preserve at least that little of the times of his prosperity and respect. Let his children have that clue to what he was. Unless my face, when I am dead, subsides into the long departed look—they say such things happen, I don't know—my children will have never seen me."

"Father, father!"

"O despise me, despise me! Look away from me, don't listen to me, stop me, blush for me, cry for me—Even you, Amy! Do it, do it! I do it to myself! I am hardened now, I have sunk too low to care long even for that."

"Dear father, loved father, darling of my heart!" She was clinging to him with her arms, and she got him to drop into his chair again, and caught at the raised arm, and tried to put it round her neck.

"Let it lie there, father. Look at me, father, kiss me, father! Only think of me, father, for one little moment!"

Still he went on in the same wild way, though it was gradually breaking down into a miserable whining.

"And yet I have some respect here. I have made some stand against it. I am not quite trodden down. Go out and ask who is the chief person in the place. They'll tell you it's your father. Go out and ask who is never trifled with, and who is always treated with some delicacy. They'll say, your father. Go out and ask what funeral here (it must be here, I know it can be nowhere else) will make more talk, and perhaps more grief, than any that has ever gone out at the gate. They'll say, your father's. Well then. Amy! Amy! Is your father so universally despised? Is there nothing to redeem him? Will you have nothing to remember him by, but his ruin and decay? Will you be able to have no affection for him when he is gone, poor castaway, gone?"

He burst into tears of maudlin pity for himself, and at length suffering her to embrace him, and take charge of him, let his grey head rest against her cheek, and bewailed his wretchedness. Presently he changed the subject of his lamentations, and clasping his hands about her as she embraced him, cried, O Amy, his motherless, forlorn child! O the days that he had seen her careful and laborious for him! Then he reverted to himself, and weakly told her how much better she would have loved him if she had known him in his vanished character, and how he would have married her to a gentleman who should have been proud of her as his daughter, and how (at which he cried again) she should first have ridden at his fatherly side on her own horse, and how the crowd (by which he meant in effect the people who had given him the twelve shillings he then had in his pocket) should have trudged the dusty roads respectfully.

Thus, now boasting, now despairing, in either fit a captive with the jail-rot upon him, and the impurity of his prison worn into the grain of his soul, he revealed his degenerate state to his affectionate child.

FRENCH PROVERB

A father is a banker provided by nature.

George and Weedon Grossmith

THE DIARY OF A NOBODY

August 4

The first post brought a nice letter from our dear son Willie, acknowledging a trifling present which Carrie sent him, the day before yesterday being his twentieth birthday. To our utter amazement he turned up himself in the afternoon, having journeyed all the way from Oldham. He said he had got leave from the bank, and as Monday was a holiday he thought he would give us a little surprise.

August 5, Sunday

We have not seen Willie since last Christmas, and are pleased to notice what a fine young man he has grown. One would scarcely believe he was Carrie's son. He looks more like a younger brother. I rather disapprove of his wearing a check suit on a Sunday, and I think he ought to have gone to church this morning; but he said he was tired after yesterday's journey, so I refrained from any remark on the subject. We had a bottle of port for dinner, and drank dear Willie's health.

He said: "Oh, by-the-by, did I tell you I've cut my first name, 'William,' and taken the second name 'Lupin'? In fact, I'm known at Oldham as 'Lupin Pooter.' If you were to 'Willie' me there, they wouldn't know what you meant."

Of course, Lupin being a purely family name, Carrie was delighted, and began by giving a long history of the Lupins. I ventured to say that I thought William a nice simple name, and reminded him he was christened after his Uncle William, who was much respected in the City. Willie, in a manner which I did not much care for, said sneeringly: "Oh, I know all about that — Good old Bill!" and helped himself to a third glass of port.

Carrie objected strongly to my saying "Good old," but she made no remark when Willie used the double adjective. I said nothing, but looked at her, which meant more. I said: "My dear Willie, I hope you are happy with your colleagues at the Bank." He replied: "Lupin, if you please; and with respect to the Bank, there's not a clerk who is a gentleman, and the 'boss' is a cad." I felt so shocked, I could say nothing, and my instinct told me there was something wrong . . .

July 1

I find, on looking over my diary, nothing of any consequence has taken place during the last month. To-day we lose Lupin, who has taken furnished apartments at Bayswater . . . at two guineas a week. I think this is most extravagant of him, as it is half his salary. Lupin says one never loses by a good address, and, to use his own expression, Brickfield Terrace is a bit "off." Whether he means it is "far off " I do not know. I have long since given up trying to understand his curious expressions. I said the neighbourhood had always been good enough for his parents. His reply was: "It is no question of being good or bad. There is no money in it, and I am not going to rot away my life in the suburbs."

We are sorry to lose him, but perhaps he will get on better by himself, and there may be some truth in his remark that an old and a young horse can't pull together in the same cart.

Gowing called, and said that the house seemed quite peaceful, and like old times. He liked Master Lupin very well, but he occasionally suffered from what he could not help — youth.

March 20

To-day being the day on which Daisy Mutlar and Mr. Murray Posh are to be married, Lupin has gone with a friend to spend the day at Gravesend. Lupin has been much cut-up over the affair, although he declares that he is glad it is off. I wish he would not go to so many music-halls, but one dare not say anything to him about it. At the present moment he irritates me by singing all over the house some nonsense about "What's the matter with Gladstone? He's all right! What's the matter with Lupin? He's all right!" I don't think either of them is. In the evening Gowing called, and the chief topic of conversation was Daisy's marriage to Murray Posh.

March 21

To-day I shall conclude my diary, for it is one of the happiest days of my life. My great dream of the last few weeks — in fact, of many years — has been realised. This morning came a letter from Mr. Perkupp, asking me to take Lupin down to the office with me. I went to Lupin's room; poor fellow, he seemed very pale, and said he had a bad headache. He had come back yesterday from Gravesend, where he spent part of the day in a small boat on the water, having been mad enough to neglect to take his overcoat with him. I showed him Mr. Perkupp's letter, and he got up as quickly as possible. I begged of him not to put on his fast-coloured clothes and ties, but to dress in something black or quiet-looking.

Carrie was all of a tremble when she read the letter, and all she could keep on saying was: "Oh, I *do* hope it will be all right." For myself, I could scarcely eat any breakfast. Lupin came down dressed quietly, and looking a perfect gentleman, except that his face was rather yellow. Carrie, by way of encouragement said: "You do look nice, Lupin." Lupin replied: "Yes, it's a good make-up, isn't it? A regular-downright-respectable-funereal-first-class-City-firm-junior-clerk." He laughed rather ironically.

In the hall I heard a great noise, and also Lupin shouting to Sarah to fetch down his old hat. I went into the passage, and found Lupin in a fury, kicking and smashing a new tall hat. I said: "Lupin, my boy, what are you doing? How wicked of you! Some poor fellow would be glad to have it." Lupin replied: "I would not insult any poor fellow by giving it to him."

When he had gone outside, I picked up the battered hat, and saw inside *Posh's Patent*. Poor Lupin! I can forgive him. It seemed hours before we reached the office. Mr. Perkupp sent for Lupin, who was with him nearly an hour. He returned, as I thought, crestfallen in appearance. I said: "Well, Lupin, how about Mr. Perkupp?" Lupin commenced his song: "What's the matter with Perkupp? He's all right!" I felt instinctively my boy was engaged. I went to Mr. Perkupp, but I could not speak. He said: "Well, Mr. Pooter, what is it?" I must have looked a fool, for all I could say was: "Mr. Perkupp, you are a good man." He looked at me for a moment, and said: "No, Mr. Pooter, you are the good man; and we'll see if we cannot get your son to follow such an excellent example." I said: "Mr. Perkupp, may I go home? I cannot work any more to-day."

My good master shook my hand warmly as he nodded his head. It was as much as I could do to prevent myself from crying in the 'bus; in fact, I should have done so, had my thoughts not been interrupted by Lupin, who was having a quarrel with a fat man in the 'bus, whom he accused of taking up too much room.

In the evening Carrie sent round for dear old friend Cummings and his wife, and also to Gowing. We all sat round the fire, and in a bottle of *Jackson Freres*, which Sarah fetched from the grocer's, drank Lupin's health. I lay awake for hours, thinking of the future. My boy in the same office as myself — we can go down together by the 'bus, come home together, and who knows but in the course of time he may take great interest in our little home. That he may help me to put a nail in here or a nail in there, or help his dear mother to hang a picture. In the summer he may help us in our little garden with the flowers, and assist us to paint the stands and pots. (By-the-by, I must get in some more enamel paint.) All this I thought over and over again, and a thousand happy thoughts beside. I heard the clock strike four, and soon after fell asleep, only to dream of three happy people — Lupin, dear Carrie, and myself.

Frederick W. Faber

When a father is indulgent, he is more indulgent than a mother. Little ones treat their mother as the authority of rule, and their father as the authority of dispensation.

Ogden Nash

I always found my daughters' beaux
Invisible as the emperor's clothes,
And I could hear of them no more
Than the slamming of an auto door.
My chicks would then slip up to roost;
They were, I finally deduced,
Concealing tactfully, *pro tem*,
Not boys from me but me from them.

Sigmund Freud

ANALYSIS OF A FIVE-YEAR-OLD BOY

FREUD: But only women have children.
HANS: I'm going to have a little girl . . .
FREUD: You'd like to have a little girl.
HANS: Yes, next year I'm going to have one . . .
FREUD: But you can't have a little girl.
HANS: Oh yes, boys have girls and girls have boys.
FREUD: Boys don't have children. Only women, only mummies have children.
HANS: But why shouldn't I?

Walt Whitman

LEAVES OF GRASS

It is I, you women, I make my way,
I am stern, acrid, large, undissuadable, but I love you,
I do not hurt you any more than is necessary for you,
I pour the stuff to start sons and daughters fit for these
    States, I press with slow rude muscle,
I brace myself effectually, I listen to no entreaties,

I dare not withdraw till I deposit what has so long
    accumulated within me.

Through you I drain the pent-up rivers of myself,
In you I wrap a thousand onward years,
On you I graft the grafts of the best-beloved of me and
    America,
The drops I distil upon you shall grow fierce and athletic
    girls, new artists, musicians, and singers,
The babes I beget upon you are to beget babes in their turn,
I shall demand perfect men and women out of my love-
    spendings,
I shall expect them to interpenetrate with others, as I and you
    interpenetrate now,
I shall count on the fruits of the gushing showers of them, as
    I count on the fruits of the gushing showers I give now,
I shall look for loving crops from the birth, life, death,
    immortality, I plant so lovingly now.

Bernard Crick

GEORGE ORWELL — A LIFE

They're awful fun in spite of the nuisance, and as they develop one has one's own childhood over again. I suppose one thing one has to guard against is imposing one's own childhood on the child, but I do think it relatively easy to give a child a decent time nowadays and allow it to escape the quite unnecessary torments that I for instance went through. I'm not sure either that one ought to trouble too much about bringing a child into a world of atomic bombs, because those born now will never have known anything except wars, rationing, etc. and can probably be quite happy against that background if they've had a good psychological start.

E. B. White

The time not to become a father is eighteen years before a world war.

Henry Miller

How can one say no to a child? How can one be anything but a slave to one's own flesh and blood?

Max Lerner

There has been a succession of women's revolutions in America. But watch out for the revolt of the father, if he should get fed up with feeding others, and get bored with being used, and lay down his tools, and walk off to consult his soul.

Henry James Sr.

It is a delight above all delights to see one's children turn out — as ours have done — all that the heart covets in children; and my delight is so full that I sometimes fancy my heart will have to burst for its own relief.

Austin O'Malley

When you are dealing with a child, keep all your wits about you, and sit on the floor.

THROUGH THE EYES OF A CHILD

> A man can deceive his fiancee or his mistress as much as he likes, and, in the eyes of a woman he loves, an ass may pass for a philosopher; but a daughter is a different matter.

> —ANTON CHEKHOV

Alice Munro

DANCE OF THE HAPPY SHADES

My father's boots went ahead. His boots were to me as unique and familiar, as much an index to himself as his face was. When he had taken them off they stood in a corner of the kitchen, giving off a complicated smell of manure, machine oil, caked black mud, and the ripe and disintegrating material that lined their soles. They were a part of himself, temporarily discarded, waiting. They had an expression that was dogged and uncompromising, even brutal, and I thought of that as part of my father's look, the counterpart of his face, with its readiness for jokes and courtesies. Nor did that brutality surprise me; my father came back to us always, to my mother and me, from places where our judgment could not follow.

Nicholas Mosley

RULES OF THE GAME

Even when my parents were at Savehay Farm they often dallied in other parts of the garden. There was a rose-garden where my father sometimes walked: he would go to and fro, up and down; preparing his speeches, I suppose, by which he might order the world. In summer he would sometimes walk there naked: Nanny would warn us — Do not go near! God walked thus, I suppose, in the Garden of Eden. So by seeing my father, or God, naked, might one know the difference between good and evil? I would creep along the passage on the first floor to where there was a window that looked over the rose-garden: this was risky because the window was in my father's bedroom: but if he was in the rose-garden he could not — or could he? — be in two places at once? However then, after all — how white and gentle and vulnerable he looked! So what was all the fuss about our not being allowed to see him in the rose-garden?

My father was, it was true, sometimes frightening. He had a way of suddenly switching from being the benign joker to someone with his chin up, roaring, as if he were being strangled. He would usually roar when he was not getting what he wanted — from servants; from my mother. Once when he was trying to work in his study and a small dog that belonged to my sister and myself was outside on the lawn barking, he leaned out of his window with his shotgun and fired off both barrels in the general direction of the dog. The dog stopped barking. My sister and Nanny were somewhat outraged at this; but I remember thinking — He would not have missed, would he, if he had been aiming at the dog? And how more efficiently do you stop a dog barking?

Nanny would tell stories of my father's terrible rudeness to servants: but she would add — "He was only once rude to me." Then she would wait, looking stern; and we children would understand that she had perhaps just looked thus at my father. She also told a story about Mabel, the parlourmaid, an equally formidable woman who was the friend of May, the gentle housemaid. Once my father had been rude to Mabel and then to her too he had never been rude again: she had answered him back with a very rude word. We knew it was no good pressing Nanny to tell us what was this word: it was something that grown-ups could tell stories about, but not utter.

My mother's and father's end of the house was somewhat secret; taboo. You went along the passage, up three steps, and were on the threshold of mysteries. My mother's bedroom was large and blue and airy and had a mass of small glass ornaments on shelves: they were of animals and birds and of a kind that would now probably be thought rather vulgar: my mother collected these when she went abroad, especially in Venice. My father's bedroom was smaller and brown and looked out on to the rose-garden: there was a scrubbed oak chest in it that was always locked. Of even deeper mystery were my mother's and father's bathrooms — there were two side by side across the passage. My mother's bathroom had the usual array of bottles and bowls and powders and creams; my father's had an enigmatic apparatus that hung on the back of the door and looked like a gutted octopus. I knew it was no use asking Nanny about this: the subject would be unmentionable like the word used by Mabel the parlourmaid. I worked out later that it was an apparatus for giving enemas.

When the children came down in the evenings at Savehay Farm we went not to the formal drawing room which was used only when guests were in the house, but to my mother's sitting room which was known as the Garden Room. This had low beams and a huge open fireplace and glass walking sticks hanging on the walls: there my mother would read to us. Once my father was persuaded to read poetry: he read Swinburne, and I fell asleep, and when I woke was covered with confusion. I wanted to ask — but might not such beautiful noises be supposed to send you to sleep?

There were certain moments of the year when it was the tradition that mothers and fathers should make special efforts with their children; the most striking of these was Christmas. After the usual opening of the stockings at Savehay Farm and the going to church with Nanny (my mother and father never went to church) and after further presents and the Christmas lunch, we had our special ritual. My father would say that he had to have a short sleep; we would exhort him not to, because after lunch was the time when Father Christmas arrived and my father might miss him. My father would promise that he would only have a nap, and be there for Father Christmas. But then at about three o'clock we would hear Father Christmas's sleigh-bells outside — this was my mother and Mabel the parlourmaid tinkling away in the garden — and we wanted to wake up my father but it was held to be too late: we were rushed out of the house by Nanny: Father Christmas was said to be already arriving at the top of the chimney. Father Christmas was of course my father, who in his study having dressed up in Father Christmas clothes complete with realistic beard and mask was now climbing up the Garden Room chimney on a stepladder held by May the housemaid while we were hoping to see him coming down from the sky at the top. We were again too late! Father Christmas was already on his way down the chimney — we were rushed back into the house just in time to see him emerge into the Garden Room down the steps held by May. All this was expertly handled by my mother — or else we children were rather thick. But my father was a very good actor: he spoke in a slow exhausted voice: poor Father Christmas! with all the other children in the world to get round to! one should not ask too many questions. And of course he had to wear a mask, to protect his face from soot. Anyway there was not much time: after we had got our presents from his sack we were rushed out of the house to see if we could catch him coming out of the roof: we just missed him again! but couldn't we hear the sleigh bells? And then after a suitable time of chasing bells around the garden there was the business of running back to my father's study and accusing him of being, yet again, so greedy and lazy that he had to go to sleep after lunch and miss Father Christmas! After a time I think I came to believe that Father Christmas must come from Harrods. Neither my sister nor I saw through my father's act while he was doing it.

There was a further ritual on Christmas evening which my father once more dominated and by which he charmed his children as indeed he charmed women. Just as my mother, when he was being loving towards her, was his mutton, his moo-moo; so were his children, as his term of endearment, porkers. When we children were making too much noise in his presence he would intone, as if it were some mystic mantra—"What is it that makes more noise than one porker stuck under a gate?"—and we would groan, because we had heard the answer so many times before: and then he would give the answer himself—"Two porkers stuck under a gate!"—and then he would laugh, with a strange clicking sound behind his teeth. On Christmas evenings, then, we would gather round the Christmas tree and we would all hold hands and my father would begin one of his mantra chants and this would go faster and faster as we went faster and faster round the tree until we all fell down and my father's chant would be just—Porker porker porker . . .

All this was rather magical for children: the gods descended, and played, and put on a tremendous performance.

Robert Morley and Sewell Stokes

ROBERT MORLEY— RESPONSIBLE GENTLEMAN

"Mother, before she married, kept house for her parents. Often when a number of her married brothers and sisters returned home with their respective families they would sit down twenty or twenty-five around the dining-room table. Mother's time was fully occupied. She had a genius for ordering meals and pacifying cooks. Those must have been the happiest days of her life. Sometimes, after her own marriage, she would return to The Grange with my sister and myself, but never, I imagine, with the same feeling of security, and never with my father who, understandably perhaps, didn't really get on with my mother's relatives. According to him, they were far too ready to criticise, and not always prepared to help with his endless financial crises as they arose. They were definitely more sober-minded than he was, but then almost anybody would be. Each was shocked at the other's attitude towards money. Father was all for spending the stuff, or giving it away to the bookmakers. But the Fass family had been brought up to conserve capital. On the whole, I believe my father was the wiser, on this point at least. Unhappiness is more often caused by having money than by trying to get hold of some. The endless hoarding of possessions, the poring over bank statements, the gloating over savings accounts, the study of market reports, all corrupt and enfeeble. There is real tragedy in the death of a rich man. Whoever said, 'Where a man's treasure is there will his heart be also,' knew what he was talking about. Too many hearts are locked up in the vaults of the great banks.

"That was one thing my father really disliked—banks. He would stand at street corners counting them and shaking his stick at them. 'You see,' he used to say to me, 'how banks flaunt themselves. All the best building sites are owned and occupied by them. Banks should be up side streets like brothels—theirs is an evil trade.' Not that my father was a moral man. I don't believe he had any particular feelings about brothels, but he found it convenient to link them with banks in order to illustrate his theory. Besides, the mention of brothels used to shock my mother's maiden sisters, for whom he affected a great dislike. If my sister Margaret and I ever annoyed him beyond endurance, he would charge us with growing up like them. 'You'll end up like your Aunt Sophie,' he'd murmur darkly; poor, blameless Aunt Sophie, who once had thrown his copy of the *Sporting Times* onto the fire, lest it should contaminate the housemaids. The row which followed that gesture lasted for ever. My father never forgave or forgot . . .

"He was a gambler, my father; a dedicated, convinced card, horses and roulette player. There wasn't a game of chance that didn't attract him, that he was able, or indeed wished, to resist. He gambled before he was twenty and was still gambling after he was seventy, with an energy and enthusiasm that, had he employed it in any other occupation, must have brought him fame, fortune, or political honour. He hardly ever won any money. It was strictly a one-way traffic. And it was when a crisis blew up that he needed the revolver. He would take to his bed and threaten to shoot himself unless someone produced the money he owed, and gave it to him at once. There actually *was* a way of getting the money, because Father's parents, realising that their son was unlikely ever to have any capital if he was able to get his fingers on it, tied up what money there was in an elaborate series of what are called 'entails.' 'There has never been an entail,' Father would boast, 'through which a good lawyer can't drive a coach and horse.' It was our job to find the coachman. What made the search so exciting was that there was always a deadline, Father having committed himself to some impossible condition, and period, for repaying the money he'd borrowed."

I asked if the family had seriously believed Major Morley would shoot himself if they let him down; if that was why they always came to his rescue in the nick of time.

"I rather think it was just that we didn't want him to let himself down by **not** shooting himself," said Morley. "In spite of the ever-recurring crises, the humiliations, the disappointments, the gradual withdrawal of his friends and relatives, who one by one refused to go on financing him, Father remained a resolute and cheerful optimist. He lived a happier life, more full of enjoyment, than many sober, honest citizens. He was always on the brink of winning a fortune. Most people are on the brink of losing one.

"Father was the kindest of men. He had immense charm, good looks, and was nearly always cheerful. Only very occasionally would he look tired or worn—a sure sign that he had had a winning day. Sometimes, during holidays abroad, he used to appear briefly on the steps of the Casino at Dieppe, or Le Touquet, clutching a thousand-franc note. 'Take this,' he would say to my sister and myself, 'before the rats get it.' Take it we did, and scooted. If we'd still been there five minutes later, he'd have been back, demanding it as a small, temporary loan.

"There were, however, times when Father temporarily abandoned the racetrack and the green baize, and explored other means of ruining himself. If Mother remonstrated with him, he used to say, 'All I'm trying to do, Daisy, is to make a few pennies for you and the children.' One of his tries was to buy a derelict tea shop, in which he served coffee made from a secret recipe of his own, and furnish the pavement outside with chairs and tables. It was to be the first of the English cafes: 'Like they have in Paris, dear,' he said. 'Later I shall get a licence, but meanwhile, if you and your sister will sit outside occasionally, and pretend to be drinking coffee, it will help to make the place look a bit fuller.' So great was his faith in my sister Margaret and myself as decoy ducks, that he imagined the public fighting for the privilege of sitting beside us. The cafe was situated off Kensington High Street. The agent who'd rented it to him estimated that some tens of thousands of people passed it every day. Unfortunately, they continued to pass. I don't know where Father made his mistake. Perhaps he chose the wrong site. Or the wrong children? Nobody seemed to want to join us. Or, of course, it could have been that people just don't care about sitting out on the pavement in the middle of December . . .

"We once had a house on the Thames with a balcony overlooking the street, on which Father used to appear opening his mouth and pretending to sing while a Caruso record spun round on the gramophone concealed in the room behind him. It was while we were here that he spent several evenings writing a long and enormously sentimental poem about a wedding. He was inordinately proud of it, and read it to us aloud. Stung perhaps by our lack of enthusiasm—a poet's relatives are seldom encouraging—he told us that not only was it a far better poem than any of us believed it to be, but that it could make him a fortune. He advertised it in the agony column of *The Times*. 'Is there,' the advertisement read, 'an After-Life? If in doubt, send three shillings to Major Morley at the address below.' The poem, which alas I no longer have, but which Father had printed on a white card, wasn't remotely connected with the promise, or indeed the threat, of an after-life, and must greatly have confused the very few people who responded to the invitation. As always, Father accepted defeat gracefully. 'It's just that very few people are interested in an afterlife,' he observed, as he rewound the gramophone.

"My natural pride in my father," Morley went on, "was strengthened by his ability, when helping himself to treacle, to stand first on a chair, then on the table itself, and with a spoon held high above his head direct the golden treacle accurately on to the roly-poly pudding. A feat I myself have never succeeded in emulating!

"It was Father, too, who walking with me one day in Hyde Park, and not paying much attention to what I was saying, gave me permission to walk fully clothed into the Serpentine. The illicit pleasure I experienced as the water soaked my sailor trousers gave way to something like panic before it reached my knees. I stood alone and dismayed in the middle of the lake, afraid to move in either direction, screaming. When I was finally hauled out by a park-keeper, the small but hostile crowd which had collected were under the impression that Father had tried to drown me — an impression he did nothing to dispel. Mother, who had been walking ahead with my sister, hurried back and asked Father what on earth he had been thinking of. 'My dear Daisy,' he said, 'it's no use trying to coddle the child, he must learn to find things out for himself.' With that he walked off briskly to his club, leaving Mother with her sodden and still screaming son to manage as best she could. Managing bravely was a habit Mother had to acquire after her marriage. To learn for the first time that dishes have to be washed after a meal, fires relighted after they've gone out, that beds require making and potatoes peeling — these are tiresome enough lessons to learn at any age. But I'm sure it was the feeling of insecurity that she came most to dread. How she ever came to marry my father, and why, were questions one longed to ask her. But somehow neither my sister nor I ever did. It would have seemed ungrateful. And I was very grateful to both my parents. They so exactly balanced each other."

Simone Signoret

NOSTALGIA
ISN'T WHAT IT USED TO BE

In 1945, after five years absence, my father reappeared. He was in uniform. His paths had taken him from London to Accra, from Accra to New York, and from New York back to London. He found his pretty child pregnant thanks to the labors of a director who had never directed anything and, just to round everything off, was the younger brother of a Colonel Allegret who was my father's direct superior in the chain of command that led to General de Gaulle. Decidedly, I was accumulating my gaffes as far as the Allegret family was concerned. His pretty child, who had been a virgin schoolgirl when he had last seen her, was now an actress without a contract, a future unwed mother . . .

My father returned to New York, where he trained most of the United Nations simultaneous interpreters. Then he went to Strasbourg, where he did the same for the Council of Europe. He is eminently respected and liked by all who have worked with him. We really missed each other, he and I. Of course, he had the joy of sharing my "triumphs," like my Oscar, but we never shared the bad times.

Don Coleman

I never saw my father nude
Because he thought it very rude.

Barbara Trapido

NOAH'S ARK

Camilla could tell that Noah was very fond of her mother. He always began his visits by kissing her on the mouth in that sloppy, wet, way that grown-ups had, which seemed to go on forever, Noah was "in love" with her mother. Camilla knew this without any doubt because there was a big new glossy book on the piano at home, of Matisse paintings, which must have cost absolutely pounds, she guessed, and inside it said "For Al, because I love her." Noah had given the book to her mother and had signed it with his name, Matisse was her mother's favourite painter, but Matisse didn't make Ali cry. Not like Schubert . . .

It was strange to think of Noah being "in love" at all, really, because he was quite old and he didn't look anything like the pictures of men in *Real Life Photo-Love Stories* which one of the girls had brought to school. In fact, he looked a bit like her father's Uncle Morrie who had used to run a men's outfitters in Southend and who used to wear those spiralled wire elasticky things like bicycle clips around his upper arms to hitch up his shirt sleeves. Noah didn't wear those, of course, and he looked more important, but he did have short arms and he did wear dowdy, old-fashioned white underpants with Y-fronts that looked huge and embarrassing on the washing line over the bath. Camilla knew it was silly and childish to react that way but the Y-fronts bothered her. There was something about them that made her squeamish — like jock straps — because they were so exclusively for men. She was not sure if Y-fronts were so that men could pee without having the bother of undoing their trousers, or whether they had to do with that other strange and dreadful thing she knew men did with that disconcerting appendage which afflicted their nether parts. Did Y-fronts mean they could do it without even taking their underpants off? Ugh!

Mervyn's underpants hadn't had Y-fronts. They had been small black bikini pants and not very different from her mother's pants really, except that the cloth had been thicker. In fact Ali had used to borrow them sometimes in cold weather which had made Mervyn furious, but then he had always been blowing-up about something or other in that scary way. Camilla's own feelings of relief about her father's departure caused her frequent nightly sessions of fear and guilt, but these had suddenly abated in Noah's house. Her father was a lot younger than Noah and he was more slim and natty-looking but for years now he had made her flinch and shrink. Camilla didn't understand about people getting married and then making each other so miserable, because in story books they got married and they lived happily and had lots of children who went on picnics and came home from boarding school — that was unless they died first. It would be lovely to get married in a long dress and have confetti and lots of children, she thought, so long as you could adopt the children and not have to do that dreadful thing together in bed every time you wanted to have another baby. But Noah wouldn't make anybody unhappy if he were married to them because he was so sensible and quiet and fair.

Bob Copper

EARLY TO RISE —
A SUSSEX BOYHOOD

Father usually made an appearance about tea-time which was heralded by a great deal of banging and foot-scraping outside before his actual arrival indoors. Having deposited in the corner of the scullery by the copper his perks for the day, a mess of rape greens, a sack of tail-corn for the chickens or a brace of rabbits — for he seldom returned home empty-handed — he would stand for a while, framed in the kitchen door-way, as if to allow time for the mutual appreciation of his homecoming to take full effect.

To me, from the level of the hearth-rug, he was a pair of huge hob-nailed boots and corduroy trousers tied in beneath the knees with leather

straps called "yorkers" and again at the waist by a stout leather belt with
a large, rectangular brass buckle, but which actually relied for suspension
upon a pair of heavy leather-thonged braces. His entrance introduced a
feeling of family completion and set the scene for an entirely different
atmosphere.

Bingo's barked greeting accompanied by ecstatic wrigglings and tail-
wagging at the sight of his master were cut short by a stern instruction,
"Box!" whereupon he would retire dutifully to his sack-upholstered bed
in the corner, lie down with his chin resting on the edge and watch
father's every move.

Father was seated again at the end of the day in his favourite fireside
chair. After removing his boots and placing them on the hearth to dry,
he would rub his feet together, as a grasshopper does his hind legs, to
remove the chaff and barley-beards that clung to the hand-knitted stitches,
then, stretching his legs out before him and wiggling his toes he would
throw back his head and let off a great sigh of satisfaction. "Aaaa-agh!
We got round ag'in, then." Something attempted, something done, he
had indeed earned a night's repose.

Taking off his yorkers to hang them on the special nail under the
mantelshelf beside the slate on which he wrote the farm orders for the
following day, and reaching for his slippers, he would wipe his sweat-
damp forehead and settle down to a large mug of tea before going into
the scullery for a great, sploshing wash under the brass tap at the sink,
puffing, snorting and blowing the air through his lips with a bubbling
sound as if he was grooming a horse. Wetting a comb under the tap he
would part his hair and smarm it down on either side, then lift the front
up into a smart and fashionable quiff. "How's that then?" he'd say,
turning to us with a caricatured grin. "Tapolene, that is. The poor man's
macassar-oil!" Then he would take up his place at the table.

As the man of the house, in those days, was the only wage-earner
and source of income, his physical welfare was a matter of great importance and so it naturally followed that father was the best-fed member
of the family. For a start, his was the largest plate and on it were placed
the choicest pieces of meat, the middle-cut of the suet pudding, the
biggest potatoes, the roundest and firmest of Brussels sprouts, the whitest
part of the cauliflower or the shapeliest carrots. As mother brought his
dinner in from the scullery and set it down before him towering high
above a moat of rich, brown gravy, it gave off delicious clouds of steam
that made us wish we hadn't had ours at midday and still had some to
come.

Like any other job he tackled, father went about eating a meal in a brisk and workmanlike manner. With the exception of a dusting of salt and pepper, he spurned the use of condiments and maintained that "hunger was the best sauce." His cutlery was highly individual. The inscription on the handle of the heavily-plated fork named its owners as "The Pullman Car Company Ltd." and his wooden-handled knife had a broad blade of pliable steel shaped rather like a miniature kukri with which, despite maternal mutterings of disapproval, he would shovel up green peas by the mouthful or scrape every vestige of gravy from his plate when the meal was finished. He had found the knife in the swill when he had been feeding the pigs so it had probably come from the kitchens of one of the big hotels in Brighton and somehow found its way into the pig bucket. No meal for father would have been the same without it and we had to give it special treatment on the knife-board on cutlery-cleaning day.

With the meal over, he would turn his chair to the fire and sometimes take me on his knee, while I explored the contours of his face, which long exposure to wind and weather was beginning to etch into countless wrinkles like sand on the foreshore at low tide. It was a familiar and reassuring landscape, the generously proportioned nose, the unobtrusive moustache, the tiny warts at the corners of the eyes and, most intriguing of all, the pupil of the right eye that was shaped like a tiny key-hole.

Evenings were not the dull affairs some younger people may imagine them to have been. Father was the type of man who could never sit idle. Though his day's work on the hills had left him physically tired, he would spend the evenings, particularly in winter, making rabbit-nets or mending watches and clocks and I was always perfectly content to sit and watch. He once made a most unusual bird-cage for a favourite bullfinch named Joey. Joey had a very smart appearance with a russet-red breast, a grey back and a neat, black skull-cap and with his engaging ways became almost like one of the family. The cage was so designed that he was unable to get to either his seed or water without considerable initiative and effort. The seed was contained in a small, four-wheeled trolley at the lower end of a sloping runway about six inches long and was attached to the wires of the cage by a fine-linked chain. Joey soon discovered that the only way to get a meal was to raise the trolley up the runway by pulling the chain with his beak and holding it fast to the perch with one of his claws to prevent it running back. On the opposite side of the cage he got his water in a similar manner through a hole in the floor of an over-hanging balcony by hauling on a chain attached to a small, silver thimble which rested in a jar of water directly beneath. He appeared to enjoy working for his living and after a cropful of rape-seed or crushed hemp washed down with a thimbleful of water he would send forth a burst of trilling song or pipe a bar or two of some tune father had painstakingly taught him.

Like as not, while busily engaged on the job in hand, while mother's knitting-needles clicked away busily on the other side of the hearth, father would break into song himself, often with one of his own father's old songs.

> Sometimes I do reap and sometimes I do mow
> At other times to hedging and to ditching I do go
> There's nothing comes amiss to me from the harrow to the
>   plough
> That's how I get my living by the sweat of my brow.

> When I get home at night just as tired as I be
> I take my youngest child and I dance him on my knee
> The others come around me with their prittle prattling toys
> And that's the only pleasure a working man enjoys.

It really was remarkable how closely cottage life at that time still resembled that depicted in those old songs many of which, even then, were well over a hundred years old.

Billie Holiday

LADY SINGS THE BLUES

Pop always wanted to blow the trumpet but he never got the chance. Before he got one to blow, the Army grabbed him and shipped him overseas. It was just his luck to be one of the ones to get it from poison gas over there. It ruined his lungs. I suppose if he'd played piano he'd probably have got shot in the hand.

Virginia Woolf

This is going to be fairly short; to have father's character done complete in it and mother's; and St. Ives and childhood; and all the usual things I try to put in — life, death, etc. But the centre is father's character, sitting in a boat, reciting "We perished, each along," while he crushes a dying mackerel.

e e cummings

MY FATHER MOVED THROUGH DOOMS OF LOVE

my father moved through dooms of love
through sames of am through haves of give,
singing each morning out of each night
my father moved through depths of height

this motionless forgetful where
turned at his glance to shining here;
that if (so timid air is firm)
under his eyes would stir and squirm

newly as from unburied which
floats the first who, his april touch
drove sleeping selves to swarm their fates
woke dreamers to their ghostly roots

and should some why completely weep
my father's fingers brought her sleep:
vainly no smallest voice might cry
for he could feel the mountains grow.

Lifting the valleys of the sea
my father moved through griefs of joy;
praising a forehead called the moon
singing desire into begin

joy was his song and joy so pure
a heart of star by him could steer
and pure so now and now so yes
the wrists of twilight would rejoice

keen as midsummer's keen beyond
conceiving mind of sun will stand,
so strictly (over utmost him
so hugely) stood my father's dream

his flesh was flesh his blood was blood:
no hungry man but wished him food;
no cripple wouldn't creep one mile
uphill to only see him smile.

Scorning the pomp of must and shall
my father moved through dooms of feel;
his anger was as right as rain
his pity was as green as grain

septembering arms of year extend
less humbly wealth to foe and friend
than he to foolish and to wise
offered immeasurable is

proudly and (by octobering flame
beckoned) as earth will downward climb,
so naked for immortal work
his shoulders marched against the dark

his sorrow was as true as bread:
no liar looked him in the head;
if every friend became his foe
he'd laugh and build a world with snow.

My father moved through theys of we,
singing each new leaf out of each tree
(and every child was sure that spring
danced when she heard my father sing)

then let men kill which cannot share,
let blood and flesh be mud and mire,
scheming imagine, passion willed,
freedom a drug that's bought and sold

giving to stead and cruel kind,
a heart to fear, to doubt a mind,
to differ a disease of same,
conform the pinnacle of am

though dull were all we taste as bright,
bitter all utterly things sweet,
maggoty minus and dumb death
all we inherit, all bequeath

and nothing quite so least as truth
—i say though hate were why men
        breathe—
because my father lived his soul
love is the whole and more than all

Francis Steegmuller

COCTEAU: A BIOGRAPHY

"I should like some Freudian to tell me the meaning of a dream I had several times a week beginning when I was ten. The dream stopped in 1912. My father, who was dead, was not dead. He had turned into a parrot in the *Pre Catelan*, one of those parrots whose squawking is always associated in my mind with the taste of foamy milk. In this dream my mother and I were about to sit down at a table in the farm of the *Pre Catelan*, which seemed to combine several farms and the cockatoo terrace of the *Jardin d'Acclimatation*. I knew that my mother knew, and that she didn't know that I knew, and it was clear to me that she was trying to discover which of the birds it was that my father had turned into, and why he had turned into that bird. I awoke in tears because of the expression on her face: she was trying to smile."

Don Coleman

I NEVER SAW MY FATHER NUDE

Going to the pictures with the old man was a treat
He'd argue with the usherette about "the bloody seat"
Then a bloke would come in, sit right in front of me
Maybe keep his hat on — so I couldn't see
Dad would tell him loudly "take off that bleedin' hat"
And I'd feel so embarrassed I'd die right where I sat

Then we'd eat our doughnuts from the shop next door
He'd drop off to sleep and wheeze and grunt and snore
All the people round us would complain about the din
And shush and tut and — Oh God! — it was bedlam there
    with him

Then the thing I dreaded most would suddenly appear
All lit up from far below the organist was here
Sitting pounding, twisting, beaming, polished organ brightly
    gleaming
All the colours of the rainbow, sounds of symbols, bells-a-
    ringing —
Then my old man started singing

How I longed for it to end, and for darkness to descend
After that the main attraction, Warner Baxter, man of action
Norma Shearer made you weep and sent the old man off to
    sleep

Then the clock said half past ten—all the lights back on
    again
Heralding *God Save the King*—a song my father didn't sing
And all the royalists would frown at my old man still sitting
    down
At last the grand finale came, get to the door down the
    fastest lane
Dodging, weaving, barging, shoving, separating couples
    loving
Must be quick—don't get in line with half an hour to
    closing time
Out of the the cinema, into the street, onto a bus—end of a
    treat!

Theodore Roethke

MY PAPA'S WALTZ

The whiskey on your breath
Could make a small boy dizzy;
But I hung on like death:
Such waltzing was not easy.

We romped until the pans
Slid from the kitchen shelf;
My mother's countenance
Could not unfrown itself.

The hand that held my wrist
Was battered on one knuckle;
At every step you missed
My right ear scraped a buckle.

You beat time on my head
With a palm caked hard by dirt,
Then waltzed me off to bed
Still clinging to your shirt.

Jan Kerouac

BABY DRIVER

Toward late fall my mother was going to court all the time to try and get child support from our fathers. She must have gotten fed up with waitressing. The day was nearing when I was to meet my father for the first time. I remember a certain gullible part of my young mind thinking that nine and a half must be the age when one was gown-up enough to meet one's father for the first time. It meant I was maturing — a big girl now. Feeling more independent than usual, I went to the pizza parlor all the way up on Fourteenth Street. I had had my hair curled for the occasion, and as I watched the guy twirl the dough, I kept looking in the mirror at my new hair, not at all sure I liked it and worrying what my father would think of me.

In Brooklyn the next day, after a long subway ride, my mother and I met Jack and his lawyer at the appointed place and went strolling down the street together. I couldn't take my eyes off my father, he looked so much like me. I loved the way he shuffled along with his lower lip stuck out.

The lawyer nervously suggested we go somewhere for lunch, and was about to walk into a restaurant when Jack saw a place he liked better, and steered us to a bar across the street, in spite of the lawyer's feeble protests. I thought it was a great idea, wanting, as I did, to be in accord with this naughty bummish fellow. We sat down in a booth, my mother and I facing the two of them, and a hamburger was ordered for me. It was the day the first astronaut went up in space, and the TV up in the corner by the ceiling was showing him up in his capsule all bundled up in glaring black and white.

My mother and father seemed to be getting along just fine, and were talking about old times.

"Yeah," he was saying into his beer, "you always used to burn the bacon," jokingly accusing her. I could see why she had been attracted to him. He was so handsome with his deep blue eyes and dark hair hanging in a few fine wisps on his forehead. I liked hearing them talk about these things they used to do. It made me feel whole, confirmed the suspicions I'd had all along that I was an official bona fide human being with two parents.

After that, we had to go get blood tests, Jack and I, to determine if he was really my father. I felt like we were special somehow, as if our blood was some precious substance the laboratory needed, and we were the only two people in the world that had it. Then we went back to my neighborhood, bringing Jack with us.

As soon as we got to the apartment, he wanted to know where the nearest liquor store was, so I took him by the hand to the one on Tenth Street, proudly walking him past kids I knew as if to say, "See — I have one too."

In the liquor store, he bought a bottle of Harvey's Bristol Cream Sherry. That name is indelibly etched in my memory. As we walked back, he talked to me but seemed shy, like a boy on his first date. I was nervous too, afraid I'd say something stupid.

Upstairs, he sat down at the kitchen table and peeled off the black plastic around the top of the bottle, as my sisters gathered around him curiously. He pointed at each little black peel and, furrowing his brow, said, "Shee im? Shs' Russian — shhs' no good!" He kept doing this, to their delight, and telling my mother, "This one has laughing eyes and this one has melting eyes."

I was a little jealous that he was paying them so much attention, but figured he didn't want to be serious, and me being older, maybe he was afraid we'd have to talk about something he didn't want to think about. So I watched his antics and smiled whenever he looked at me.

To my sisters, he was just another funny guy that came over to visit and entertain them, like Ray Gordon or Pete Rivera. But to me he was something special, he was my very own funny man out of all the others—like their father, Don Olly, was to them.

When he left, leaving the empty bottle surrounded by its debris on the table, I watched him go through the battered old door into the dark hallway, sitting still and staring at his vanishing point almost as if I knew he was coming right back. A few seconds later, he stuck his head back in and said, "Whoops, I forgot my survival hat."

I looked and found his funny smashed blue hat under the chair and handed it to him. He slapped it on his head and turned around to leave again.

"See ya in Janyary!" he called down the hall.

After that meeting with my father, things went on as always, except that the twins and I were closer, having spent the summer together on the Cape. I did my homework every night to the radio, and hung out in the candy stores by day, and every once in a while I'd take out my one souvenir of his visit—the cork from the bottle of sherry—and stare at it, wishing it would hurry up and be Janyary.

Mordecai Richler

HOME SWEET HOME

After the funeral, I was given my father's talis, his prayer shawl, and (oh my God) a file containing all the letters I had written to him while I was living abroad, as well as carbon copies he had kept of the letters he had sent to me.

> December 28, 1959: "Dear Son, Last week I won a big Kosher Turkey, by bowling, when I made the high triple for the week. How I did it I do not know, I guess I was lucky for once, or was it that the others were too sure of themselves, being much better at the game than I am."

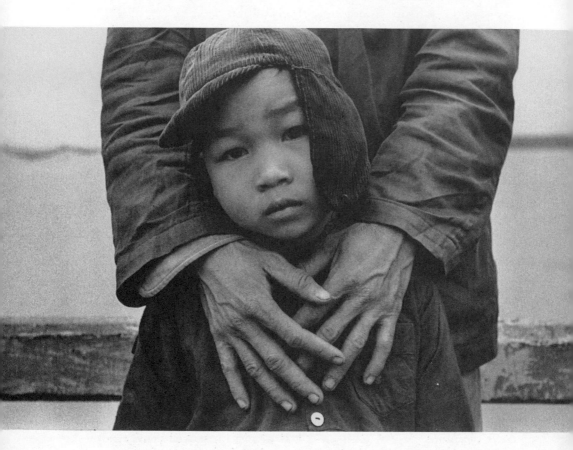

February 28, 1963: "This month has been a cold one, making it difficult, almost impossible to work outside. Yes! it's been tough. Have you found a title for your last novel? What can you do with a title like this? UNTIL DEBT DO US PART?"

His letter of February 28, 1963, like so many others written that year begins, "Thanks for the cheque." For by that time we had come full circle. In the beginning it was my father who had sent checks to me. Included in the file I inherited were canceled checks, circa 1945, for $28 monthly child support, following the annulment of my parents' marriage. A bill dated January 15, 1948, for a Royal portable, my first typewriter; a birthday gift. Another bill, from Bond Clothes, dated August 21, 1950, on the eve of my departure for Europe, for "1 Sta. Wag. Coat, $46.49."

My own early letters to my father, horrendously embarrassing for me to read now, usually begin with appeals for money. No, *demands*. There is also a telegram I'd rather forget. March 11, 1951. IMPERATIVE CHECK SENT PRONTO MADRID C O COOKS WAGON LITS ALCALA NR 23 MADRID, BROKE, MORDECAI.

Imperative, indeed.

I was also left a foot-long chisel, his chisel, which I now keep on a shelf of honour in my workroom. Written with a certain flourish in orange chalk on the oak shaft is my father's inscription:

Used by M I Richler
Richler Artificial Stone Works
1922
De La Roche Street
NO SUCCESS.

My father was twenty years old then, younger than my eldest son is now. He was the firstborn of fourteen children. Surely that year, as every year of his life, on Passover, he sat in his finery at a dining-room table and recited, "We were once the slaves of Pharaoh in Egypt, but the Lord our God brought us forth from there with a mighty hand and an outstretched arm." But, come 1922, out there in the muck of his father's freezing backyard on De La Roche Street in Montreal — yet to absorb the news of his liberation — my father was still trying to make bricks with insufficient straw.

Moses Isaac Richler.

Insufficient straw, NO SUCCESS, was the story of his life. Neither of his marriages really worked. There were searing quarrels with my older brother. As a boy, I made life difficult for him. I had no respect. Later, officious strangers would rebuke him in the synagogue for the novels I had written. Heaping calumny on the Jews, they said. If there was such a thing as a reverse Midas touch, he had it. Not one of my father's penny mining stocks ever went into orbit. He lost regularly at gin rummy. As younger, more intrepid brothers and cousins began to prosper, he assured my mother, "The bigger they come, the harder they fall."

My mother, her eyes charged with scorn, laughed in his face. "You're the eldest and what are you?"

Nothing.

After his marriage to my mother blew apart, he moved into a rented room. Stunned, humiliated. St. Urbain's cuckold. He bought a natty straw hat. A sports jacket. He began to use aftershave lotion. It was then I discovered that he had a bottle of rye whiskey stashed in the glove compartment of his Chevy. My father. Rye whiskey. "What's that for?" I asked, astonished.

"For the femmes!" he replied, wiggling his eyebrows at me. "It makes them want it."

I remember him as a short man, squat with a shiny bald head and big floppy ears. Richler ears. My ears. Seated at the kitchen table at night in his Penman's long winter underwear, wetting his finger before turning a page of the *New York Daily Mirror*, reading Walter Winchell first. Winchell, who knew what's what. He also devoured *Popular Mechanics*, *Doc Savage* and *Black Mask*. And, for educational purposes, *Reader's Digest*. My mother, on the other hand, read Keats and Shelley. *King's Row*. *The Good Earth*. My father's pranks did not enchant her. A metal ink spot on her new chenille bedspread. A felt mouse to surprise her in the larder. A knish secretly filled with absorbent cotton. Neither did his jokes appeal to her. "Hey, do you know why we eat hard-boiled eggs dipped in salt water just before the Passover meal?"

"No, Daddy. Why?"

"To remind us that when the Jews crossed the Red Sea they certainly got their balls soaked." . . .

He was stout, he was fleshy. But in the wedding photographs that I never saw until after his death the young man who was to become my father is as skinny as I once was, his startled brown eyes unsmiling behind horn-rimmed glasses. Harold Lloyd. Allowed a quick no-promises peek at the world and what it had to offer, but clearly not entitled to a place at the table.

My father never saw Paris. Never read Yeats. Never stayed out with the boys drinking too much. Never flew to New York on a whim. Nor turned over in bed and slept in, rather than report to work. Never knew a reckless love. What did he hope for? What did he want? Beyond peace and quiet, which he seldom achieved, I have no idea. So far as I know he never took a risk or was disobedient . . .

My father was afraid of his father. He was afraid of my unhappy mother, who arranged to have their marriage annulled when I was thirteen and my brother eighteen. He was also afraid of his second wife. Alas, he was even afraid of me when I was a boy. I rode streetcars on the Sabbath. I ate bacon. But nobody was ever afraid of Moses Isaac Richler. He was far too gentle . . .

My father never talked to me about anything. Not his own boyhood. His feelings. Or his dreams. He never even mentioned sex to me until I was nineteen years old, bound for Paris to try to become a writer. Clutching my Royal portable, wearing my Sta. Wag. coat. "You know what safes are. If you have to do it — and I know you — use 'em. Don't get married over there. They'd do anything for a pair of nylon stockings or a Canadian passport."

Hot damn, I hoped he was right. But my father thought I was crazy to sail for Europe. A graveyard for the Jews. A continent where everything was broken or old. Even so, he lent me his blue steamer trunk and sent me $50 a month support. When I went broke two years later, he mailed me my boat fare without reproach. I told him that the novel I had written over there was called *The Acrobats* and he immediately suggested that I begin the title of my second novel with a B, the third with a C, and so on, which would make a nifty trademark for me. Writing, he felt, might not be such a nutty idea after all. He had read in *Life* that this guy Mickey Spillane, a mere goy, was making a fortune. Insulted, I explained hotly that I wasn't that kind of writer. I was a serious man.

"So?"

"I only write out of my obsessions."

"Ah, ha," he said, sighing, warming to me for once, recognizing another generation of family failure . . .

So many things about my father's nature still exasperate or mystify me.

All those years he was being crushed by his own father, nagged by my mother, teased (albeit affectionately) by his increasingly affluent brothers and cousins, was he seething inside, plotting a vengeance in his diary. Or was he really not so sweet-natured at all, but a coward? Like me. Who would travel miles to avoid a quarrel. Who tends to remember slights—recording them in my mind's eye—transmogrifying them—finally publishing them in a code more accessible than my father's. Making them the stuff of fiction.

Riddles within riddles . . .

We endured some rough passages together. Shortly after the marriage annulment, I fought with my father. Fists flew. We didn't speak for two years. Then, when we came together again, meeting once a week, it wasn't to talk, but to play gin rummy for a quarter of a cent a point. My father, I began to suspect, wasn't reticent. He didn't understand life. He had nothing to say to anybody.

In 1954, some time after my return to Europe, where I was to remain rooted for almost two decades, I married a *shiksa* in London. My father wrote me an indignant letter. Once more, we were estranged. But no sooner did the marriage end in divorce than he pounced: "You see, mixed marriages never work."

"But, Daddy, your first marriage didn't work either and Maw was a rabbi's daughter."

"What do you know?"

"Nothing," I replied, hugging him.

When I married again, this time for good, but to another *shiksa*, he was not overcome with delight, yet neither did he complain. For after all the wasting years, we had finally become friends. My father became my son. Once, he had sent money to me in Paris. Now, as the scrapyard foundered, I mailed monthly checks to him in Montreal. On visits home, I took him to restaurants. I bought him treats. If he took me to a gathering of the Richler clan on a Sunday afternoon, he would bring along a corked bottle of 7-Up for me, filled with scotch whisky. "There'll be nothing for you to drink there, and I know you."

"Hey, Daddy, that's really very thoughtful."

During the Sixties, on a flying trip to Montreal, my publishers put me up at the Ritz-Carlton Hotel, and I asked my father to meet me for a drink there.

"You know," he said, joining me at the table, "I'm sixty-two years old and I've never been here before. Inside, I mean. So this is the Ritz."

"It's just a bar," I said, embarrassed.

"What should I order?"

"Whatever you want, Daddy."

"A rye and ginger ale. Would that be all right here?"

"Certainly . . ."

What I'm left with are unresolved mysteries. A sense of regret. Anecdotes for burnishing.

My wife, a proud lady, showing him our firstborn son, his week-old howling grandchild, saying, "Don't you think he looks like Mordecai?"

"Babies are babies," he responded, seemingly indifferent.

Some years later my father coming to our house, pressing chocolate bars on the kids. "Who do you like better," he asked them, "your father or your mother?"

In the mid-Sixties, I flew my father to London. He came with his wife. Instead of slipping away with him to the Windmill Theatre or Raymond's Revue Bar, another strip joint, like a fool I acquired theatre tickets. We took the two of them to *Beyond the Fringe*. "What did you think?" I asked as we left the theatre.

"There was no chorus line," he said.

Following his last operation for cancer, I flew to Montreal, promising to take him on a trip as soon as he was out of bed. The Catskills. Grossinger's. With a stopover in New York to take in some shows. Back in London, each time I phoned, his doctor advised me to wait a bit longer. I waited. He died. The next time I flew to Montreal it was to bury him.

Anne Frank

I'm not jealous of Margot [her sister], never have been. I don't envy her good looks or her beauty. It is only that I long for Daddy's real love: not only as his child, but for me — Anne, myself.

Robert Lynd

Happy is the child whose father acquits himself with credit in the presence of its friends.

Robert Drewe

THE MANAGERESS
AND THE MIRAGE

My father wasn't in his element in party hats. His head was too big; the mauve crepe-paper crown stretched around his wide forehead looked neither festive nor humorous, just faintly ridiculous. Annie and David and I sat embarrassed in silly hats as well. They were compulsory fun, Dad was definite about them. We'd always worn them at home and the normal Christmas dinner routine was being followed wherever possible.

There was one major difference this Christmas: because our mother had died in July we were having dinner at the Seaview Hotel instead of at home. Consequently we were observing several other minor variations on our traditional dinner — we ate roast turkey instead of the usual chicken and ham, we children were allowed glasses of pink champagne alongside our glasses of lemonade, and the plum pudding contained plastic tokens like Monopoly symbols — obviously poked into the pudding later — rather than real threepences and sixpences cooked into it.

When Dad suggested that we eat dinner at the hotel we agreed readily enough. Since July we'd had a middle-aged woman, Gladys Barker, housekeeping for us. Dad called her Glad to her face, but to us he sometimes called her Gladly—as in the hymn "Gladly My Cross I'd Bear"—because of her sighs around the house and air of constant martyrdom. We thought this was funny, but at the time we thought he was saying "Gladly, My Cross-Eyed Bear" so we had it wrong for five or six years. Glad's cooking was unexceptional, a depressing prospect for Christmas dinner, and anyway, without anyone spelling it out, this Christmas we wanted to keep the family unit tight and self-contained.

I caught Annie's and David's eyes from time to time, but they showed only a vague self-consciousness as we sat in the hotel dining room in our party hats and school uniforms, picking at our meals, gingerly sipping pink champagne and pulling crackers. Dad was becoming increasingly amiable, however, even hearty. It was clear to us that he was making an effort. He made jokes and we laughed at them, for him rather than with him, out of mutual support.

"Remember I was travelling the other week to a sales conference down at Albany?" he said. "Well, I stopped overnight at Mount Barker. I went down to dinner in the hotel dining room and on the menu was rabbit casserole. I said to the waitress, 'Excuse me, dear, is that with or without myxomatosis?'

" 'I wouldn't know,' she said, very po-faced, 'it's all in the gravy.' "

He was trying hard for all our sakes. It had not dawned on me before that I loved him and the realisation was slightly embarrassing.

Soon he became the dining room's focus of attention. Selecting a plastic whistle from the cracker debris, he blew it gamely. Other nearby guests, observing us and seeing the lie of the land, smiled encouragingly at us and followed suit. An old fellow gave Annie his cracker toy. A fat man tickled his wife's nose with a feathered whistle; she balanced a champagne cork on his sunburnt head. Crackers popped and horns tooted. Above these antics a fan slowly revolved.

Beyond the high expanse of windows the ocean glistened into the west, where atmospheric conditions had magically turned Rottnest Island into three distinct islands. Annie was struck by the mysterious asymmetry of this illusion.

"It's gone wrong," she said loudly, pointing out to sea. The other guests began murmuring about the phenomenon. Annie's plaits looked irregular; one was thicker than the other; Dad still hadn't mastered them. "The lighthouse has gone," she said.

"No, it's still there," Dad said, and tried to explain mirages, mentioning deserts and oases, with emphasis on the Sahara. I knew the horizon was always twelve miles away, but I couldn't grasp the idea of shifting islands or the creation of non-existent ones. So thirsty people in deserts saw visions of water—why would people bursting with food and drink see visions of land?

As our plates were being removed our table drew special attention from the hotel manageress. A handsome dark-haired woman in her thirties, she clapped her hands authoritatively for more champagne, and more crackers for us to pull, and joined us for a drink, inquiring about our presents with oddly curious eyes. Dad introduced us.

She announced to me, "You do look like your father, Max." She remarked on Annie's pretty hair and on the importance of David looking after his new watch. Sportively, she donned a blue paper crown and looked at us over the rim of her champagne glass. As the plum pudding was being served she left the table and returned with gifts for us wrapped in gold paper—fountain pens for David and me, a doll for Annie. Surprised, we looked to Dad for confirmation.

He showed little surprise at the gifts, however, only polite gratitude, entoning several times, "Very, very kind of you."

"Rex, it gave me pleasure," the manageress said. "They're a credit to you." She called him Rex, not Mr. Lang. His eyes were moist at her compliment. He lit a cigar and leaned back in his seat, crown askew, like Old King Cole.

After the plum pudding (he and the manageress had brandies instead) and another cracker pulling we thanked her again for our presents, on his instructions, and he sent us outside while he paid the bill.

"Get some fresh air, kids," he said.

We trooped out to the car park. Before today the car park had been the only part of the Seaview Hotel familiar to us. Sometimes on Saturday mornings we'd languished there, watching the ocean swells roll in, dying for a swim, squabbling in the Ford's back seat or desultorily reading Shell road maps from the glovebox while Dad had a drink or two.

"I have to see a chap about something," he'd say, bringing us out glasses of raspberry lemonade. A frightening hubbub sounded from the bar, yet he would turn and stride back into this noise and smoke and beer-smell with all the cheer in the world.

Outside, the mirage persisted. Rottnest was still three oddly attenuated islands which seemed to be sailing south. The afternoon sea breeze was late and the temperature lingered in the nineties. The heat haze smudged the definition of the horizon and the Indian Ocean stretched flat and slick to Mauritius and beyond before curving into the sky.

David said, "Did you smell her perfume?" and made a face. He loosened his tie and farted from the champagne. Annie poked at her doll's eyes. "I've got one like this called Amanda," she said. We presumed who had given her the other doll yet by unspoken agreement no one mentioned her. I knew the others were thinking that normally at this time we'd be unwrapping presents from the tree. She would play cheery Christmas records on the radiogram and run from the kitchen bringing us mints and nuts and little mince pies.

Eyes remained dry as we walked to the car. The car park was almost empty because of the bars being closed for Christmas. Asphalt bubbled, a broken beer glass from Christmas Eve sat on the verandah rail and the smell of stale beer settled over the beer garden. Around the garden's dusty, worn lawn, red and yellow hibiscuses wilted in the heat. Christmas was running short of breath. One after another, David, Annie and I snatched off our party hats, crumpled them and threw them on the ground.

The imaginary islands, showing smoky silhouettes of hills and tall trees, kept sailing south. From the car you could see into the manageress's office. She was combing his hair where his party hat had ruffled it. He came out whistling "Jingle Bells" and the stench of his cigar filled the car.

Randolph S. Churchill

TWENTY-ONE YEARS

It was at this time that I first discovered in a rather macabre way that my father was different from other fathers and was a great man. I was about five years old at the time and I said to a little boy at school (it makes me blush to recall the episode), "Will you be my chum?" He said, "No." I said, "Why not?" He said, "Your father murdered my father." I said: "What do you mean?" He said, "At the Dardanelles." So when I got home I told this to my mother who was naturally distressed at what had happened and explained to me about the Dardanelles. I am sorry to say it made me feel immensely proud for I realised my father was a boss man who could order other fathers about.

My discovery that my father had exceptional powers was reinforced in a more mundane matter. Often my mother and father were not at Lullenden for many weeks. He was making munitions and she was running a lot of canteens for munition workers. One day we heard that my father was coming down that afternoon at tea time. We had run out of jam. My father has never had tea as a meal in his life. He had always said, "I don't believe in eating between meals." However, we thought that perhaps he would come and sit with us children while we had our tea. So with a precocious sense of propaganda I collected ten or twelve empty jam pots and put them on the tea table. My father is not particularly observant about these sort of things but a collection of twelve empty jam pots caught his eye. He was horrified to learn that we had no jam. The next day several jars arrived.

He seemed to me a very powerful man. He could order the fathers of other boys into battle and could produce jam.

Harold Acton

NANCY MITFORD — A MEMOIR

Her attitude towards her irascible father was ambivalent. Thanks to her strong sense of humour she was able to laugh at his foibles with a secret admiration for the vigorous eccentricity of his character, the externals of which she borrowed for "General Murgatroyd" in her early novel *Highland Fling*, and again for the unforgettable "Uncle Matthew" in *The Pursuit of Love*: "Much as we feared, much as we disapproved of, passionately as we sometimes hated Uncle Matthew, he still remained for us a sort of criterion of English manhood; there seemed something not quite right about any man who greatly differed from him." Uncle Matthew "never altered his first opinion of people . . . his favourites could commit nameless crimes without doing wrong in his eyes . . . He always liked people who stood up to him." An arrant chauvinist, he declared: "I loathe abroad, nothing would induce me to live there, I'd rather live in the game keeper's hut in Hen's Grove, and, as for foreigners, they are all the same, and they make me sick . . ." His fits of temper were profitable to dentists as he invariably ground his false teeth. "There was a legend in the family that he had already ground away four pairs in his rages." Apparently his addiction to literature was limited; "I have only read one book in my life, and that is *White Fang*. It's so frightfully good I've never bothered to read another."

An endearing quality of Lord Redesdale was that far from being offended by this caricature, he was amused by it.

Sue Townsend

THE SECRET DIARY OF ADRIAN MOLE AGED 13¾

Sunday April 12th
Palm Sunday

This weekend with Nigel has really opened my eyes! Without knowing it I have been living in poverty for the past fourteen years. I have had to put up with inferior accommodation, lousy food and paltry pocket money. If my father can't provide a decent standard of living for me on his present salary, then he will just have to start looking for another job. He is always complaining about having to flog electric storage heaters anyway. Nigel's father has worked like a slave to create a modern environment for *his* family. Perhaps if *my* father had built a formica cocktail

bar in the corner of *our* lounge my mother would still be living with us. But oh no. My father actually boasts about our hundred-year-old furniture.

Yes! Instead of being ashamed of our antiques, he is proud of the clapped-out old rubbish.

My father should take lessons from Great Literature. Madame Bovary ran away from that idiot Doctor Bovary because he couldn't supply her needs.

LADIES' HOME JOURNAL

[November 1946]

"My daddy doesn't work, he just goes to the office; but sometimes he does errands on the way home."

Geoffrey Willans

HOW TO BE TOPP

Another thing about xmas eve is that your pater always reads the xmas carol by c. dickens. You cannot stop this aktually although he pretend to ask you whether you would like it. He sa:

Would you like me to read the xmas carol as it is xmas eve, boys?
We are listening to the space serial on the wireless, daddy.
But you cannot prefer that nonsense to the classick c. dickens?
Be quiet. He is out of control and heading for jupiter.
But—
He's had it the treen space ships are ataking him ur–ur–ur–whoosh. Out of control limping in the space vacuum for evermore unless they can get the gastric fuel compressor tampons open.
I—
Why don't they try Earth on the intercom? They will never open those tampons with only a z-ray griper. They will—
Father thwarted strike both boys heavily with loaded xmas stoking and tie their hands behind their backs. He cart them senseless into the sitting room and prop both on his knees. Then he begin:

THE XMAS CAROL by C. DICKENS

(published by grabber and grabber)
Then he rub hands together and sa You will enjoy this boys it is all about ghosts and goodwill. It is tip-top stuff and there is an old man called scrooge who hates xmas and canot understand why everyone is so mery. To this you sa nothing except that scrooge is your favourite character in fiction next to tarzan of the apes. But you can sa anything chiz. Nothing in the world in space is ever going to stop those fatal words:

MARLEY WAS DEAD

Personaly i do not care a d. whether Marley was dead or not it is just that there is something about xmas Carol which makes paters and grown-ups read with grate XPRESION, and this is very embarassing for all. It is all right for the first part they just roll the r's a lot but wate till they come to scrooge's nephew. When he sa Mery Christmas uncle it is like an H-bomb xplosion and so it go on until you get to Tiny Tim chiz chiz chiz he is a weed. When Tiny Tim sa God bless us every one your pater is so overcome he burst out blubbing. By this time boys hav bitten through their ropes and make good their escape so 9000000000 boos to bob cratchit.

PROVERB

[16th century]

It is a wise child that knows its own father.

Alex Haley

THE AUTOBIOGRAPHY OF MALCOLM X

After that, my memories are of the friction between my father and mother. They seemed to be nearly always at odds. Sometimes my father would beat her. It might have had something to do with the fact that my mother had a pretty good education. Where she got it I don't know. But an educated woman, I suppose, can't resist the temptation to correct an uneducated man. Every now and then, when she put those smooth words on him, he would grab her.

My father was also belligerent toward all the children, except me. The older ones he would beat almost savagely if they broke any of his rules — and he had so many rules it was hard to know them all. Nearly all my whippings came from my mother. I've thought a lot about why. I actually believe that as anti-white as my father was, he was subconsciously so afflicted with the white man's brainwashing of Negroes that he inclined to favour the light ones, and I was his lightest child. Most Negro parents in those days would almost instinctively treat any lighter children better than they did the darker ones. It came directly from the slavery tradition that the "mulatto," because he was visibly nearer to white, was therefore "better."

Isadora Duncan

As my mother had divorced my father when I was a baby in arms, I had never seen him. Once, when I asked one of my aunts whether I ever had a father, she replied, "Your father was a demon who ruined your mother's life." After that I always imagined him as a demon in a picture book, with horns and tail, and when other children at school spoke of their fathers, I kept silent.

Sylvia Lady Brooke

QUEEN OF THE HEAD HUNTERS

I think Reginald Baliol Brett will be remembered as one of the geniuses of his time, not in any particular capacity but as a poet, a musician, a litterateur, a polished diplomat, and a brilliant statesman. He could have filled almost any post, but he preferred to be free.

You can imagine the feeling of having a father as fantastic as this; it was like being related to the Encyclopaedia Britannica. In my mother's heart there was no-one greater than Reginald Baliol Brett, except God. What Reggie said, where Reggie went, how Reggie felt, were of the utmost importance to her; the very air she breathed was enchanted by Reggie's rose-tipped cigarettes. He was the substance and body of her existence, her *raison d'être*.

What incredible children should have been born from such a union, instead of the disappointing brood my poor little mother gave birth to!

We were left very much to ourselves in those early days for our parents were too preoccupied—he with his affairs of State, and she with her wifely adoration. So we quarrelled and fought like a litter of small puppies, and bit and scratched our way through the toddling age into the bewilderments of adolescence.

Children should never be left alone to steep their small souls in doubts and fears and torn emotions. Youth should be such a joyous thing; confident and carefree, without panic or dismay, but it was by no means so with me. I was tormented by imaginative fears. I felt that nobody loved me and that I was the cuckoo in this illustrious family nest. It even seemed to me that my father's voice altered when he spoke to me, as if he were forcing his words through cubes of ice. My mother, my dear possessed mother with her compliant love for Reggie, noticed nothing; her children's emotions were totally unable to break into the absorption of her wifely concern. I spent a great deal of my childhood crying my eyes out in a ten-foot by twelve ivy-papered lavatory at the top of the house.

Ted Hughes

MY FATHER

Some fathers work at the office, others work at the store,
Some operate great cranes and build up skyscrapers galore,
Some work in canning factories counting green peas into
    cans,
Some drive all night in huge and thundering removal vans.

But mine has the strangest job of the lot.
My Father's the Chief Inspector of—What?
O don't tell the mice, don't tell the moles,
My Father's the Chief Inspector of HOLES.

It's a work of the highest importance because you never
     know
What's in a hole, what fearful thing is creeping from below.
Perhaps it's a hole to the ocean and will soon gush water in
     tons,
Or maybe it leads to a vast cave full of gold and skeletons.

Though a hole might seem to have nothing but dirt in it,
Somebody's simply got to make certain.
Caves in the mountain, clefts in the wall,
My father has to inspect them all.

That crack in the road looks harmless. My Father knows it's
     not.
The world may be breaking into two and starting at that
     spot.
Or maybe the world is a great egg, and we live on the shell,
And it's just beginning to split and hatch: you simply cannot
     tell.

If you see a crack, run to the phone, run;
My Father will know just what's to be done.
A rumbling hole, a silent hole,
My father will soon have it under control.

Keeping a check on all these holes he hurries from morning
     to night.
There might be sounds of marching in one, or an eye shining
     bright.
A tentacle came groping from a hole that belonged to a
     mouse,
A floor collapsed and Chinamen swarmed up into the house.

A Hole's an unpredictable thing—
Nobody knows what a Hole might bring.
Caves in the mountain, clefts in the wall,
My father has to inspect them all!

PATERNAL GUIDANCE

The words a father speaks to his children in the privacy of the home are not overheard at the time, but, as in whispering galleries, they will be clearly heard at the end and by posterity.

—RICHTER

John Cheever

BULLET PARK

When the extremely shabby scene in the living room ended, Nellie went upstairs and washed away her tears. Then she served dinner so that Tony would not suspect there was anything wrong. At the end of dinner Nailles asked: "Have you done your homework?"

"It's all done," Tony said. "I had two study halls."

"Shall we play some golf?"

"Sure."

Nailles got some putters and balls out of the hall closet and they drove to a miniature golflinks off Route 64. The links, Nailles guessed, had been built in the thirties. There were deep water traps, bridges and a windmill. The place had long ago gone to seed and had then been abandoned. The water traps were dry, the windmill had lost its sails and the greens were bare concrete but most of the obstacles were intact and on summer nights men and boys still played the course although there were no trespassing signs all over the place. There were no lights, of course, but that was a summer night and there was light in the sky. A little wind was blowing from the west and there was thunder across the river. When Nailles described the scene to himself, as he would a hundred times or more, his description followed these lines.

"I was ashamed of having quarreled with Nellie and I kept blaming the whole thing on psychological motives and mouthwash. If I hadn't gone to Westfield none of this would have happened. Tony led off and I remember feeling very happy to be with him. I taught him how to putt and he has a nice stance. I gave up golf four years ago but I thought I might take it up again. We would play together. I know he isn't handsome—his nose is too big and he had a bad color—but he's my

son and I love him. Well, it was windy and there was some thunder on
the other side of the river. I remember the thunder because I remember
thinking how much I liked the noise of thunder. It seems to me a very
human sound, much more human than the sound of jet planes; and
thunder always reminds me of what it felt like to be young. We used to
belong to the country club when I was a kid and I went to all the
dances — assemblies — and when I hear the music we used to dance to
— 'Rain' and 'The Red, Red Robin' — and so forth I remember what it
felt like going to dances when you're seventeen and eighteen, but thunder
refreshes my memory much better. It isn't that I feel young when I hear
thunder, it's just that I can remember what it felt like to be young. We
shot the second hole at par and on the third hole you're supposed to
make your ball loop through an old automobile tire. I had some trouble
with this. Tony said: 'You know what, Dad?' and I said, 'What?' and
he said, 'I'm going to leave school.'

"Well this got me off-guard. It really spilled me. The idea had never
crossed my mind. The first thing I figured out was that I mustn't lose
my temper. I must be reasonable and patient and so forth. He was only
seventeen. I worked out a reasonable and a patient character like a character in a play. Then I tried to act the part. What it really felt like was
that patience was this big woolly blanket and I was wrapping myself up
in it but it kept slipping. So I said very patiently, 'Why, Tony?' and he
said because he wasn't learning anything. He said that French was all
grief and English was even worse because he read more than the teacher.
Then he said that astronomy was just a gut course and that his teacher
was senile. He said that whenever the teacher turned off the lights for a
film strip everybody took naps and threw spitballs and that once the
teacher cried when they piled out of the class in the middle of a sentence.
He said that when he got to the door he looked back and saw the teacher
crying. So he went up to him and explained that they didn't mean to be
rude, they just didn't want to be late for the next class, and then he said
that the teacher said that nobody understood him, that he loved his
students, he loved them all. Then Tony said he didn't think too much
of a teacher who cried. Well, then we played the fifth hole where you
have to get your ball through a gate. I did this in par but he was three
over and we went on talking. I said that he had to get his diploma. I
asked him what he was planning to do without a diploma and he said
he thought he might do some social work in the slums. He said there
was this place for children with disturbed parents and he thought he
might work there. Well, I was having trouble with my patience, my

woolly blanket. It kept slipping. I said that if he wanted to do social work that was all right with me and I felt sure it would be all right with his mother but first he had to get his diploma. I said I guessed that social work like everything else needed training and preparation and that after he got his diploma I and his mother would be happy to send him on to some college where he could get training as a social worker. So then he said he couldn't see what was the good of a diploma if he wasn't learning anything. He said it was just a phony, just a phony scrap of paper like a phony treaty. Then I said that phony or not you had to observe some of the rules of the game. I said that trousers, for instance, weren't perhaps the most comfortable form of clothing but it was one of the rules of the game that you wear trousers. I asked him what would happen if I went to the train bare-ass and he said he didn't care if I went to the train bare-ass. He said I could go to the train bare-ass as far as he was concerned. By this time we'd stopped playing and that was when these other men, men or boys, asked if they could play through and we said yes and stood aside.

"It was windy, as I say, and there was more thunder and it looked like rain and the light on the course was failing so you really couldn't see the faces of the men who played through. They were high school kids, I guess, slum kids, hoods, whatever, wearing tight pants and trick shirts and hair grease. They had spooky voices, they seemed to pitch them in a way that made them sound spooky, and when one of them was addressing the ball another give him a big goose and he backed right into it, making groaning noises. It isn't that I dislike boys like that really, it's just that they mystify me, they frighten me because I don't know where they come from and I don't know where they're going and if you don't know anything about people it's like a terrible kind of darkness. I'm not afraid of the dark but there are some kinds of human ignorance that frighten me. When I feel this I've noticed that if I can look into the face of the stranger and get some clue to the kind of person he is I feel better but, as I say, it was getting dark and you couldn't see the faces of any of these strangers as they played through. So they played through and we went on talking about his diploma and the rules of the game. I said that whatever he wanted to do he had to train himself for it, he had to prepare himself. I said that even if he wanted to be a poet he had to prepare himself to be a poet. So then I said to him what I've never said before. I said: 'I love you, Tony.'

"So then he said, 'The only reason you love me, the only reason you think you love me is because you can give me things.' Then I said this wasn't true, that the only reason I was a generous father was because my own father hadn't given me very much. I said that because my own father had been so tight was why I wanted to be generous. So then he said: 'Generous, generous, generous, generous.' He said he knew I was generous. He said that he heard about how generous I was practically every day in the year. So then he said, 'Maybe I don't want to get married. I wouldn't be the first man in the world who didn't want to get married, would I? Maybe I'm queer. Maybe I want to live with some nice, clean faggot. Maybe I want to be promiscuous and screw hundreds and hundreds of women. There are other ways of doing it besides being joined in holy matrimony and filling up the cradle. If having babies is so great why did you only have one? Why just one?' I told him then that his mother had nearly died when he was born. 'I'm sorry,' he said. 'I didn't know that.' So then he said that I had got to understand that he might not want to come home at dusk to a pretty woman and play softball with a bunch of straight-limbed sons. He said he might want to be a thief or a saint or a drunkard or a garbage man or a gas pumper or a traffic cop or a hermit. Then I lost my patience, my woolly blanket, and said that he had to get off his ass and do something useful and he said: 'What? Like pushing mouthwash.' Then I lifted up my putter and I would have split his skull in two but he ducked and threw down his club and ran off the links into the dark.

"So there I was on this ruined miniature golf course having practically murdered my son but what I wanted to do then was to chase after him and take another crack at him with the putter. I was very angry. I couldn't understand how my only son, whom I love more than anything in the world, could make me want to kill him. So then I picked up his putter and walked back to the car. When I got home I told Nellie that I'd had a fight with Tony but she sympathized with him, of course, because I'd already had a fight with her. Then I had a drink and looked at television—there wasn't anything else to do. I sat there in front of the set until about midnight when he came in. He didn't speak to me and I didn't speak to him. He went upstairs to bed and I went up a little later.

"He's been in bed ever since."

Ogden Nash

to his daughter

Dearest Isabel,

I gather that by now you have decided Mr. X is too old for you, as well as being a very silly man, but I am not pleased by the episode and I trust that by now you aren't either. The propensity of old men for flirting with young girls has been the object of coarse merriment since primeval days, as I should think your reading, if nothing else, should have told you.

You should be intelligent enough to know that in various eras of history it has been fashionable to laugh at morals, but the fact of the matter is that Old Man Morals just keeps rolling along and the laughers end up as driftwood on a sandbar. You can't beat the game, because morals as we know them represent the sum of the experience of the race. That is why it distressed me to find you glibly tossing off references to divorce. You surely have seen enough of its effects on your friends to know that it is a tragic thing even when forced on one partner by the vices of the other.

Read the marriage vows again—they are not just words, not even just a poetic promise to God. They are a practical promise to yourself to be happy. This I know from simply looking around me.

It bothers me to think that you may have sloppy—not sophisticated but sloppy—ideas about life. I have never tried to blind you to any side of life, through any form of censorship, trusting in your intelligence to learn of, and to recognize, evil without approving or participating in it. So please throw Iris March and all the golden doomed Bohemian girls away and be Isabel—there's more fun in it for you.

Keep on having your gay time, but just keep yourself in hand, and remember that generally speaking it's better to call older men Mister.

I love you tremendously,
Daddy

A Nineteenth Century Father

to his daughter

My dear Sophia,

Your mother does not object to your going to the ball; I may add that I not only do not object, but approve of it, as you go in a party in whom I can place the utmost confidence. It is rather too soon for you to go to such places, which are neither to be eagerly sought after, nor to be fastidiously rejected. Though I was early initiated into the mysteries of dancing, and by a residence in France, before I went to College, acquired a somewhat greater skill in capering than the generality of young men of my age, yet I did not go to a ball, except in vacation times in the country, till I had taken my first degree. Young as you are, yet I can trust you in a ball-room without any fears of your being guilty of impropriety; yet there are a few things worth your knowing, and some against which you should be on your guard. The main point is to avoid affectation of every kind, whether in walk, gesture, or talk.

In the common modes of dancing you have had instruction enough, and of them I say nothing. Anything like romping in dancing is to be carefully avoided. There is a certain distance to be moved over in a given time. I have seen girls scurrying through twice that distance, and thinking they had done a great feat; but, in fact, they only made themselves ridiculous, and looked like hoydens. Mind your time and the figure of the dance, and should you ever in the latter be set right by your neighbour, take it in good part, and be sure you make him or her sensible you feel obliged to them. I perceive by your letter that you already have two partners, but should you have any other, which I don't object to, don't stand like a statue, but converse with him freely, if he is so inclined; but beware of making any remark that is to the disadvantage of any person in the room.

Use your eyes well; look about you and notice those who appear to be the most graceful in their gestures and manner of conversation.

You may probably have some people of rank there, ladies who discredit by their rude, dashing behaviour, and others who do credit to their station by propriety of conduct. There is an awkward bashfulness and a bold look of self-importance, between which is the happy medium which distinguishes a well-bred woman. Few are there that can make either a good bow or a good curtsey. I care not whether it is a low one, as in my time, or a nod, or a slip, as is now the fashion; there is grace in doing either, which, if you cannot attain, still the extreme may be avoided. Observe what is done by others, but avoid imitation; what may be graceful in one may not suit another. Each has a suitable modification peculiar to himself which, if it is changed by affectation, makes him ridiculous.

The great secret, however, is to carry with you a cheerful and innocent heart, desirous of giving and receiving all the satisfaction which the amusement is capable of affording, wishing no ill to your neighbours, passing over their faults, and highly regarding their excellences.

Eric Newby

A TRAVELLER'S LIFE

He was a rowing man before everything, even before his business. So great was his passion for rowing that he had left his newly married wife (my mother-to-be) at the wedding reception at Pagani's in Great Portland Street on learning that it was just coming on to high water at Hammersmith and had gone down to the river by cab for what he described as "a jolly good blow" in his double-sculler with his best man, who eventually became my godfather, returning hours later to his flat to find his bride in tears and having missed the boat train for Paris where the honeymoon was to be spent at the Lotti. His ambition was that I should win the Diamond Sculls at Henley, and in this ambition he was aided and abetted by my godfather, a crusty old Scot if ever there was one, who had himself won the Diamonds and the Stockholm Olympics in 1912.

To help me to victory in this and life's race my father insisted that my bowels should open at precisely the same moment every morning (this was at a time when certain Harley Street surgeons were advocating the removal of whole stretches of their patients' digestive tracts in the belief that whatever was passing through would emerge at the other end with as little delay as possible and thus avoid "poisoning" the owner). In addition, he made me sniff up salt and water so that my nasal passages might remain equally clear, and have a cold bath each morning, winter and summer.

Evelyn Waugh

BRIDESHEAD REVISITED

There was only ten days of term to go; I got through them somehow and returned to London as I had done in such different circumstances the year before, with no plans made.

"That very good-looking friend of yours," asked my father. "Is he not with you?"

"No."

"I quite thought he had taken this over as his home. I'm sorry, I liked him."

"Father, do you particularly want me to take my degree?"

"I want you to? Good gracious, why should I want such a thing? No use to me. Not much use to you either, as far as I've seen."

"That's exactly what I've been thinking. I thought perhaps it was rather a waste of time going back to Oxford."

Until then my father had taken only a limited interest in what I was saying: now he put down his book, took off his spectacles, and looked at me hard.

"You've been sent down," he said. "My brother warned me of this."

"No, I've not."

"Well, then, what's all the talk about?" he asked testily, resuming his spectacles, searching for his place on the page. "Everyone stays up at least three years. I knew one man who took seven to get a pass degree in theology."

"I only thought that if I was not going to take up one of the professions where a degree is necessary, it might be best to start now on what I intend doing. I intend to be a painter."

But to this my father made no answer at the time.

The idea, however, seemed to take root in his mind; by the time we spoke of the matter again it was firmly established.

"When you're a painter," he said at Sunday luncheon, "you'll need a studio. I'm not going to have you painting in the gallery."

"No. I never meant to."

"Nor will I have undraped models all over the house, nor critics with their horrible jargon. And I don't like the smell of turpentine. I presume you intend to do the thing thoroughly and use oil paint?" My father belonged to a generation which divided painters into the serious and the amateur, according to whether they used oil or water.

"I don't suppose I should do much painting in the first year. Anyway, I should be working at a school."

"Abroad?" asked my father hopefully. "There are some excellent schools abroad, I believe."

It was all happening rather faster than I intended.

"Abroad or here. I should have to look round first."

"Look round abroad," he said.

"Then you agree to my leaving Oxford?"

"Agree? Agree? My dear boy, you're twenty-two."

"Twenty," I said, "twenty-one in October."

"Is that all? It seems much longer."

John Osborne

A BETTER CLASS OF PERSON

My father had once attempted to give me a very straightforward account of the whole reproductive process. He drew two detailed male and female figures and began explaining the functions of both at length but simply. The diagrams and the unlikely enormity of it all were too much for me. To his amusement, I rushed out of the room to be sick before he was half-finished. "What did you want to go and start telling him all that for?" said my mother. "You know what he's like." He never brought the subject up again.

Ralph Schoenstein

TELL ME, DADDY, ABOUT THE BEES AND THE FLEAS

The sexual briefing that I got from my father was memorable for the way that it avoided textbook jargon and came directly to the point: he took me into the library one day when I was twelve and solemnly told me that the time had come for me to know that I was never to use a men's room in the Broadway subway. Since this dissertation left a certain gap in the story of procreation, my mother tried to fill in by also taking me to the library, this time the public one, where she spent more than an hour trying to find a book that explained how I'd been brewed; but

in those dark days, the secret was never published for tiny eyes . . .

It remained for a pal named Mickey Higgins to take me into an alley one day during the Battle of Midway and reveal the facts of life in all their ageless beauty.

"It's somethin' your mother 'n' father do to each other," said Mickey, carefully choosing his words. "Your mother 'n' father — they're definitely the ones involved. Y'see . . . well, y'see . . ." And here he smiled with embarrassment and disbelief. "Well, this is gonna kill ya 'cause believe me it's really stupid . . ."

The story didn't kill me, but it left me with a wound, for the earthy scholarship of that little curbstone Kinsey moulded my view of *amour*. Perhaps it was Mickey's Rabelaisian presentation or perhaps his story was inherently silly: I only know that no matter how sweetly the violins are playing, I can never approach love without also approaching laughter . . .

Although Mickey's romantic tale fell somewhat short of *Ivanhoe*, it was good that he told me how the population explodes because I went on to have two little pops of my own. By loosely following his instructions, I managed to sire two daughters, one of whom has just requested the flaming facts from *me*, the facts that every father hates to declassify. One day last week, Eve-Lynn, my eight-year-old, came to me and said, "Daddy, what's *mating*?"

There it was: the new American trigger word; and for a moment I felt like joining the militants called POSE: Parents Opposing Sex Education. I was silent for several seconds after Eve-Lynn's question, but not because I didn't know if some racy little two-reeler from the Board of Education — perhaps something called *I, A Mommy* — was already playing in her classroom. And so I made a quick decision: I would explain only *external* fertilization and let all other thrills come from the teacher.

"Honey," I said, "mating is when two bees or fleas or fish decide to make more bees and fleas and fish." It was hardly a marriage manual, but it was prettier than Mickey's tale. Carefully remaining on a low zoological level, I went on to deliver a veterinary *Kama Sutra*, shrewdly avoiding pauses for questions; and by the time that I was done, Eve-Lynn knew exactly how to keep herself from ever being compromised by a lobster.

I couldn't have gone any further and still protected the American way of life, for I've recently learned from leading conservatives that sex education was invented by Karl Marx to wreck the family unit, corrupt the young, and destroy the domino theory. Moreover, it has now been established that for the past two decades, the Communists have been following a programme of conquest by pornography, distributing French postcards whenever political subversion has failed, while Americans in the silent majority have looked to prayer and impotence for a patriotic counter-attack.

"The long-range plan to bring sex education into the American public schools for children from kindergarten to the twelfth grade is part of a giant Communist conspiracy," says the Reverend Billy Hargis, for whom POSE also means Preacher Opposing Socialist Erotica.

And so I gave Eve-Lynn just enough information to satisfy her curiosity while still keeping her loyal. All the naughtier details will have to come from the Vietcong.

Unfortunately, however, I now have a problem with my older daughter, Jill, who may well be headed down the road to socialised hormones. Yesterday Jill's class saw a movie that told how cows are born. When I asked her about it, she said she'd explain the whole business to me when I take all the THINK AMERICA stickers off her books.

Gail Sheehy

PASSAGES

Margaret Hennig combed *Who's Who in America*, *Who's Who of American Women*, and the annual reports of the top 500 corporations. She found 100 women who hold positions as presidents or vice-presidents of large business and financial corporations. She traced the lives of twenty-five of them, and her findings are fascinating.

All these women saw marriage and career as an either-or choice. They chose to reach for more than the traditional woman's role would allow and in their twenties put aside most of their romantic yearnings.

Hennig set out to learn whether that was a fixed character type, the stock figure of woman as male copy, or a developmental stage that might lead to a resolution later on.

Every one of her subjects enjoyed the position of being the firstborn child. They liked being girls and objected only to people saying there were certain things girls didn't do. Their fathers, however, encouraged them to resist such constraints. This clear and early conflict between the culture's instructions and the freedom encouraged at home, Hennig observed, figured largely in the formula that brought these women to success.

In early adolescence they resisted the Oedipal loop that would have sent them back to identification with their mothers. They envied the more active and exciting existence of men. Hennig observes that the envy phenomenon here did not seem fraught with any murky Freudian fears. It was the straightforward desire of human beings who had enjoyed early experiences of freedom and wanted to retain that freedom all their lives.

None of their mothers had particularly magnetic personalities. They were classic caregivers who tried to teach their daughters to be the same. When those daughters entered the crucial period between 11 and 14, they resisted being turned into "young ladies," moved away from their mothers, and found their fathers to be the port in the storm. But there is no evidence that the fathers treated their little girls *as* boys. Instead, a unique element was described by all the subjects in the dynamic between father and daughter. The relationship transcended both of their sexes.

The fathers did not in any way reject the femininity of these girls. They did emphasize skills and abilities rather than any sex role. It was common for the two to play tennis or sail together and to talk about Dad's business. One has the feeling these men were seeking in their daughters the comradeship they couldn't have with their more limited wives. Although their wives were definitely expected to be noncompetitive and nonachieving, the men took pride in a competitively successful daughter. Such a daughter is often the favorite because she, unlike a son, can reflect well on him without becoming a rival. And encouraging her will not mean losing the services of a wife.

When Hennig's outstandingly successful women were questioned about the family romance, the very notion that they might have had to rival their mothers for their fathers' attentions struck them as foreign. Their mothers were felt to be no threat at all. Dad had been won over years before.

The relationship between father and daughter remained constant throughout the tempest of adolescence: Their fathers confirmed the girls' self-worth and became their chief source of rewards.

The consistency with which these women chose to handle their midlife crisis is truly remarkable. All twenty-five took a moratorium for a year or two. They continued to work, but much less strenuously. With devil-may-care exuberance they all did things like buying flirtatious new wardrobes and having their hair restyled. They let themselves have fun again and freed time to enjoy the sexual part of their beings.

Almost half the women married a professional man they met during this period. Their nurturing side came into play too. Though none had natural children, all those who married became stepmothers.

The other half apparently did not meet anyone they could marry; when this momentous change caught them by surprise, they had literally no social life. But the fact of marrying or not marrying proved to make little difference. The women who remained single, no less than the others, realized they could not go on without making a basic shift in emphasis. They, too, became more outgoing, more responsive to people, and often, for the first time, were willing to become mentors themselves.

Two years or so after their moratoria, all the women recommitted to a goal of working toward top management. But their behavior and sense of self had undergone a profound change. They weren't acting a stock part in some early Joan Crawford film anymore. Their exchanges with people had become more honest and spontaneous. Where formerly they had felt segmented, they now began to feel more nearly integrated. And instead of describing themselves as they did in earlier stages, as "satisfied" or "rewarded," for the first time they all added the word "happy."

"It was never a simple case of what others did to them which made so much conflict in their lives," Hennig concludes, "but very much a case of what they did with the duality within themselves. Clearly, this process was made more difficult . . . because of societal and cultural attitudes about women who seek executive careers. Yet it was much easier for them to find ways to avoid those external conflicts than to overcome their internal ones."

A not-so-happy ending awaited a control group of women who got frozen in middle management. When Dr. Hennig compared them to the major research group, she found that the parental situation had been very different: These fathers had treated their daughters not *like* they might have treated a son, but as sons. Their femininity was virtually denied; some were even called boys' names. As they moved up in occupational life, these women formed only "buddy" relationships at work. Perhaps most important, they never allowed themselves a crisis, not even in midlife. Whatever gates had been latched inside they left latched. None married. This group tended to remain dependent on their mentors until the mentors dropped them. They did not proceed to the top, but arrived in their fifties lonely as women, second-best as executives, feeling bitter and cheated as people. It was the businesswomen who did bring to the surface in midlife an emotional, sexual, and nurturing side that had been left behind who easily outgrew their mentors shortly thereafter, broke out of middle management, and went on to the president's or vice-president's chair and a triumph of personal integration.

Jane Austen

PRIDE AND PREJUDICE

"Oh! Mr. Bennet, you are wanted immediately; we are all in an uproar. You must come and make Lizzy marry Mr. Collins, for she vows she will not have him, and if you do not make haste he will change his mind and not have *her*."

Mr. Bennet raised his eyes from his book as she entered, and fixed them on her face with a calm unconcern which was not in the least altered by her communication.

"I have not the pleasure of understanding you," said he, when she had finished her speech. "Of what are you talking?"

"Of Mr. Collins and Lizzy. Lizzy declares she will not have Mr. Collins, and Mr. Collins begins to say that he will not have Lizzy."

"And what am I to do on the occasion?—It seems an hopeless business."

"Speak to Lizzy about it yourself. Tell her that you insist upon her marrying him."

"Let her be called down. She shall hear my opinion."

Mrs. Bennet rang the bell, and Miss Elizabeth was summoned to the library.

"Come here, child," cried her father as she appeared. "I have sent for you on an affair of importance. I understand that Mr. Collins has made you an offer of marriage. Is it true?" Elizabeth replied that it was. "Very well—and this offer of marriage you have refused?"

"I have, sir."

"Very well. We now come to the point. Your mother insists upon your accepting it. Is it not so, Mrs. Bennet?"

"Yes, or I will never see her again."

"An unhappy alternative is before you, Elizabeth. From this day you must be a stranger to one of your parents. Your mother will never see you again if you do *not* marry Mr. Collins, and I will never see you again if you *do*."

Elizabeth could not but smile at such a conclusion of such a beginning; but Mrs. Bennet, who had persuaded herself that her husband regarded the affair as she wished, was excessively disappointed.

"What do you mean, Mr. Bennet, by talking in this way? You promised me to *insist* upon her marrying him."

"My dear," replied her husband, "I have two small favours to request. First, that you will allow me the free use of my understanding on the present occasion; and secondly, of my room. I shall be glad to have the library to myself as soon as may be."

Paul Mann

I'LL NEVER FORGET WHAT MY FATHER TOLD ME

I have just finished reading one of my father's diaries dealing with the final months of World War Two. My father was a wireless and telegraph operator in the Royal Navy, having joined up at the outbreak of war in 1939 and leaving as a petty officer in 1946. He saw more than his fair share of action, was in at the sinking of the *Bismarck*, served aboard corvettes on the Murmansk Run and on the North Atlantic convoys. He was on one of the ships ferrying reinforcements to Juno Beach on the second day of the Normandy landings and I remember him telling me years later that the Germans were putting up such a good show he thought the invasion might be stopped.

In the last months of the war he was aboard the corvette, *HMS Poppy*, again escorting convoys across the North Atlantic hoping he wouldn't be torpedoed with peace just in sight. On Wednesday, April 11, 1945, *HMS Poppy* and two other warships surprised a U-boat on the surface, attacked and destroyed it.

Naturally, reading this diary rekindled childhood memories of my father although it added nothing substantive to my perceptions of him. I can't remember when my father stopped being a god-like figure to me but I do know it was early. I suspect I was a demanding kid and I looked to him for demonstration of qualities which he never really possessed. I further suspect he was never aware of my disappointment.

At first I looked to him as some kind of ally against the overpowering eccentricity of my mother, . . . but he turned out to be the kind of man who would do anything for a bit of peace and quiet. Perhaps surviving the war exhausted all his inner resources of strength and stamina and when confronted by my mother's tantrums he found it easier to surrender quietly.

He was one of those many hen-pecked suburban husbands who would rather slink off down to the pub for a soothing beer than have a stand-up brawl with his wife.

At first, judging him with the fascist simplicity of youth, I thought him weak but it was more complicated than that. After leaving the navy he had joined the police force which, in England, . . . was a respectable occupation. I learned, usually by eavesdropping on the conversations of off-duty policemen visiting our home, that he was a tough copper, not afraid of a fight. His toughness it seemed, dissipated when he crossed the threshold of his own home. He was simply a soft husband and father, no more, no less.

After this realisation I became less judgemental but while I understood I could not look to him for a display of firmness against the temperamental excesses of my mother I continued to look to him as a source of parental wisdom. He was, after all, a worldly man, was he not? Brave but compassionate, strong but sensitive. He had travelled, seen history as it was made, observed human behaviour in all its extremes. Surely, I thought, he must have formed many profound opinions about human nature which he might be able to share with me to my enlightenment.

As much as I secretly longed for my mother to be like Lauren Bacall I longed with equal intensity for my father to be like Gary Cooper. To the qualities I knew my father already possessed would be added Coop's sense of honour, his humanity and his wonderfully dry, dignified, masculine humour. Like Coop, I thought, my father was probably capable of delivering profound insights with very few words. I waited and waited as the years passed and I entered my teens. I was right in one sense . . . my father was a man of few words.

He shirked his duty in other areas too. We never had a heart to heart about sex, for instance. I had to learn all about that from Isabel, my first girlfriend. Mostly I learned that girls get skidmarks on their knickers too.

Then, when I was 14 years old, something happened that was to affect me for the rest of my life.

Though I didn't appreciate it at the time it was to teach me a lesson: A Great Truth About Life. I was to learn a great deal in the one hit, all about grace under pressure, courage in the face of hopeless odds, dignity under duress and the worth of it all. And, indirectly at least, I could thank my father.

I had come home from school one day to find the house empty, both my parents still at work. Still wearing my school uniform I went out to lark about with some other kids in the woods nearby. There was a big grassy knoll in a clearing in the woods and some of the older kids had just invented grass hill tobogganing. It involved sliding down the steep, grassy hillside on a battered old drinks tray at a fair rate of knots.

When it came to my turn I thought I was doing pretty well until, part way down I hit a bump, the tray went one way and I went the other on the seat of my pants. Unfortunately for me I wasn't to have a soft landing. Instead I slid over a jagged rock and gouged a lump of flesh out of my left buttock. I got shakily to my feet and could already feel the warm rush of blood down my leg. I took off in the direction of home as quickly as I could, dramatically bow legged and walking like one of those speeded up cowboys in a silent movie. The other kids, displaying all the customary sympathy of youth, were quadriplegic with laughter.

By the time I got home my left trouser leg was stained maroon.

My father was back from work, ordered me to drop my trousers, took a quick look and pronounced that stitches would be necessary. We drove to the doctor's surgery in the family Ford, me riding tenderly on the right buttock, the gash in the left buttock temporarily stuffed with a lump of bandage.

When we reached the doctor's surgery the real horror began. Parents and doctors are hopelessly insensitive to the self-consciousness of adolescents and, caught up in the hormonal maelstrom of puberty, I was painfully self-conscious about my changing body. Learning to cope with body hair, alternating voice pitch and importunate erections was bad enough but having to succumb to close examination of my teenage bum was mortification beyond belief.

The doctor ordered me to take off my trousers and underpants and climb up on the examination couch. I rested there on all fours wearing only shirt, tie, jacket and socks, head lowered, face flushed with embarrassment, bare bleeding backside reared high in the air for all the world to see.

Stitches indeed, confirmed the doctor. He assembled his needle and catgut, announced he wouldn't bother with a local anesthetic because it would only take him a minute and, hang on, he said, he had better get his assistant in to shine the table lamp helpfully on the wounded area while he worked. She came in all starched linen, bright eyed and brisk, a very pretty 17-year-old nurse whom I recognised as a former student from my school. Not a girl I would have chosen to meet in my present position.

She dutifully held the lamp close to the wound, her pretty face mere centimetres from my bare bottie, her eyes no doubt fixed on a view of me that had only previously been seen by the toilet seat. If it were possible for anyone to die of shame that is when it would have happened to me. Words do not exist to describe the epic nature of my humiliation. Death would have been blissful relief.

The doc smartly inserted half-a-dozen stitches into my left cheek, sewing the ugly flap of skin neatly back in place. Meanwhile, how was I getting along, asked the nurse and wasn't I a brave boy? I knew then that, rather than risk meeting that girl again, I would have to leave home, the town, England. Perhaps Australia was far enough away.

At last they had finished and they allowed me to climb down and get dressed. I was numb with misery and the nurse avoided my eyes.

I tottered stiffly back to the car, face and bum burning. I said nothing. My father said nothing. We drove home in deafening silence until, turning into the street that led to our house my father glanced over at me with a smile that seemed at once worldly and reassuring.

"Well, son," he said with what sounded like genuine respect in his voice, "I'll say one thing for you."

I looked at him hungrily, expectantly, eager to hear the words that would save my shattered pride.

"You've got a really hairy arse," he said.

Damon Runyan

to his son

July 3, 1945

My dear Son:
I was delighted to hear from you and greatly relieved as I did not know just where you were or what you were doing.

To say that I am pleased with your good report is putting it very mildly. It is the best news I have heard in a long time.

I think the samples of your work that you sent are excellent reporting with a swell human interest touch. I have always thought you could write and it has always been my hope that you would carry on what I think is an honorable name in the newspaper game, the greatest profession in the world.

You will improve the more you write. Good writing is simply a matter of application but I learned many years ago that words will not put themselves down on paper in dreams or in conversations . . .

I know more about Alcoholics Anonymous than you might think. I read a great deal about the organization and I had several contacts with active participants on the Pacific Coast. One worked at Fox when I was making *Irish Eyes Are Smiling*.

I think it may be one of the great movements of all time and I am extremely pleased that it has aroused your interest.

Surely by this time you must have learned that you were not cut out for a drinking man. Drinking is not hereditary as some rumpots like to alibi, but I think there are certain strains that are allergic to alcohol and you seem to carry that strain.

You ask me about my own experiences. I quit drinking thirty-five years ago in Denver and have not had a drink since. I quit because I realized that I got no fun out of drinking. Liquor only gave me delusions of grandeur that got me into trouble. It never made me happy and bright and sparkling as it does some people. It made me dull and stupid and quarrelsome, It made me dreadfully ill afterwards. I did not have the constitution to drink. It rendered me helpless. It destroyed my pride, my sense of decency.

I quit because I saw that I was not going to get anywhere in the world if I didn't, and I wanted to go places. I was sorely tempted many times, usually in moments of elation over some small triumph or when I was feeling sorry for myself, a strong characteristic of the drinker, but I managed to stand it off.

It was never taking that first drink that saved me.

I had to endure loneliness and even derision as a result of my abstinence for some years but it eventually became a matter of such general knowledge that no one pressed me to take a drink any more and finally I became positively famous for hanging out with drunks and never touching a drop.

We could have saved many a great career with an organisation like the AA's in the old days when a lush was shunned even more than he is today.

You stick to your organization and try to help other fellows unfortunate enough to be under the spell of old John Barleycorn. No good ever comes of drinking and I don't think any bad ever comes of not drinking.

So much for my temperance lecture, except that I have only a little time left as you may surmise from my ailment, but I will go happy if I know that you have conquered your enemy. If you have gone eight months without drinking, you would be a fool to ever start again, knowing what you know . . .

Your AA's should give you something you never had — sympathy for your fellow man. It was not your fault that you didn't have it. It was just the way you were gaited.

That is one element a writer must have to be a good writer — sympathy. What we call "Heart" . . .

I will not again write to you at this length. But I am so glad to hear that you are getting along all right I am a little windier than usual.

I am quite pleased that we are in opposing papers. I have been in the *Enquirer* off and on for years — usually off. You are with a fine outfit, the Scripps-Howard. I think it is better for a young writer than any other. The kind of work you are doing is exactly the kind you need because it gives you human contact and a knowledge of how people live.

You say that you don't know if you will ever be anything more than a better-than-average reporter. Well, my boy, I think that is better than being king. I do indeed.

Mary sends her love and I sign myself in deepest affection.

Dad

William Carlos Williams

to his son

March 13, 1938

Dearest Bill:

This I can say for certain, you seem not far different from what I was myself at your age. I don't mind saying I went through hell . . . what with worrying about my immortal soul and my hellish itch to screw almost any female I could get my hands on — which I never did. I can tell you it is almost as vivid today as it was then when I hear you speak of it. Everything seems upside down and one's self the very muck under one's foot.

It comes from many things, my dear boy, but mostly from the inevitable maladjustment consequent upon growing up in a more or less civilized environment . . . But more immediately, your difficulties arise from a lack of balance in your daily life, a lack of balance which has to be understood and withstood — for it cannot be avoided for the present.

I refer to the fact that your intellectual life, for the moment, has eclipsed the physical life, the animal life, the normal he-man life, which every man needs and craves. If you were an athlete, a powerful body, one who could be a hero on the field or the diamond, a *Big Hero*, many of your mental tortures would be lulled to sleep. But you cannot be that—so what? You'll have to wait and take it by a different course.

You, dear Bill, have a magnificent opportunity to enjoy life ahead of you. You have sensibility (even if it drives you nuts at times) which will be the source of keen pleasures later and the source of useful accomplishments too. You've got a brain, as you have been told *ad nauseam*. But these are things which are tormenting you, the very things which are your most valuable possessions and which will be your joy tomorrow. Sure you are sentimental, sure you admire a man like Wordsworth and his *Tintern Abbey*. It is natural, it is the correct reaction of your age to life. It is also a criticism of Wordsworth as you will see later. All I can say about that is, wait! Not wait cynically, idly, but wait while looking, believing, getting fooled, changing from day to day. Wait with the only kind of faith I have ever recognized, the faith that says I wanna know! I wanna see! I think I will understand when I do know and see. Meanwhile I'm not making any final judgments. Wait it out. Don't worry too much. You've got time. You're all right. You're reacting to life in the only way an intelligent, sensitive young man in college can. In another year you'll enter another sphere of existence, the practical one. The knowledge, abstract now, which seems unrelated to sense to you (at times) will get a different color . . .

Mother and I both send love. Don't let *anything* get your goat and don't think you have to duck anything in life. There is a way out for every man who has the intellectual fortitude to go on in the face of difficulties.

Yours,
Dad

Prince Philip

It's no use saying do this, do that, don't do that . . . it's very easy when children want something to say *no* immediately. I think it's quite important not to give an unequivocal answer at once. Much better to think it over. Then, if you eventually say *no*, I think they really accept it.

Jean Renoir

MY LIFE AND MY FILMS

My father's influence on me is undeniable, but it is manifest principally in the details of my everyday life. The truth is, I think, that the influence of one person on another can never be defined. It has to do with the smell of the body, the colour of the hair, the bearing and above all the kind of invisible and unanalysable wireless in which I firmly believe and of which the effects are beyond scientific explanation.

Although he did not seek to influence his children my father did most decidedly influence us by the magic of the pictures covering the walls of our home. We came unconsciously to believe that his was the only possible kind of painting. I can only remember one occasion when Renoir uttered what might pass for a word of advice from master to pupil. He was talking to a young friend of his, the painter Albert Andre. "One has to fill out," he said. "A good painting, a good novel or a good opera makes its subject burst at the seams." Albert Andre observed that there were splendid pictures with empty spaces in them, in particular those by painters at the beginning of the Italian Renaissance. Renoir's reply to this was that what Albert Andre supposed to be empty spaces were as filled with life as the parts crammed with matter. A pause in music can be as resonant as a fanfare by a dozen military bands. This law of content enclosed in a containing framework is one of the few pieces of artistic advice that my father gave me, albeit indirectly, and it astonishes me that my young mind, stuffed with nonsense about the *Soltats t'l'Empire* and the Musketeers, should have remembered it.

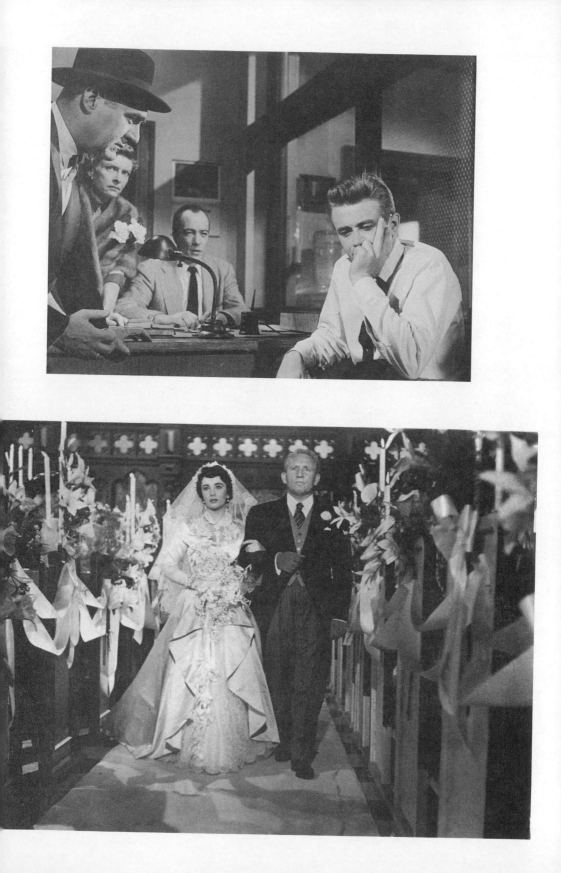

Leopold Mozart

to his son

My Son! You are hot-tempered and impulsive in all your ways! Since your childhood and boyhood your whole character has changed. As a child and a boy you were serious rather than childish, and when you sat at the clavier or were otherwise intent on music, no one dared to make the slightest jest. Why, even your expression was so solemn that, observing the early efflorescence of your talent and your ever grave and thoughtful little face, many discerning people of different countries sadly doubted whether your life would be a long one. But now, as far as I can see, you are much too ready to retort in a bantering tone to the first challenge — and that, of course, is the first step towards undue familiarity, which anyone who wants to preserve his self-respect will try to avoid in this world. A goodhearted fellow is inclined, it is true, to express himself freely and naturally; nonetheless it is a mistake to do so. And it is just your good heart which prevents you from detecting any shortcomings in a person who showers praises on you, has a great opinion of you and flatters you to the skies, and who makes you give him all your confidence and affection; whereas as a boy you were so extraordinarily modest that you used to weep when people praised you overmuch. The greatest art of all is *to know oneself* and then, my dear son, to do as I do, that is *to endeavour to get to know others through and through*. This, as you know, has always been my study; and certainly it is a fine, useful and indeed most necessary one.

As for your giving lessons in Paris, you need not bother your head about it. *In the first place*, no one is going to dismiss his master at once and engage you. *In the second place*, no one would dare to ask you, and you yourself would certainly not take on anyone except possibly some lady who is already a good player and wants to take lessons in interpretation, which would be easy work for good pay. For instance, would you not have gladly undertaken to give Countess von Lutzow and Countess Lodron two or three lessons a week at a fee of two or three *louis d'or* a month, the more so as such ladies also put themselves to much trouble to collect subscribers for the engraving of your compositions? In Paris everything is done by these great ladies, many of whom are devoted lovers of the clavier and in some cases excellent performers. These are the people who can help you. As for composition, why, you could make money and gain a great reputation by publishing works for the clavier, string quartets, and so forth, symphonies and possibly a collection of melodious French arias with clavier accompaniments like the one you sent me, and finally operas. Well, what objection have you to raise now? But you want everything to be done at once, before people have even seen you or heard any of your works. Read my long list of the acquaintances we had in Paris at that time. All, or at least most of them, are the leading people in that city and they will all be both delighted and interested to see you again. Even if only six of them take you up (and indeed one single one of the most influential of them would be enough), you would be able to do whatever you pleased.

Sydney Smith

to his daughter

London 22 July 1835

Lucy, Lucy, my dear child, don't tear your frock: tearing frocks is not in itself a proof of genius; but write as your mother writes, act as your mother acts; be frank, loyal, affectionate, simple, honest; and then integrity or laceration of frock is of little import.

And Lucy, dear child, mind your arithmetic. You know, in the first sum of yours I ever saw, there was a mistake. You had carried two (as a cab is licensed to do) and you ought, dear Lucy, to have carried but one. Is this a trifle? What would life be without arithmetic, but a scene of horrors?

You are going to Boulogne, the city of debts, peopled by men who never understood arithmetic; by the time you return, I shall probably have received my first paralytic stroke, and shall have lost all recollection of you; therefore I now give you my parting advice. Don't marry anybody who has not a tolerable understanding and a thousand a year, and God bless you, dear child!

Shakespeare

HAMLET
Act 1 Scene 3

POLONIUS:
Yet here, Laertes! aboard, aboard, for shame!
The wind sits in the shoulder of your sail,
And you are stayed for: there — my blessing with you!
And these few precepts in thy memory
Look thou character. Give thy thoughts no tongue
Nor any unproportion'd thought his act.
Be thou familiar, but by no means vulgar.
The friends thou hast, and their adoption tried,
Grapple them to thy soul with hooks of steel;
But do not dull thy palm with entertainment
Of each new-hatch'd, unfledg'd comrade. Beware
Of entrance to a quarrel: but, being in,
Bear it that the opposer may beware of thee.
Give every man thine ear, but few thy voice:
Take each man's censure, but reserve thy judgment.
Costly thy habit as thy purse can buy,
But not express'd in fancy; rich, not gaudy:
For the apparel oft proclaims the man;
And they in France, of the best rank and station,
Are most select and generous, chief in that.

Neither a borrower nor a lender be:
For loan oft loses both itself and friend;
And borrowing dulls the edge of husbandry.
This above all, — to thine own self be true;
And it must follow, as the night the day,
Thou canst not then be false to any man.
Farewell; my blessing season this in thee!

Prince Charles

If your children want to alter society, listen to their reasons and the idealism behind them. Don't crush them with some clever remark straight away.

Nigel Nicolson

PORTRAIT OF A MARRIAGE

My darling Benzie,

I thought your sonnet excellent — really good. And the absurd thing is that the "swallow" passage, which you made up yourself, was far the best passage in the whole thing. The rest was a clever imitation and adaptation. But the swallows were observed.

I think that your weakness in writing is not technique but originality. You need not bother about writing well. That comes naturally to you.

But you must bother about thinking well. That has not come to you yet. I sometimes wish that you did not agree with Mummy and me so much. Of course, *of course*, we are always right. But a boy of your age should sometimes think us wrong.

It is no use *trying* to be original. That ends by being merely contradictory—and people who are merely contradictory are the worst of all sorts of bore. But you should think things out for yourself. Do not start merely by disagreeing in principle with whatever other people think. They are probably right. But work out slowly, carefully, quietly, your own ideas about everything.

I think in some ways you have an original and courageous mind. You were very good indeed about confirmation and Holy Communion. That was the real Ben. It was not *just* trying to be original: it was a deliberate and perfectly sensible attitude or gesture of thought. Now that you are becoming less bothered about what Hanbury thinks, or Sevelode thinks, or Tiddliumpty thinks, you might begin to be bothered about what Ben thinks.

My darling, I am so glad that you are less bored at Eton and less unhappy. Seek out the things you enjoy and forget the things you hate. You are beginning to realize that your independence is not just because you are a freak, but because you are a person. The same idea is occurring to your contemporaries. Go on being the same, only with a smile on your lips. They may tease you about it, but at the bottom of their hearts they respect you. Being "odd," being "different," is a sign of individuality. It exposes you, when a young boy among other young boys, to the jeers of the herd. But the herd is growing older even as you are growing older. They will come to look on you with a "vague surmise" (or is it "a wild surmise"?). They will begin to wonder whether after all Nicolson *ma* is not Benedict Nicolson—a person, who in spite of much suffering, has emerged as himself from the crude machinery, the crushing uniformity, of the lower boy ideals. You may find that the stand you have taken, which seemed so odd to them at first, seems to them now a rather courageous thing—a thing far finer than their own subservience to the course of the stream.

I repeat, be nice to the lower boys. I know that this may expose you to misunderstanding, and I do not wish you to flaunt intimacy with the more handsome youths of fourteen. But I beg you, when you see a person as shy and as unhappy as you were yourself, to give him a kind word, a look of understanding. You will answer, "Daddy doesn't know the conditions at Eton." I reply, "Yes, I do." They were just the same in my day at Wellington. Human nature doesn't change. And I know that in my case I found that when I got to your position in my house, the opportunity of being kind to little miseries, made up for all the unkindness and cruelty which I had received myself.

Boys are generally insensitive. You are far too sensitive. One act or word of kindness on your part will compensate you for all the jeers of the worthless people who have laughed at you in the past. Try it and see. It will give you a warm feeling inside, in place of that cold sore feeling which you know.

> Bless you, my own darling. Your very loving,
> H G N

Viscount Archibald Wavell

One word of command from me is obeyed by millions . . . but I cannot get my three daughters, Pamela, Felicity and Joan, to come down to breakfast on time.

Charles Dickens

to his son

My dearest Plorn,
I write this note today because your going away is much upon my mind, and because I want you to have a few parting words from me to think

of now and then at quiet times. I need not tell you that I love you dearly, and am very, very sorry in my heart to part with you. But this life is half made up of partings, and these pains must be borne. It is my comfort and sincere conviction that you are going to try the life for which you are best fitted. I think its freedom and wildness more suited to you than any experiment in study or office would ever have been; and without that training, you could have followed no other suitable occupation.

What you have already wanted until now has been a set, steady, constant purpose. I therefore exhort you to persevere in a thorough determination to do whatever you have to do as well as you can do it. I was not so old as you are now when I first had to win my food, and to do this out of determination, and I have never slackened in it since.

Never take a mean advantage of anyone in any transaction, and never be hard upon people who are in your power. Try to do to others, as you would have them do to you, and do not be discouraged if they fail sometimes. It is much better for you that they should fail in obeying the greatest rule laid down by your Saviour, than that you should.

I put a New Testament among your books, for the very same reason, and with the very same hopes that made me write an easy account of it for you, when you were a little child; because it is the best book that ever was or ever will be known in the world, and because it teaches you the best lessons by which any human creature who tries to be truthful and faithful to duty can possibly be guided. As your brothers have gone away, one by one, I have written to each such words as I am now writing to you, and entreated them all to guide themselves by this book, putting aside the interpretations and inventions of men.

You will remember that you have never at home been wearied about religious observances or mere formalities. I have always been anxious not to weary my children with such things before they are old enough to form opinions respecting them. You will therefore understand the better that I now must solemnly impress upon you the truth and beauty of the Christian religion, as it came from Christ Himself, and the impossibility of your going far wrong if you humbly but heartily respect it.

Only one thing more in this head. The more we are in earnest as to feeling it, the less we are disposed to hold forth about it. Never abandon the wholesome practice of saying your own private prayers, night and morning. I have never abandoned it myself, and I know the comfort of it.

I hope you will always be able to say in after life, that you had a kind father. You cannot show your affection for him so well, or make him so happy, as by doing your duty.

Your affectionate Father

George Sitwell

to his son

My dearest Osbert,

As I fear a line sent to Chelsea Barracks may not reach you before you leave tomorrow, I write to you, care of your regiment, B.E.F. so that you may find a letter from me waiting for you when you arrive in the trenches. But I had wanted if possible to give you a word of advice before you left. Though you will not, of course, have to encounter anywhere abroad the same weight of gunfire that your mother and I had to face here — it has been my contention for many years that there were no guns in the world to compare for weight and range with the great German naval guns, and that our own do not come anywhere near them — yet my experience may be useful to you. Directly you hear the first shell, retire, as I did, to the Undercroft [cellar], and remain there quietly until all firing has ceased. Even then, a bombardment, especially as one grows older, is a strain upon the nervous system — but the best remedy for that, as always, is to keep warm and have plenty of plain, nourishing food at frequent but regular intervals. And, of course, plenty of rest. I find a nap in the afternoon most helpful, if not unduly prolonged, and I advise you to try it whenever possible.

— Ever your loving father, George R. Sitwell.

Eric Nichol

LETTERS TO MY SON

Desert Springs, 8 December

My dear Son:

Somebody, perhaps one of your sisters, has sent me a newspaper clipping, a photo in which you are identifiable as one of the youths skirmishing with police during the Grey Cup festivities.

As I have not heard from you regarding paying a fine, I assume that you were let off with a warning, in the spirit of the occasion. Canada's Grey Cup football game and its attendant fiesta are not reported in the American press, hence my vagueness.

This is the first time, to my knowledge, that you have shown an interest in sport since you were ten. Your golden years as an athlete were between seven and nine, you'll recall. Those were the three years during which you played soccer in the 8th Division of the Fairburn Junior Soccer League, as a member of the team whose uniforms were sponsored by the Pink Lady Beauty Salon. Do you remember that every Saturday morning I drove you to the school soccer pitch, and cheered your team on?

"Go, go, go, Pink Lady!" I yelled. Strange, it didn't seem undignified at the time. I wanted to show that I was cheering for the whole team, not just you. I didn't want to act like a Little League father, bullying his son to perform better and gratify the parental ego. Looking back, I know that I was a happy man for those Saturday mornings, that I enjoyed standing in a puddle, and slicing the eight oranges into halves for Pink Lady's half-time pick-me-up.

On the right wing, you always showed a real burst of speed, breaking for the oranges. I sometimes wondered if your team would have been more strongly motivated if they were chasing a ball that gave juice.

Even though Pink Lady Beauty Salon didn't win a game for the first two seasons, you scored one of the two goals of your team's season total. I was very proud of you.

I can tell you now that your sparkling play was enhanced by the presence on the sidelines of a mother who attended most games — Mrs. Corelli. Mrs. Corelli, all black hair and white skin, wore a velvet pantsuit that defined her figure in terms that a layman could understand. To share with her the shelter of her umbrella, her black boots nudging my galoshes, watching you skirmish pluckily in the mud, made for spectator sport at its best.

It was only towards the end of the last season that I learned that Mrs. Corelli was a scout for a team in the 7th Division. She was actually more interested in your potential than she was in mine. This came as a blow to my self-esteem, and may have been a factor in my getting on your back a bit about your play, about your standing around chatting with your check during play, that sort of thing.

When you said to me: "Gee, Daddy, it's only a game," I wanted to slap your face. I remembered who had told you that soccer was only a game — me. But I didn't hit you. I somehow found the self-restraint to play out the remainder of the season. And you played one of your best games as the closer, with my saying not a word. You had distinguished yourself so well in the 8th Division that I thought they should retire your orange peel, ha, ha.

But you never went on to the 7th Division, despite your endorsement by Mrs. Corelli. You quit soccer at nine years of age, your best years behind you.

In high school the closest you got to organized games was when you turned out as male cheer leader — for the ping-pong team. I gathered that you were trying to make some obscure point about competitive sport. And you may have been trying to get back at me, because you knew I played league-class table tennis as a young man and I won the cup, for runner-up, in the Vancouver city open championship. I guess a psychologist would explain it as part of your effort to chuck my authority and emerge as a full-blown adult. But it turned my stomach to see you practicing cartwheels in a short pleated skirt.

The tragedy is that you have missed a wonderful outlet for the aggressive instinct. Waterloo was won on the playing fields of Eton, but the detente with Red China rolled off a ping-pong table.

Although I didn't understand what was happening at the time of my league play, it is more salutary to break a ping-pong ball than somebody's head. I admit that I have not noticed any aggressive instinct in you, till I got this news photo. I thought you were dedicated to peaceful violence. That is, you only put up a fight to prevent bloodshed. Or something like that—I don't pretend to understand the love generation.

Just a short note from you, to enlighten me about the Grey Cup incident, will be gratefully received by—

your loving Dad.

J. R. Ackerley

MY FATHER AND MYSELF

Another disadvantage to which he may be thought to have put himself in regard to us children was that throughout our formative years he was what may be called a "weekend" father, if as frequent as that. Having accidentally produced us all and concealed us, first in Herne Hill, where I was born, then in Herne Bay, where my sister was born two years later, he removed us again, at the turn of the century, to Bowdon in Cheshire, his own homeland, where we were accidentally discovered by his business friends. He himself was working in Covent Garden and had a flat in Marylebone where, according to Aunt Bunny, he led a gay free bachelor's life—"all the fun of the fair," as she put it—and to which my mother was never invited. We were therefore brought up and surrounded by women, my mother, aunt, grandmother, his sisters, old Sarah and various nurses, governesses, and maids, while he himself was an irregular weekend visitor: in 1900, for instance, eighteen months after my sister's birth, he departed with Stockley for Jamaica on a business trip. It was not until 1903, when he removed us again, this time to the first of the three houses we were to occupy in Richmond, Surrey, that he lived with us and we became a united family.

Such a father might well be an awe-inspiring figure to small children, and that was the aspect he sometimes assumed. For of course we were as naughty and disobedient as children are likely to be when reared almost entirely by sweet, kind, doting women in whom all sense of discipline is lacking. My poor, dear, scatter-brained mother to whom, in particular, we paid so little heed, would sometimes be driven by our unruliness, impertinence, or downright cruelty to say, "I shall have to tell your father when he comes," and occasionally, provoked beyond endurance, she did — and that was how I got my beatings. The dogs too. We always had household dogs, and my father was dispenser of justice to them also, for no one but he would "rub their noses in it" to house-train them, or take punitive action against them, the "good hiding," for other offences. It is fair to say that he came to us generally in the guise of Father Christmas, loaded with presents; but if we or the dogs were in disgrace he came as a figure of retribution, and it may be that, for this reason, he did not perfectly earn his way into my childish heart. But I would not care to make too much of all this as affecting the confidential relationship he himself offered my brother and me some years later.

It must have been about the year 1912, when I was turned sixteen, that he invited the two of us into the billiard-room of Grafton House, the second and largest of our three Richmond residences, for a "jaw," which could hardly be called "pi" and which he himself described as "man to man." We were both at the age when boys have normally discovered the pleasures of masturbation, and if that delightful pastime can be overworked, no doubt we were overworking it. Probably we both looked a trifle yellow and my father thought the moment had come for a friendly chat. The precise way he approached this delicate subject I don't recall; I am sure he did it as decently as could be done in the circumstances — the circumstances being that he had left it all rather late. The ground for such intimacies needs some preparation, and in common with many English children of our class and time our education in such matters had been totally neglected. Worse than neglected, I, at least, had been misled and reached my preparatory school supposing that I had been delivered to my parents by a stork, a naivety that won me the ridicule of other boys. Indeed, considering what I afterwards learnt of my father's behaviour, and of the licence and impropriety of his relationship with my mother, I think it a trifle dishonest of them to have excluded me so completely from that freedom of thought in which they themselves seem to have indulged. At any rate, by the age of sixteen, such knowledge of sex as I had gained I had gained for myself, and it had become tinged with slyness and guilt.

F. Scott Fitzgerald

to his daughter

Dear Pie:

I feel very strongly about your doing duty. Would you give me a little more documentation about your reading in French? I am glad you are happy — but I never believe much in happiness. I never believe in misery either. Those are things you see on the stage or the screen or the printed page, they never really happen to you in life.

All I believe in in life is the rewards for virtue (according to your talents) and the *punishments* for not fulfilling your duties, which are doubly costly. If there is such a volume in the camp library, will you ask Mrs. Tyson to let you look up a sonnet of Shakespeare's in which the line occurs *Lilies that fester smell far worse than weeds*.

Have had no thoughts today, life seems composed of getting up a *Saturday Evening Post* story. I think of you, and always pleasantly; but if you call me "Pappy" again I am going to take the White Cat out and beat his bottom *hard, six times for every time you are impertinent*. Do you react to that?

I will arrange the camp bill.

Half-wit, I will conclude. Things to worry about:

Worry about courage

Worry about cleanliness

Worry about efficiency

Worry about horsemanship . . .

Things not to worry about:

Don't worry about popular opinion

Don't worry about dolls

Don't worry about the past

Don't worry about the future

Don't worry about growing up

Don't worry about anybody getting ahead of you

Don't worry about triumph

Don't worry about failure unless it comes through your own fault

Don't worry about mosquitoes
Don't worry about flies
Don't worry about insects in general
Don't worry about parents
Don't worry about boys
Don't worry about disappointments
Don't worry about pleasures
Don't worry about satisfactions
Things to think about:
What am I really aiming at?
How good am I in comparison to my contemporaries in regard to:
(a) Scholarship
(b) Do I really understand about people and am I able to get along
with them?
(c) Am I trying to make my body a useful instrument or am I
neglecting it?

With dearest love

Lewis J. Paper

THE PROMISE
AND THE PERFORMANCE

After entering the White House, John Kennedy reminisced with Arthur
Schlesinger Jr., one night . . .

My father wasn't around as much as some fathers when I was young,
but, whether he was there or not, he made his children feel that they
were the most important things in the world to him. He was so terribly
interested in everything we were doing. He held up standards for us,
and he was very tough when we failed to meet those standards . . .

Kennedy's father, much more than his mother, believed that one's level of achievement was very dependent on an individual's determination, that success rarely was a result of chance. Joseph Kennedy therefore encouraged his children, but especially his sons, to thrive on competition. When Kennedy and his older brother, Joe Jr., participated in sports contests, for example, their father would take a special interest in the effort they expended to be first. Rose Kennedy remembered a typical exchange after the elder Kennedy had watched his sons in a sailing race: He didn't know anything about sailing, and he'd say, "Why was your sail not as large as the other one? Why was it flapping when the other one was straight, and the other one won the race and you didn't?" And then the boys would say, "Well, we bought our sails three years ago." And their father would say, "Well, why don't you tend to those things and find out what's going on? If you're in a race, do it right. Come in a winner; second place is no good." The ambition Joseph Kennedy tried to instill in his sons was epitomized by his remark to *New York Times* columnist Arthur Krock: "For the Kennedys, it's the [outhouse] or the castle—nothing in between." In a word, Joseph Kennedy conveyed an aura of ambition and high-mindedness in his family, an aura not without effect on all the children and particularly on the sons.

Sue Townsend

THE SECRET DIARY OF ADRIAN MOLE AGED 13 ¾

Sunday February 8th
Fifth after Epiphany

My father came into my bedroom this morning, he said he wanted a chat. He looked at my Kevin Keegan scrapbook, screwed the knob of my wardrobe door back on with his Swiss army knife, and asked me about school. Then he said he was sorry about yesterday and the shouting, he said my mother and him are "going through a bad patch." He asked me if I had anything to say. I said he owed me thirty-two pence for the Chinese chips and soy sauce. He gave me a pound. So I made a profit of sixty-eight pence.

Dame Nellie Melba

MELODIES AND MEMORIES

Throughout my life there has always been one man who meant more than all others, one man for whose praise I thirsted, whose character I have tried to copy—my father . . .

My father was never a great talker. He was very reserved, very Scotch and, you might think, very shy. He did not talk so much as twinkle. He could say more with his eyes than most men with their lips. And he admired reserve in others as much as he practised it in himself. I remember, long afterwards, when I came back to Australia in 1902, he took me aside and said, "Well—have you saved any money?"

MYSELF (hesitating): "Yes, a little."

FATHER: "How much?"

MYSELF (fibbing): "Perhaps 20,000 pounds."

FATHER: "Well, lass, you're much richer than I am."

There was a pause, and he solemnly winked at me, and I winked at him; then, taking me by the arm, he said: "You're quite right, lassie. Never tell anybody what you've got. Not even me."

My father shared my love of life in the open air—riding, fishing, tramping through the bush. Many were the rides I went with him, and though he never gave me much encouragement, he was a good master. If my hat blew off, he never paused to allow me to pick it up, but rode steadily on until I galloped up, very out of breath, to apologise for my foolishness. If I was ever one minute late, he went without me and turned a deaf ear to all excuses.

But if he was a stern master, I was a willing pupil. When I was twelve years old, I had already developed a positive passion for playing the organ, and every week on Tuesdays and Fridays I used to take lessons at St. Peter's. My father never told me that I played well, nevertheless he spurred me on in his way. "Learn twelve pieces by heart, lass," he said to me, "and I'll give you a gold watch." I learnt the twelve pieces in as many days, and sure enough the watch was mine, for my father never broke a promise. But I fear I broke the watch. Running home one day in the brief twilight of the Australian autumn, I dropped the watch in a gutter, and when I went back to look for it, dark had already come. It was found, weeks later, by a detective and returned to me, ruined. I shall never forget the look of black disapproval on Daddy's face when he saw the ruins of the watch in my hand. "You will never get another from me," he said. And I never did, but I keep that old watch to this day in one of the drawers reserved for happy memories.

Elihu Burritt

"Yes, they are good boys," I once heard a kind father say. "I talk to them very much, but do not like to beat my children—the world will beat them." It was a beautiful thought, though not elegantly expressed.

J. B. Priestley

To show a child what has once delighted you, to find the child's delight added to your own, so that there is now a double delight seen in the glow of trust and affection, this is happiness.

FATHER'S
FOOTSTEPS

*Greatness of name in the father often times over-
whelms the son; they stand too near one another.
The shadow kills the growth.*

—BEN JONSON

Christopher Milne

THE ENCHANTED PLACES

If the Pooh books had been like most other books — published one year, forgotten the next — there would have been no problem. If I had been a different sort of person there might well have been no problem. Unfortunately the fictional Christopher Robin refused to die and he and his real-life namesake were not always on the best of terms. For the first misfortune (as it sometimes seemed) my father was to blame. The second was my fault.

Actually it was not one but two problems. First: Christopher Robin and the Schoolboy; secondly: Chrisopher Robin and the Man. The two are separated not just in time but by the fact that two quite different sides of my personality were the cause.

Take the Schoolboy first. This was by far the lesser of the two. It was a problem caused by my shyness. I have already said that this was Grandfather Milne's responsibility rather than my father's: that I would have been plagued by shyness anyway, Christopher Robin or no. Nevertheless, Christopher Robin undoubtedly made things worse, though perhaps less so than might have been supposed. His appearances at school were few. Mostly we were occupied with other things, other anxieties, other delights. Fridays, for instance, were clouded by the thought of Latin, Latin, Maths, Soup, Fish, Biscuits, P.T., History, French. If I fussed over the Fish and dreaded the History this had nothing to do with a boy and his bear. Nevertheless, Christopher Robin was beginning to be what he was later to become, a sore place that looked as if it would never heal up. To begin with it was only sometimes sore; at other times it was quite the reverse. It would depend, of course, on the intentions of the person who raised the subject. If he intended to hurt, he could do so quite easily, for I was very vulnerable. I vividly recall how intensely painful it was to me to sit in my study at Stowe while my neighbours played the famous—and now cursed—gramophone record remorselessly over and over again. Eventually, the joke, if not the record, worn out, they handed it to me, and I took it and broke it into a hundred fragments and scattered them over a distant field. But mostly I had other things to think about and didn't bother about being Christopher Robin one way or the other, And because I spent so much time at school not bothering, it never occurred to me that perhaps I ought to be blaming somebody for it all. In fact I blamed nobody. I felt no resentment. My relations with my father were quite unaffected.

Christopher Robin and the Man is a less happy story. Here the cause of the trouble was jealousy.

My father was lucky in that this was something that could have clouded, but in fact did not, his earlier relations with his brother, Ken. Alan, sixteen months his junior, was intellectually his superior. Ken was clever, Alan cleverer. Ken was successful, Alan even more successful. All through their very happy lives together Alan was always to beat Ken, yet Ken was never to feel resentment. How fortunate for the two of them that the talents had been dealt out in this way, that if one of them had to suffer jealousy it was Alan (who didn't need to), *not* Ken. How nice if, when my turn came, I could have been another Ken. How sad that I wasn't.

As a schoolboy my jealousy was directed mainly against my contemporaries. I was jealous when Tompkins minor made more runs than I did and got into the Second Eleven while I remained in the Third. But luckily I was brainier than he and this consoled me. At home I was only jealous of my father when he beat me at golf. The rest of the time we were not rivals but friends. The sun shone equally upon us both. Neither stood in the other's shadow.

But in 1947 all this changed. Up to then we had run neck and neck. He had been the better cricketer but I had been the better mathematician. We had both done equally badly at Cambridge, but I—with a six-year break for the war—could offer the better excuse. We had both been equally indifferent soldiers, but I had at least started from the ranks; and a wound in the head was surely more glorious than trench fever. We had been companions, but now our ways were to part. Admittedly fortune had then smiled on him. He had been "not wholly the wrong person in the right spot at the right time." Admittedly fortune was now frowning on me. I was the wrong person in the wrong place with qualifications nobody wanted. But this didn't alter the fact that he had pressed on to become a famous writer and here was I staring up at him, filled with resentment. Other fathers were reaching down helping hands to their sons. But what was mine doing? What, to be fair, could mine do? He had made his own way by his own efforts and he had left behind him no path that could be followed. But were they entirely his own efforts? Hadn't I come into it somewhere? In pessimistic moments, when I was trudging London in search of an employer wanting to make use of such talents as I could offer, it seemed to me, almost, that my father had got to where he was by climbing upon my infant shoulders, that he had filched from me my good name and had left me with nothing but the empty fame of being his son.

This was the worst period for me. It was a period when, suitably encouraged, my bitterness would overflow. On one or two occasions it overflowed more publicly than it should have done, so that there seemed to be only one thing to do: to escape from it all, to keep out of the limelight. Sorry, I don't give interviews. Sorry, I don't answer letters. It is better to say nothing than to say something that I might regret.

That is how I saw it, looking up at him. How did he see it, looking down at me? Neither of us knew what the other thought. We could only guess. Did he guess right? Did he sympathize? Was he resentful? Did he have any feelings of guilt? Well, he had his own battles to fight and, curiously, they were not dissimilar from mine. If I was jealous of him, he was no less jealous of himself. If I wanted to escape from Christopher Robin, so, too did he.

> *It is easier in England* (he wrote) *to make a reputation than to lose one. I wrote "Children's books," containing altogether, I suppose, 70,000 words—the number of words in the average-length novel. Having said good-bye to all that in 70,000 words, knowing that as far as I was concerned the mode was out moded, I gave up writing children's books. I wanted to escape from them as I had once wanted to escape from* Punch; *as I have always wanted to escape. In vain. . . . As a discerning critic pointed out: the hero of my latest play, God help it, was "just Christopher Robin grown up." So that even when I stop writing about children I still insist on writing about people who were children once. What an obsession with me children are become!*

He was forty-six when *The House at Pooh Corner* was published. Up to then his star had been steadily ascending: editor of *Granta*, assistant editor of *Punch*, successful playwright, and now author of four brilliant

children's books. But *The House at Pooh Corner* was to mark his meridian. After that came the decline. He was writing just as fluently, just as gracefully. But fluency and grace were not enough: the public wanted stronger meat. His last play was put on in 1938: it was a failure. During the war he returned to light verse, and for a number of weeks A.A.M. was back again in *Punch*. His skill had not deserted him, but his public had; and eventually the editor, E.V. Knox, wrote to tell him so. After the war he turned to short stories. He had always written what he had wanted to write. His luck was that this was also what the public wanted to read. Now his luck was deserting him. People didn't want books of short stories. Nor did they want long philosophical poems. Nor even collections of random reflections. He at the top of the hill, I at the bottom: we each had our sorrows, our moments of disillusion. We were both of us unwanted.

Well, if nobody wanted me, if nobody was looking for a very shy young man who had once been quite good at solving differential equations, who had scraped a third class Honours Degree in English Literature, and who was handy with a tenon saw, if nobody would employ me, I must employ myself. I toyed with the idea of making furniture. In the end I decided to sell books.

"I would have thought," said my mother, who always hit the nail on the head no matter whose fingers were in the way, "I would have thought that this was the one thing you would have absolutely hated. I thought you didn't like 'business.' You certainly didn't get on at John Lewis. And you're going to have to meet Pooh fans all the time. Really it does seem a very odd decision." She was quite right, of course. I was no businessman. There were certainly drawbacks to the idea. However hard I tried to play down Christopher Robin, however little space I allowed on my shelves to the Pooh Books, people would inevitably think of mine as "The Christopher Robin Bookshop." However much I wanted to succeed as a bookseller on my own merits, people would inevitably conclude that I was succeeding partly at least on my father's reputation. They might even think (wrongly) that my father's money was subsidising the venture and that—unlike other less fortunate booksellers—I did not really need to make ends meet. "It's easy for him," they might say. And to some small extent this might be true, though I would do my utmost to make it as little true as possible.

On the other hand there were compensations. For here was something my wife and I could do together as partners; here was something we could do in a part of England of our own choosing; and if I wasn't too happy about four of the books, there were still plenty of others.

So in 1951 we left London for Dartmouth; and twenty-one years later we celebrated our coming of age. If, immediately after the war, fortune had frowned, from 1951 onwards it smiled. We had had the good luck to be not wholly the wrong people opening the right shop at the right time in the right town.

Of course, Christopher Robin has intruded, however hard I have tried to keep him at bay; and he still fills me with acute embarrassment.

"So this is the original. Well, well! Come over here a minute, Mandy love. Come and say how-do-you-do to Christopher Robin. Come on. Don't be shy. Shake hands with the gentleman. There now. You can tell your little friends that you've shaken hands with Christopher Robin." After years of practice I am still terribly bad at this sort of thing.

Many years ago a woman followed me into our office (if you can call it that) at the back of the shop. She leaned over my desk. "What are you writing?" she asked with a coy little smile. "An invoice," I said. "Oh." Her face fell. "I thought it might have been a book."

No. Booksellers don't often write books. They know only too well that there are already far too many books. They also haven't the time. Writing a book is not the sort of thing one can do (or rather not the sort of thing I can do) in the office between serving a customer and preparing an invoice. If by any chance a bookseller does write a book, it is because he feels he must: because the urge and the opportunity combine to say "Now! This is the moment. Take your typewriter and away to the attic with you!" Ripeness — as anyone who has had to study King Lear for his English Tripos will tell you — is all.

The first fairy to visit the cradle had said "He shall have his father's brains and his mother's hands." When she had vanished a second fairy appeared. "And his name shall be famous throughout the world." Yes, it was another one of those cryptic spells that fairies have always been so good at, those spells that sound like a blessing but are in fact something of a curse. To be fair, in my particular case, it was again a bit of both. It is tempting, but of course quite impossible, to try and separate the blessing from the curse, to weigh them up and calculate which has been the greater. Tempting but impossible, and I shall never know whether or not I would have been better off as Charles Robert — or even Rosemary.

Some years ago I had a letter from a small child in America. She was very, very angry with me because — so she had heard — I didn't like being Christopher Robin. If she had been Christopher Robin, she told me, she would have been VERY PROUD, and I ought to be ashamed of myself for not feeling proud, too. It was a "Wol" letter, naturally: I doubt if she expected it to be otherwise. She will be older now. Older, wiser, more tolerant. And if she happens on this book she may perhaps understand just how and why it all came about.

"Pooh," said Christopher Robin earnestly, "if I—if I'm not quite—" he stopped and tried again—"Pooh, whatever happens, you will understand, won't you?"

I like to think that Pooh understood. I hope that now others will understand too.

Friedrich Nietzsche

What the father hath hid cometh out in the son; and oft have I found in the son the father's revealed secret.

Randolph S. Churchill

TWENTY-ONE YEARS

IRVING: Did you find it very difficult to assert some kind of separate personality from your father's, although you in fact believed in the same ideals?

CHURCHILL: Well, yes, I suppose that was partly my trouble really. Much as I revered and reverenced him I wasn't prepared just to be an ADC and go along, I wanted to have a show of my own. So, struggling to establish my own individuality and personality I often said and wrote rather reckless things, which I suppose if I hadn't felt this frustration I would have tempered down. I suppose I am a markedly extrovert person and I like to cultivate and display my own personality. I try and think things out for myself. Substantially I went along with my father all the way, but I was always looking for opportunities to establish an individual position, and it's very hard to do so, obviously, when you're living under the shadow of the great oak tree—the small sapling, so close to the parent tree, doesn't perhaps receive enough sunshine. Of course, I had wonderful opportunities and to begin with everyone was very kind and helpful to me. But I became sort of bloody-minded, I suppose, and wanted to strike out on my own and adopted possibly rather an arrogant attitude towards people and institutions at a time when I didn't really have the ammunition or the skill to hit the target. But I hold neither guilt feelings nor reproaches about that. I think anyone can see that there were difficulties naturally inherent in the situation.

John Mortimer

CLINGING TO THE WRECKAGE

"Mr. Justice Cunningham gave custody of the two children to the father. It was proved to his satisfaction that the mother went out to tea dances."

"That's terrible!"

"Well, I was extremely angry at first. You never like to go down in a case, but you'll find this when you're at the bar. You'll have forgotten all about it by the time you slide tape off your next brief."

"I mean, it's terrible to lose your children, just for going to tea dances."

"She went on her own, you see. I suppose the implication was, she danced with gigolos."

"What's a gigolo?"

"I don't think," my mother said, "that's very suitable."

"Mr. Justice Cunningham didn't think it was suitable either." My father shook his head sadly.

"That Judge sounds an absolute swine. He ought to be locked up. Taking away people's children. Just for dancing!"

"Mr. Justice Cunningham is a hard man, old boy," my father agreed. "But it's just part of the rough and tumble in the Probate, Divorce and Admiralty Division. No real fun in winning if it's all too easy. You'll find that."

"I'm not sure I want to. Go to the bar, I mean."

"How is the *viburnum fragans* Kath? Paint me a picture."

How many choices do we make in a lifetime? Even the selection of a wife or a lover is severely limited by the number of people of a vaguely appropriate age, sex and physical appearance you happen to meet at a given moment who may possibly fancy you, a field, as far as most marriages are concerned, of three or four possible candidates. If I had been born into one of those solidly conservative criminal families of London burglars I was later to defend, my career would have been mapped out for me by a father when he was home from the Nick. He would have planned an apprenticeship in Takings and Drivings Away, a little minor Warehouse Breaking and finally the responsibility of Look-out-Man for a firm of bank robbers. Was my life decided when I was a child, bathed and put to bed by the wife of a lawyer's clerk, given bedtime stories from the Divorce Court? I could have chosen not to be a barrister, but every time my father changed the subject I remained on my pre-determined path. If I'm still an agnostic on the subject of Free Will, it operates, I am sure, within the narrowest of limits. We spend our time punishing criminals or rewarding heroes, not for the great decisions they have taken for good or evil but for proceeding, with more or less dedication, in the direction in which they were pointed. At the time my father told me about the custody case and *thé dansants* my cards had no doubt been dealt, a mixed hand adding up to a bid as a barrister and a writer.

Oscar Wilde

to Lord Alfred Douglas

And the curious thing to me is that you should have tried to imitate your father in his chief characteristics. I cannot understand why he was to you an exemplar, where he should have been a warning, except that whenever there is hatred between two people there is bond or brotherhood of some kind. I suppose that, by some strange law of the antipathy of similars, you loathed each other, not because in so many points you were so different, but because in some you were so like. In June 1893 when you left Oxford, without a degree and with debts, petty in themselves, but considerable to a man of your father's income, your father wrote you a very vulgar, violent and abusive letter. The letter you sent him in reply was in every way worse, and of course far less excusable, and consequently you were extremely proud of it. I remember quite well your saying to me with your most conceited air that you could beat your father "at his own trade." Quite true. But what a trade! What a competition! You used to laugh and sneer at your father for retiring from your cousin's house where he was living in order to write filthy letters to him from a neighbouring hotel. You used to do just the same to me. You constantly lunched with me at some public restaurant, sulked or made a scene during luncheon, and then retired to White's Club and wrote me a letter of the very foulest character. The only difference between you and your father was that after you had dispatched your letter to me by special messenger, you would arrive yourself at my rooms some hours later, not to apologise, but to know if I had ordered dinner at the Savoy, and if not, why not. Sometimes you would actually arrive before the offensive letter had been read . . .

You went quite beyond your father in such habits, as you did in others. When his revolting letters to you were read in open Court he naturally felt ashamed and pretended to weep. Had your letters to him been read by his own Counsel still more horror and repugnance would have been felt by everyone.

Homer

Few sons, indeed, are like their fathers. Generally they are worse; but just a few are better.

Bruce Page

PHILBY—THE SPY WHO BETRAYED A GENERATION

In 1960 he [Philby's father] visited Russia as a guest of the Royal Geographical Society and returned via London, where he made a great show of displaying a medal Khrushchev had given him. He took his grandchildren on a fortnight's holiday to Falmouth . . . Then he stopped off at Beirut on his way back to Riyadh and stayed with Kim. The reunion was gay and hectic. On 29 September, after a particularly heavy party, St. John had a heart attack and was taken to hospital unconscious. Kim sat with him throughout the night. In the morning St. John regained consciousness briefly, looked vaguely around the ward and then focused on his son. His last words, worthy of any deathbed anthology, were: "God, I'm bored."

He was buried with simple Muslim rites the following day. Kim, who had a tombstone placed on his father's grave with the inscription THE GREATEST EXPLORER OF THEM ALL, was strongly affected by his father's death. Their relationship had been a complicated one. In the early years St. John had alternated a smothering affection with public humiliation until Kim lost an important factor in a child's development—the certainty of parental love. After St. John had repeatedly belittled his son in front of others, Kim reached a stage where he could not speak to his father without having difficulty in getting the words out. It seems highly probable that Kim's stammer stems from this period and that St. John was to blame. On the other hand St. John was every boy's dream of the romantic parent. While other fathers went to the City or toiled in banks, St. John strode ten feet tall across the Empty Quarter, glory and honour by his side. There is no doubt that Kim hungered to follow in his father's footsteps and that St. John's influence was a powerful motive for Kim. So was Kim's final rejection of Britain an extension of his father's rejection? The similarity of their lives certainly suggests it. Yet in his later years St. John seemed to mellow towards his country. He even became perversely proud of Kim's appointment as First Secretary in Washington and told his friends that he was certain Kim would one day become Ambassador.

What then would he have felt about Kim's defection? One reverts to an impression which outweighs all others: St. John Philby was a man who listened to a different drum and the sense of individual purpose that this gave him was his son's strongest inheritance. If St. John had known the nature of the game which Kim had chosen, with its years on lonely and dangerous paths, one feels he might not have approved but he would most certainly have understood.

DISAGREEMENTS

There is no good father, that's the rule. Don't lay the blame on men but on the bond of paternity, which is rotten.

—JEAN-PAUL SARTRE

Mark Twain

My father and I were always on the most distant terms when I was a boy—a sort of armed neutrality, so to speak. At irregular intervals this neutrality was broken, and suffering ensued; but I will be candid enough to say that the breaking and suffering were always divided with strict impartiality between us—which is to say, my father did the breaking and I did the suffering.

Osbert Sitwell

LAUGHTER IN THE NEXT ROOM

Only one good thing for me, I believe, had come out of the interplaying forces at work in my home life: they had developed to the highest degree a sense of mutual confidence and interdependence among my brother, my sister and myself, from earliest years devoted to one another. We formed a closed corporation, whose other members wrote to me while I was at the war with the greatest regularity, so that I knew from them exactly what was happening, and how it was happening. I think no brother could have two more sensitive and percipient correspondents. My mother also wrote at frequent intervals: as did my father, and for the most part kindly. Yet though primogeniture luckily afforded me, as

I have before indicated, my own *ex-officio* position in the universe, and though undoubtedly he worried about me, yet in a letter written to me at this time he announced that, finding himself compelled to reduce expenditure, and because, as he said, I was in the trenches and therefore could have no need for money, he had decided as a measure of economy to cut off my allowance. And this despite the fact that he was under the impression—created, I must confess, by myself—that I was receiving no Army pay: for, after he had told me that, when it reached me, he would deduct an equivalent sum from the amount he first gave me and then continually snatched from me, I decided to lie, knowing that no lie was too absurd for him to believe—indeed, it had to be ridiculous for him to be taken in by it. Accordingly I declared that no sums were ever paid to my account by the authorities, and maintained this deception stoutly to the end of my military career. When he from time to time asked about it, and if all my other brother-officers were in the same unfortunate predicament, I said, yes, that it was a current scandal, widely commented on. (I am not trying to justify my attitude or conduct, no doubt both to my discredit, but before passing to the result, which was so disconcerting that I must record it, let me urge on my own behalf that I had been given some provocation, and that to a certain degree a sense of fun inspired me.) I was, however, most acutely embarrassed when, while standing for Parliament in 1918, I learnt from my father that he had consulted a cousin, in strict confidence, on what should be done to remedy the shocking state of public affairs I had so innocently revealed, and that, on this man's advice, he had gone to a firm of private detectives, and employed them to set on sleuths to watch the Army Pay Department and to make enquiries in general of the clerk:. The detectives, however, had obtained no satisfaction, and had been received, when in the end they had to become more direct in their questions, at first with bewilderment, and then with anger . . . I thought it best now to admit the whole of my iniquity, i.e. that I had kept the money I had earned, and which, if I had admitted to receiving it, I had realised, would have been taken away from me. And not the least singular part of the story is that my father seemed in no way put out by my confession; if anything, on the contrary, rather pleased . . . I felt some shame at what I had done, but at times, when I thought of those long months in 1918 during which detectives had been watching the Army Pay Department, laughter would sweep away all other sensations.

However, we are still only in 1914; I am at the Front, and though my father sent me there—as well as letters—hampers, wading boots and various necessities of life, yet he had been as good as his word, and had proceeded to retrench in his favourite and familiar style. I did not know where to turn for money, but at the same time a certain ludicrous side to it, and perhaps a love of adventure, forbad me to take the matter too seriously—although I was resolved to give my father a fright and regain my allowance. Moreover, I had already learnt a lesson: always, in any disagreement with my father, to be inventive, to view the question in dispute from an altogether novel angle, and whenever possible to indulge in a high degree of fantasy. (This was a rule by which, more and more, in the coming years I guided my dealings with him, and it proved invaluable by its results.) Now a year or two before the war my father had started to farm in a small way, and had latterly expanded the scope of his operations, into which he had thrown himself with a kind of fury. Before long the area had amounted to no less than two thousand acres, and he had founded a company, of which, since some of the land it worked belonged to me, I had been made a director . . . He started, of course, with no knowledge of agriculture, but he was keen on fault-finding. I was away, and in the circumstances this new occupation afforded him the fullest outlet for it. He drove about, balanced on his British-Museum air-cushion in a pony cart—a tub, smartly painted in green and yellow, and drawn by a skewbald pony—criticising to the top of his bent. Fortunately, Maynard Hollingworth, who made the plans and carried them out, was an expert in farming; and on his advice my father had particularly specialised in pigs and potatoes. I have mentioned that recently, where certain ideas, not political or esthetic, were concerned, he had rather unexpectedly shown himself liable to be very easily influenced by the press. Thus, in the years immediately preceding 1914, he had become an enthusiastic advocate of Standard Bread and paper-bag cookery, when those two objects or ideals were written up in rival daily papers. It happened that lately a correspondence had been published in *The Times*, concerning the possible benefits to be derived from reviving the medieval habit of payment in kind. My father had thoroughly enjoyed, and pondered on, these letters, and had determined that his approval of ancient ways should find a practical application. He had returned to Renishaw in January 1915, and late that month or early in February had sent a letter to my brother's housemaster at Eton, to intimate that, having been particularly hard hit by the war, he could not afford to pay the usual fees at the end of the term in money, but instead would deliver to their value pigs and potatoes. The housemaster was, it can be imagined, perturbed by the novelty of the suggestion and when the story transpired it created much interest. Sacheverell, whose life had been made by no whit easier as a result, appeared far from enthusiastic about the scheme when he wrote to tell me of it. His letter reached me at the Front, at about the same time as that from my father in which he had cut off my allowance, and from this conjunction an idea came to me . . . I was shortly due to proceed on leave and, after all, I remembered, I was a director of the Sitwell Farming Company!

I wrote to my father in the following terms, and without showing any sign of resentment.

My Dearest Father,

Thank you for your letter. I well understand that your present position forces you to make economies, because I am obliged to do the same. I come home on leave in about a fortnight, and, as I have no allowance now, I have been able to arrange, I am glad to say, with the guard on the leave-train to accept potatoes instead of my fare. — Ever your loving son, Osbert.

In his reply to me, my father did not even permit himself to allude to the subject of my letter, and for a while I feared it had fallen flat: but not many more days had passed before, without a word of explanation, my allowance was restored in full.

On my return I learned more, and that my ruse had been successful: for Maynard Hollingworth described to me the following scene.

"One day Sir George rushed up to the office, waving a letter in his hand and shouting, '*What does the boy mean*? They're not *HIS* potatoes: they're *MY* potatoes!' "

"I said to him, 'If you'd let me see the letter, Sir George, perhaps I might be able to help' . . . He gave it to me and after reading it, I said, 'It's nothing, Sir George; it's Mr. Osbert's chaff!' But he tore it out of my hand, and dashed out of the room again, crying, 'Oh no, it's not. *HE would do it!*' "

In the end it had only been by stressing the improbability of there being guards on trains near the fighting, and the difficulties I should undoubtedly encounter in securing the transport requisite for moving the crop from Renishaw to the Front, that Hollingworth had been able to allay, though not to dispel, my father's fears . . .

The London house he had taken at this time seemed to Edith [his sister] and me to be full of a highly coloured, evil levity of spirit, so strong as almost to have a presence and become a haunting. When I arrived from Flanders, I was put in a bedroom on the ground floor, but entirely cut off from the rest of the house. It was dark and inconvenient, and I slept badly in it. I asked if I could be moved. My father, however, had read in the papers that the troops in the trenches were infested with lice, and he now explained to me that he had selected a room far away on purpose, in case I was acting as host to a pack of these vermin, since the distance made it less likely that they would attack him — for if they did, it might, he pointed out, entail very serious consequences! When I became angry, for personal cleanliness has always been something of an obsession with me, and protested that if thus afflicted I should not go to stay in any house and that it was a slur on me to suggest it, he fluttered his hand at me condescendingly, and replied, "Not at all, my dear boy. It's no disgrace. Any primitive form of life is most interesting!"

Anais Nin

I never could dance around you, my father. No one ever danced around you. As soon as I left you, my father, the whole world swung into a symphony.

Edith Sitwell

My maddening old father is in Italy; and has sent through a message to say that if we cannot send money through to him by December, he will be starving. What an end and climax to a life in which one has been a constant nuisance to one's off-spring!

Stephen Leacock

THE BOY I LEFT BEHIND ME

My father, as he drank more, changed towards us from a superman and hero to a tyrant, from easy and kind to fits of brutality. I was small enough to escape from doing much of the farm chores and farm work. But I carry still the recollection of it — more, no doubt, than Jim or Dick ever did. In fact the sight and memory of what domestic tyranny in an isolated, lonely home, beyond human help, can mean helped to set me all the more firmly in the doctrine of the rights of man and Jefferson's liberty.

Sylvia Plath

DADDY

You do not do, you do not do
Any more, black shoe
In which I have lived like a foot
For thirty years, poor and white,
Barely daring to breathe or Achoo.

Daddy, I have had to kill you.
You died before I had time—
Marble-heavy, a bag full of God,
Ghastly statue with one grey toe
Big as a Frisco seal

And a head in the freakish Atlantic
Where it pours bean green over blue
In the waters off beautiful Nauset.
I used to pray to recover you.
Ach, du.

In the German tongue, in the Polish town
Scraped flat by the roller
Of wars, wars, wars.
But the name of the town is common.
My Polack friend

Says there are a dozen or two.
So I never could tell where you
Put your foot, your root,
I never could talk to you.
The tongue stuck in my jaw.

It stuck in a barb wire snare.
Ich, ich, ich, ich,
I could hardly speak.
I thought every German was you.
And the language obscene

An engine, an engine
Chuffing me off like a Jew.
A Jew to Dachau, Auschwitz, Belsen.
I began to talk like a Jew.
I think I may well be a Jew.

The snows of the Tyrol, the clear beer of
        Vienna
Are not very pure or true.
With my gypsy ancestress and my weird
        luck
And my Taroc pack and my Taroc pack
I may be a bit of a Jew.

I have always been scared of you,
With your Luftwaffe, your gobbledygoo.
And your neat moustache
And your Aryan eye, bright blue.
Panzer-man, panzer-man, O You—

Not God but a swastika
So black no sky could squeak through.
Every woman adores a Fascist,
The boot in the face, the brute
Brute heart of a brute like you.

You stand at the blackboard, daddy,
In the picture I have of you,
A cleft in your chin instead of your foot
But no less a devil for that, no not
Any less the black man who

Bit my pretty red heart in two.
I was ten when they buried you.
At twenty I tried to die
And get back, back, back to you.
I thought even the bones would do.

But they pulled me out of the sack,
And they stuck me together with glue.
And then I knew what to do.
I made a model of you,
A man in black with a Meinkampf look

And a love of the rack and the screw.
And I said I do, I do.
So daddy, I'm finally through.
The black telephone's off at the root,
The voices just can't worm through.

If I've killed one man, I've killed two—
The vampire who said he was you
And drank my blood for a year,
Seven years, if you want to know.
Daddy, you can lie back now.

There's a stake in your fat black heart
And the villagers never liked you.
They are dancing and stamping on you.
They always *knew* it was you.
Daddy, daddy, you bastard, I'm through.

Virginia Woolf

Father's birthday. He would have been 96, 96, yes, today; and could have been 96, like other people one has known: but mercifully was not. His life would have utterly ended mine.

Margaret Laurence

THE STONE ANGEL

Father took such a pride in the store—you'd have thought it was the only one on earth. It was the first in Manawaka, so I guess he had due cause. He would lean across the counter, spreading his hands, and smile so wonderfully you'd feel he welcomed the world.

Mrs. McVitie, the lawyer's wife, bonneted garishly, smiled back and asked for eggs. I remember so well it was eggs she asked for— brown ones, which she thought more nourishing than the white-shelled kind. And I, in black buttoned boots and detested mauve and beige striped stockings worn for warmth and the sensible long-sleeved navy-blue serge dress he ordered each year from the East, poked my nose into the barrel that housed the sultanas, intending to sneak a handful while he was busy.

"Oh, look! The funniest wee things, scampering—"

I laughed at them as they burrowed, the legs so quick and miniature you could hardly see them, delighted that they'd dare appear there and flout my father's might, mustache and his ire.

"Mind your manners, miss!"

The swipe he caught me then was nothing to what I got in the back of the store after she'd left.

"Have you no regard for my reputation?"

"But I saw them!"

"Did you have to announce it from the housetops?"

"I didn't mean—"

"No good to say you're sorry when the damage is done. Hold out your hands, miss."

I wouldn't let him see me cry, I was so enraged. He used a foot ruler, and when I jerked my smarting palms back, he made me hold them out again. He looked at my dry eyes in a kind of fury, as though he'd failed unless he drew water from them. He struck and struck, and then all at once he threw the ruler down and put his arms around me. He held me so tightly I was almost smothered against the thick mothball smelling roughness of his clothes. I felt caged and panicky and wanted to push him away, but didn't dare. Finally he released me. He looked bewildered as though he wanted to explain but didn't know the explanation himself.

"You take after me," he said, as though that made everything clear. "You've got backbone, I'll give you that."

He sat down on a packing-case and took me on his knee.

"What you must realize," he said, speaking softly, hastily, "is that when I have to take the ruler to you, it hurts me just as much as it does you." I'd heard that before, many times. But looking at him then from my dark bright eyes, I knew it was a barefaced lie. I did take after him, though—God knows he wasn't wrong in that.

I stood in the doorway, poised and ready to run.

"Are you going to throw them away?"

"What?"

"The sultanas. Are you going to throw them away?"

"You mind your own business, miss," he snapped, "or I'll—"

Sir Richard Livingstone

So long as there is life in the world, each generation will react against its predecessor, correct it, go beyond it. The house that accommodates the fathers never quite suits the children.

Charles Dickens

DOMBEY AND SON

There were some children staying in the house. Children who were as frank and happy with fathers and with mothers as those rosy faces opposite home. Children who had no restraint upon their love, and freely showed it. Florence sought to learn their secret; sought to find out what it was she had missed; what simple art they knew, and she knew not; how she could be taught by them to show her father that she loved him, and to win his love again.

Many a day did Florence thoughtfully observe these children. On many a bright morning did she leave her bed when the glorious sun rose, and walking up and down upon the river's bank, before anyone in the house was stirring, look up at the windows of their rooms, and think of them, asleep, so gently tended and affectionately thought of. Florence would feel more lonely then, than in the great house all alone; and would think sometimes that she was better there than here, and that there was greater peace in hiding herself than in mingling with others of her age, and finding how unlike them all she was. But attentive to her study, though it touched her to the quick at every little leaf she turned in the hard book, Florence remained among them, and tried with patient hope, to gain the knowledge that she wearied for.

Ah! how to gain it! how to know the charm in its beginning! There were daughters here, who rose up in the morning, and lay down to rest at night, possessed of fathers' hearts already. They had no repulse to overcome, no coldness to dread, no frown to smooth away. As the morning advanced, and the windows opened one by one, and the dew began to dry upon the flowers and grass, and youthful feet began to move upon the lawn, Florence, glancing round at the bright faces, thought what was there she could learn from these children? It was too late to learn from them; each could approach her father fearlessly, and put up her lips to meet the ready kiss, and wind her arm about the neck that bent down to caress her. *She* could not begin by being so bold. Oh!

could it be that there was less and less hope as she studied more and more!

She remembered well, that even the old woman who had robbed her when a little child—whose image and whose house, and all she had said and done, were stamped upon her recollection, with the enduring sharpness of a fearful impression made at that early period of life—had spoken fondly of her daughter, and how terribly even she had cried out in the pain of hopeless separation from her child. But her own mother, she would think again, when she recalled this, had loved her well. Then sometimes, when her thoughts reverted swiftly to the void between herself and her father, Florence would tremble, and the tears would start upon her face, as she pictured to herself her mother living on, and coming also to dislike her, because of her wanting the unknown grace that should conciliate that father naturally, and had never done so from her cradle. She knew that this imagination did wrong to her mother's memory, and had no truth in it, or base to rest upon; and yet she tried so hard to justify him, and to find the whole blame in herself, that she could not resist its passing, like a wild cloud, through the distance of her mind.

There came among the other visitors, soon after Florence, one beautiful girl, three or four years younger than she, who was an orphan child, and who was accompanied by her aunt, a grey-haired lady, who spoke much to Florence, and who greatly liked (but that they all did) to hear her sing of an evening, and would always sit near her at that time, with motherly interest. They had only been two days in the house, when Florence, being in an arbour in the garden one warm morning, musingly observant of a youthful group upon the turf, through some intervening boughs, and wreathing flowers for the head of one little creature among them who was the pet and plaything of the rest, heard this same lady and her niece, in pacing up and down a sheltered nook close by, speak of herself.

"Is Florence an orphan like me, aunt?" said the child.

"No, my love. She has no mother, but her father is living."

"Is she in mourning for her poor Mama, now?" inquired the child quickly.

"No; for her only brother."

"Has she no other brother?"

"None."

"No sister?"

"None."

"I am very, very sorry!" said the little girl.

As they stopped soon afterwards to watch some boats, and had been silent in the meantime, Florence, who had risen when she heard her name, and had gathered up her flowers to go and meet them, that they might know of her being within hearing, resumed her seat and work, expecting to hear no more; but the conversation recommenced next moment.

"Florence is a favourite with everyone here, and deserves to be, I am sure," said the child, earnestly. "Where is her Papa?"

The aunt replied, after a moment's pause, that she did not know. Her tone of voice arrested Florence, who had started from her seat again; and held her fastened to the spot, with her work hastily caught up to her bosom, and her two hands saving it from being scattered on the ground.

"He is in England, I hope, aunt?" said the child.

"I believe so. Yes; I know he is, indeed."

"Has he ever been here?"

"I believe not. No."

"Is he coming here to see her?"

"I believe not."

"Is he lame, or blind, or ill, aunt?" asked the child.

The flowers that Florence held to her breast began to fall when she heard those words, so wonderingly spoken. She held them closer; and her face hung down upon them.

"Kate," said the lady, after another moment of silence, "I will tell you the whole truth about Florence as I have heard it, and believe it to be. Tell no one else, my dear, because it may be little known here, and your doing so would give her pain."

"I never will!" exclaimed the child.

"I know you never will," returned the lady. "I can trust you as myself. I fear then, Kate, that Florence's father cares little for her, very seldom sees her, never was kind to her in her life, and now quite shuns her and avoids her. She would love him dearly if he would suffer her, but he will not — though for no fault of hers; and she is greatly to be loved and pitied by all gentle hearts."

More of the flowers that Florence held fell scattering on the ground; those that remained were wet, but not with dew; and her face dropped upon her laden hands.

"Poor Florence! Dear, good Florence!" cried the child.

"Do you know why I have told you this, Kate?" said the lady.

"That I may be very kind to her, and take great care to try to please her. Is that the reason, aunt?"

"Partly," said the lady, "but not all. Though we see her so cheerful; with a pleasant smile for everyone; ready to oblige us all, and bearing her part in every amusement here: she can hardly be quite happy, do you think she can, Kate?"

"I am afraid not," said the little girl.

"And you can understand," pursued the lady, "why her observation of children who have parents who are fond of them, and proud of them — like many here, just now — should make her sorrowful in secret?"

"Yes, dear aunt," said the child, "I understand that very well. Poor Florence!"

More flowers strayed upon the ground, and those she yet held to her breast trembled as if a wintry wind were rustling them.

"My Kate," said the lady, whose voice was serious, but very calm and sweet, and had so impressed Florence from the first moment of her hearing it, "of all the youthful people here, you are her natural and harmless friend; you have not the innocent means, that happier children have—"

"There are none happier, aunt!" exclaimed the child, who seemed to cling about her.

"—As other children have, dear Kate, of reminding her of her misfortune. Therefore I would have you, when you try to be her little friend, try all the more for that, and feel that the bereavement you sustained — thank Heaven! before you knew its weight — gives you claim and hold upon poor Florence."

"But I am not without a parent's love, aunt, and I never have been," said the child, "with you."

"However that may be, my dear," returned the lady, "your misfortune is a lighter one than Florence's; for not an orphan in the world can be so deserted as the child who is an outcast from a living parent's love."

King George V

My father was frightened of his father, I was frightened of my father, and I am damned well going to see to it that my children are frightened of me.

Harry Graham

THE STERN PARENT

Father heard his children scream,
So he threw them in the stream,
Saying, as he drowned the third,
"Children should be seen, not heard!"

Elizabeth Barrett Browning

The bitterest "fact" of all is, that I had believed Papa to have loved me more than he obviously does: but I never regret knowledge—I mean I never would *unknow* anything—even were it the taste of apples by the Dead Sea—and this must be accepted like the rest.

Alexandre Dumas

to his son

[January 1840]

It is not my fault, but yours, that the relationship between us is no longer that of father and son. You came to my house, where you were well received by everyone, and then, suddenly, acting upon whose advice I do not know, decided no longer to recognize the lady whom I regarded as my wife, as should have been obvious from the fact that I was living with her. From that day, since I had no intention of taking advice (even indirectly) from you, the situation of which you complain, began and has lasted, much to my sorrow, for six years.

It can cease whenever you wish. You have only to write a letter to Madam Ida, asking her to be to you what she is to your sister; you will then be always, and eternally welcome. The happiest thing that could happen to you is that this liaison should continue, since, having had no child for six years, I am now certain that I never shall have any, so that you are now not only my eldest, but my only, son.

I have nothing else to tell you. All that I would have you consider is this, that, should I marry any woman other than Madam Ida, I might well have three or four more children, whereas with her, I shall have none.

I trust that in all this you will consult your heart rather than your interests, though this time—contrary to what usually happens—the two are in agreement. I embrace you with all my heart.

Shakespeare

KING LEAR

LEAR: Know that we have divided
In three our kingdom: and 'tis our fast intent
To shake all cares and business from our age;
Conferring them on younger strengths, while we
Unburden'd crawl toward death. Our son of Cornwall.
And you, our no less loving son of Albany,
We have this hour a constant will to publish
Our daughters' several dowers, that future strife
May be prevented now. The princes, France and Burgundy,
Long in our court have made their amorous sojourn,
And here are to be answer'd. Tell me, my daughters,
(Since now we will divest us, both of rule,
Interest of territory, cares of state)
Which of you, shall we say, doth love us most?
That we our largest bounty may extend
Where merit doth most challenge it. Goneril,
Our eldest-born, speak first.

GONERIL: Sir, I
Do love you more than words can wield the matter;
Dearer than eyesight, space, and liberty;
Beyond what can be valued, rich or rare;
No less than life, with grace, health, beauty, honour:
As much as child e'er loved, or father found;
A love that makes breath poor, and speech unable;
Beyond all manner of so much I love you.

CORDELIA: [Aside.] What shall Cordelia do?
Love and be silent.

LEAR: Of all these bounds, even from this line to this,
With shadowy forests and with champains rich'd,

With plenteous rivers and wide-skirted meads,
We make thee lady: to thine and Albany's issue
Be this perpetual. — What says our second daughter,
Our dearest Regan, wife to Cornwall? Speak.

REGAN: I am made of that self metal as my sister,
And prize me at her worth. In my true heart
I find she names my very deed of love;
Only she comes too short, — that I profess
Myself an enemy to all other joys,
Which the most precious square of sense possesses;
And I find I am alone felicitate
In your dear highness' love.

CORDELIA: [Aside.] Then, poor Cordelia!
And yet not so; since I am sure my love's
More richer than my tongue.

LEAR: To thee and thine, hereditary ever,
Remain this ample third of our fair kingdom;
No less in space, validity, and pleasure,
Than that confirm'd on Goneril. — Now, our joy,
Although the last, not least; to whose young love
The vines of France and milk of Burgundy
Strive to be interess'd: what can you say, to draw
A third more opulent than your sister? Speak.

CORDELIA: Nothing, my lord.

LEAR: Nothing?

CORDELIA: Nothing.

LEAR: Nothing can come of nothing: speak again.

CORDELIA: Unhappy that I am, I cannot heave
My heart into my mouth: I love your majesty
According to my bond; nor more nor less.

LEAR: How, how, Cordelia! mend your speech a little,
Lest it may mar your fortunes.

CORDELIA: Good my lord,
You have begot me, bred me, loved me. I

Return those duties back as are right fit,
Obey you, love you, and most honour you.
Why have my sisters husbands, if they say
They love you all? Haply, when I shall wed,
That lord, whose hand must take my plight, shall carry
Half my love with him, half my care and duty:
Sure, I shall never marry like my sisters,
To love my father all.

LEAR: But goes this with thy heart?

CORDELIA: Ay, good my lord.

LEAR: So young, and so untender?

CORDELIA: So young, my lord, and true.

LEAR: Let it be so. — Thy truth, then, be thy dower:
For, by the sacred radiance of the sun,
The mysteries of Hecate, and the night;
By all the operations of the orbs
From whom we do exist, and cease to be;
Here I disclaim all my paternal care,
Propinquity and property of blood,
And, as a stranger to my heart and me,
Hold thee from this, for ever. The barbarous Scythian,
Or he that makes his generation messes
To gorge his appetite, shall to my bosom
Be as well neighbour'd, pitied, and relieved,
As thou my sometime daughter.

KENT: Good my liege, —

LEAR: Peace, Kent!
Come not between the dragon and his wrath.
I loved her most, and thought to set my rest
On her kind nursery. [To Cordelia] Hence, and avoid my
    sight! —
So be my grave my peace, as here I give
Her father's heart from her! — Call France; — who stirs?
Call Burgundy. Cornwall, and Albany,
With my two daughters' dowers digest this third:
Let pride, which she calls plainness, marry her.

I do invest you jointly with my power,
Pre-eminence, and all the large effects
That troop with majesty. Ourself, by monthly course,
With reservation of a hundred knights,
By you to be sustain'd, shall our abode
Make with you by due turns. Only we still retain
The name, and all the additions to a king;
The sway, revenue, execution of the rest,
Beloved sons, be yours: which to confirm,
This coronet part between you.

Ben Fong-Torres and Kurt Loder

MARVIN GAYE: 1939–1984

Marvin Gaye was home at last, but somehow things weren't the same. He was back near his mother again, and he was glad for that. He was close again, too, with his brothers and sisters and children. But his father? The righteous disciplinarian of his youth? Yes, there was the problem. "We don't communicate like before," Marvin said.

It was shortly before noon on April 1st, 1984, when the argument began that ended Marvin Gaye's life. Gaye and his seventy-one-year-old mother, Alberta, were talking in his upstairs bedroom in the family's two-story Los Angeles home. The pair heard an unintelligible shout from downstairs: It was Marvin's seventy-year-old father, Marvin Gaye Sr. He was upset because he couldn't find some letters pertaining to an insurance policy.

Gaye Sr. yelled at his wife again. Marvin was peeved at his father's tone of voice and called to him to come upstairs so that his mother could understand what he was saying. When the elder Gaye entered his son's room, he shouted a third time at his wife. Marvin exploded. "You can't talk to my mother that way," he said sternly. A loud exchange ensued.

Marvin told his father to get out of the bedroom. He refused. Marvin pushed his father into the hallway, where the argument continued. Finally, Alberta intervened; the father stormed off, and the son and the mother returned to the bedroom.

By now, Marvin Gaye Sr. wasn't trying to find insurance papers. He was looking for a gun, and he found one: a .38-caliber revolver. He reentered his son's bedroom, and from a distance of four to six feet, Marvin Gaye Sr. shot his son in the chest. The bullet tore through Marvin's heart. A few seconds passed. The father moved closer to his dying son, and as his mother looked on, shot him once more, point-blank, in the left shoulder.

Then Marvin Gaye Sr. walked downstairs, left the house, tossed the gun onto the lawn, took a seat on the porch and waited for the police to arrive . . .

Father and son had quarreled frequently during Marvin Jr.'s youth. "Marvin told me he never got the love from his father that he wanted," said Shaw. "He told me, 'He doesn't accept my love.' "

Love and respect from his father were paramount concerns of Marvin's. When the time had come to renew his contract with Motown in 1978, Marvin demanded a million-dollar signing bonus — delivered in cash in a briefcase to him. Motown refused. "I told Marvin, 'Are you crazy?' " recalled Shaw. "And Marvin said, 'I want a million dollars cash so I can take it to my father and say, See that? That's a million dollars. I just want you to know how successful I am.' " . . .

Upon his arrest, Marvin Gaye Sr. expressed no emotion whatsoever. At his April 4th arraignment on a charge of murder, his attorney asked for a postponement because his client was not "mentally competent" to stand trial.

"I wish it were out in the open what his mental state really is," said Banks, "because he's really been through a lot. He's been through a lot of easy times, really. He didn't have to do nothing all his life. He didn't have the responsibilities Marvin had. So, you know, his attitude was just as cocky as Marvin's sometimes. It's like teacher and student. Clever people."

One theory holds that the singer may have intentionally hastened his own death. "Marvin felt it was his time," said a close friend. "He was tired of running. By him pushing his dad, his dad was forced to do something."

"It's possible that was the case," said Anna Gordy. "I knew when I heard [about Marvin's death] that it was God's will. I thought about the fact that, oddly and ironically, the very person who helped bring him into this world . . . [that] God had the same person take him out of this world. There is probably something there." . . .

"Do you love your father?" I asked Marvin. "Yes," he answered in a voice light as a spring breeze. "Then why don't you tell him?" I challenged. "I can't," he said.

T. Campbell

LORD ULLIN'S DAUGHTER

A Chieftain to the Highlands bound
Cries "Boatman, do not tarry!
And I'll give thee a silver pound
To row us o'er the ferry!"

"Now who be ye, would cross Lochgyle.
This dark and stormy water?"
"O I'm the chief of Ulva's isle,
And this, Lord Ullin's daughter.

"And fast before her father's men
Three days we've fled together,
For should he find us in the glen,
My blood would stain the heather.

"His horsemen hard behind us ride—
Should they our steps discover,
Then who will cheer my bonnie bride,
When they have slain her lover?"

Out spoke the hardy Highland wight,
"I'll go, my chief, I'm ready:
It is not for your silver bright,
But for your winsome lady:

"And by my word! the bonny bird
In danger shall not tarry;
So though the waves are raging white
I'll row you o'er the ferry."

By this the storm grew loud apace,
The water-wraith was shrieking;
And in the scowl of Heaven each face
Grew dark as they were speaking.

But still as wilder blew the wind,
And as the night grew drearer,
Adown the glen rode armed men,
Their trampling sounded nearer.

"O haste thee, haste!" the lady cries,
"Though tempests round us gather;
I'll meet the raging of the skies,
But not an angry father."

The boat has left a stormy land,
A stormy sea before her, —
When, oh! too strong for human hand
The tempest gather'd o'er her.

And still they row'd amidst the roar
Of waters fast prevailing:
Lord Ullin reached that fatal shore, —
His wrath was changed to wailing.

For, sore dismay'd, through storm and shade
His child he did discover: —
One lovely hand she stretched for aid,
And one was round her lover.

"Come back! come back!" he cried in grief,
"Across this stormy water:
And I'll forgive your Highland chief,
My daughter! — Oh, my daughter!"

'Twas vain: the loud waves lash'd the shore,
Return or aid preventing:
The waters wild went o'er his child,
And he was left lamenting.

Harry Graham

L'ENFANT GLACÉ

When Baby's cries grew hard to bear
I popped him in the Frigidaire.
I never would have done so if
I'd known that he'd be frozen stiff.
My wife said: "George, I'm so unhappe!
Our darling's now completely *frappé*!"

Antony Alpers

THE LIFE
OF KATHERINE MANSFIELD

The notebook then turns to Kathleen's parents. They are worse than she had even expected, and her father's appearance fills her with disgust: "His hands, covered with long sandy hair, are absolutely cruel hands. A physically revolted feeling seizes me." He has spoken of her returning to England as "Damned rot," saying, "look here, he wouldn't have me fooling round in dark corners with fellows." But it isn't only fellows: there is something about Kathleen that attracts women as well as men, and her parents are aware of it. Her mother is always watching her, "constantly suspicious, constantly overbearingly tyrannous"; and as for her father: "I cannot be alone or in the company of women for half a minute—he is there, eyes fearful, attempting to appear unconcerned, pulling at his long drooping red-grey moustache with his hairy hands. Ugh!"

This was the low point of Kathleen's comments on her parents. Although the torrent of egotism continued for some time in various notebooks, she was never again quite so nasty about her father as she was during this hateful, confined, symbolic journey out, this journey to "home" from the other place called "Home" that was now her spiritual home . . .

[Dying, Katherine finally writes to her father] . . .

It is plain—most painfully plain—that when Katherine wrote it her heart was full of affection for the father she had spurned in her adolescence, and that *her* main concern was to regain whatever of love might be regained before her death; but in trying for that she was forced to speak of what she had been told about his begrudging her allowance.

It is equally plain—and as painfully too, from the strokes of his sharp steel businessman's nib—that when Beauchamp read the letter ten weeks later, it was the money question that touched him most deeply, at least in private. What he wrote to her on 7 January cannot be known . . . What he wrote to himself—diagonally across the top of the letter, in his firm, businessman's hand—was this: "R[eceived]. 7/1/22. A[nswered]. Idem." And on reflection two days later: "I can emphatically state that in *thought, word, & deed* I have never begrudged any of my children the amounts I have paid them by way of allowances. On the contrary, I have always considered it a *pleasure* and a *privilege* to do everything possible for their comfort, happiness & worldly advancement. H.B. 9/1/22." In the vigorous strokes, and the stab of the nib in the inkwell—how she knew that inkwell in his office!—one sees as nowhere else what it was that Kass had been afraid of all these years. On the later pages of the letter Beauchamp also made the two marginal notes . . .

Confidential

I

xi

1921

Chalet des Sapins
Montana-sur-Sierre
(Valais)
Switzerland

Father darling,

I must get over this fear of writing to you because I have not written for so long. I am ashamed to ask for your forgiveness and yet how can I approach you without it? Every single day I think and wonder how I can explain my silence. I cannot tell you how often I dream of you. Sometimes night after night I dream that I am back in New Zealand and sometimes you are angry with me and at other times this horrible behaviour of mine has not happened and all is well between us. It is simply agony *not* to write to you. My heart is full of you. But the past rises before me, when I have promised not to do this very thing that I have done and it's like a wall that I can't see over.

The whole reason for my silence has been that, in the first weeks I was ill and waited until I was better. And then events conspired to throw me into a horrible depression that I could not shake off. Connie and Jinnie made me understand how very much you considered you were doing for me. They made me realise that for you to give me 300 pounds a year [In the margin at this point: "Quite Untrue. H.B."] was an extreme concession and that as a matter of fact, my husband was the one who ought to provide for me. Of course I appreciate your great generosity in allowing me so much money. And I know it is only because I am ill in the way that I am that you are doing so. But it is highly unlikely that I shall live very long and consumption is a terribly expensive illness. I thought that you did not mind looking after me to this extent. And to feel that you did — was like a blow to me. I couldn't get over it. I feel as though I didn't belong to you, really. If Chaddie or Jeanne had developed consumption husbands or no husbands they would surely have appealed to you. One does turn to one's father however bad one is. Have I forfeited the right to do so? Perhaps . . . There is no reason, Father dear, that you should go on loving me through thick and thin. I see that. And I have been an extraordinarily unsatisfactory and disappointing child.

But in spite of everything, one gets shot in the wing and one believes that "home" will receive one and cherish one.

When we were together in France I was happy with you as I had always longed to be but when I knew that you grudged me the money [In the margin at this point: "Quite untrue. Never made such a statement to anyone. H.B."] it was simply torture.

I did not know what to say about it. I waited until I saw if I could earn more myself at that time. But it was not possible. Then I had waited so long that it seemed impossible to write. Then I was so seriously ill that I was not in a state to write to anybody. And by the time that crisis was over it seemed to me my sin of silence was too great to beg forgiveness, and so it has gone on.

But I cannot bear it any longer. I must come to you and at least acknowledge my fault. I must at least tell you, even though the time has passed when you wish to listen, that never for a moment, in my folly and my fear, have I ceased to love and to honour you. I have punished myself so cruelly that I couldn't suffer more.

Father don't turn away from me, darling. If you cannot take me back into your heart believe me when I say I am

Your devoted deeply sorrowing child
Kass

Keith Sagar

THE LIFE OF D. H. LAWRENCE

Lawrence and his sister could not bear to watch the pointless suffering of their mother. They put morphine in her milk. Three days later she died.

An advance copy of *The White Peacock* had been rushed through to Lawrence. He had put it into his mother's hands, but she had been beyond reading it. After the funeral, his father "struggled through half a page, and it might as well have been Hottentot":

"And what dun they gi'e thee for that, lad?"

"Fifty pounds, father."

"Fifty pounds!" He was dumbfounded, and looked at me with shrewd eyes, as if I were a swindler. "Fifty pounds! An' tha's niver done a day's hard work in they life."

The death of his mother did not soften Lawrence's detestation of his father. The following month he wrote of him to the minister Robert Reid as "disgusting, irritating, and selfish as a maggot. Yet I am sorry for him: he's old, and stupid, and very helpless and futile."

William Carlos Williams

A man wants to protect his son, wants to teach him the things he, the father, has learned or thinks he has learned. But it's exactly that which a child resents. He wants to know but he wants to know on his own— and the longer the paternal influence lasts the harder it is to break down and the more two individuals who should have much in common are pushed apart. Only a sudden enforced break can get through that one.

Clarence Day

LIFE WITH FATHER

There was a time in my boyhood when I felt that Father had handicapped me severely in life by naming me after him, "Clarence." All literature, so far as I could see, was thronged with objectionable persons named Clarence. Percy was bad enough, but there had been some good fighters named Percy. The only Clarence in history was a duke who did something dirty at Tewkesbury, and who died a ridiculous death afterwards in a barrel of malmsey.

As for the Clarences in the fiction I read, they were horrible. In one story, for instance, there were two brothers, Clarence and Frank. Clarence was a "vain, disagreeable little fellow," who was proud of his curly hair and fine clothes, while Frank was a "rollicking boy who was ready to play games with anybody." Clarence didn't like to play games, of course. He just minced around looking on.

One day when the mother of these boys had gone out, this story went on, Clarence "tempted" Frank to disobey her and fly their kite on

the roof. Frank didn't want to, but Clarence kept taunting him and daring him until Frank was stung into doing it. After the two boys went up to the roof, Frank got good and dirty, running up and down and stumbling over scuttles, while Clarence sat there, giving him orders, and kept his natty clothes tidy. To my horror, he even spread out his handkerchief on the trapdoor to sit on. And to crown all, this sneak told on Frank as soon as their mother came in.

This wasn't an exceptionally mean Clarence, either. He was just run-of-the-mill. Some were worse.

So far as I could ever learn, however, Father had never heard of these stories, and had never dreamed of there being anything objectionable in his name. Quite the contrary. And yet as a boy he had lived a good rough-and-tumble boy's life. He had played and fought on the city streets, and kept a dog in Grandpa's stable, and stolen rides to Greenpoint Ferry on the high, lurching bus. In the summer he had gone to West Springfield and had run down Shad Lane through the trees to the house where Grandpa was born, and had gone barefoot and driven the cows home just as though he had been named Tom or Bill.

He had the same character as a boy, I suppose, that he had as a man, and he was too independent to care if people thought his name fancy. He paid no attention to the prejudices of others, except to disapprove of them. He had plenty of prejudices himself, of course, but they were his own. He was humorous and confident and level-headed, and I imagine that if any boy had tried to make fun of him for being named Clarence, Father would simply have laughed and told him he didn't know what he was talking about.

I asked Mother how this name had ever happened to spring up in our family. She explained that my great-great-grandfather was Benjamin Day, and my great-grandfather was Henry, and consequently my grandfather had been named Benjamin Henry. He in turn had named his eldest son Henry and his second son Benjamin, The result was that when Father was born there was no family name left. The privilege of choosing a name for Father had thereupon been given to Grandma, and unluckily for the Day family she had been reading a novel, the hero of which was named Clarence.

I knew that Grandma, though very like Grandpa in some respects, had a dreamy side which he hadn't, a side that she usually kept to herself, in her serene, quiet way. Her romantic choice of this name probably made Grandpa smile, but he was a detached sort of man who didn't take small matters seriously, and who drew a good deal of private amusement from the happenings of everyday life. Besides, he was partly to blame in this case, because that novel was one he had published himself in his magazine.

I asked Mother, when she had finished, why I had been named Clarence too.

It hadn't been her choice, Mother said. She had suggested all sorts of names to Father, but there seemed to be something wrong with each one. When she had at last spoken of naming me after him, however, he had said at once that that was the best suggestion yet — he said it sounded just right.

Father and I would have had plenty of friction in any case. This identity of names made things worse. Every time that I had been more of a fool than he liked, Father would try to impress on me my responsibilities as his eldest son, and above all as the son to whom he had given his name, as he put it. A great deal was expected, it seemed to me, of a boy who was named after his father. I used to envy my brothers, who didn't have anything expected of them on this score at all.

I envied them still more after I was old enough to begin getting letters. I then discovered that when Father "gave" me his name he had also, not unnaturally I had to admit, retained it himself, and when anything came for Clarence S. Day he opened it, though it was sometimes for me.

He also opened everything that came addressed to Clarence S. Day, Jr. He didn't do this intentionally, but unless the "Jr." was clearly written, it looked like "Esq," and anyhow Father was too accustomed to open all Clarence Day letters to remember about looking carefully every time for a "Jr." So far as mail and express went, I had no name at all of my own.

For the most part nobody wrote to me when I was a small boy except firms whose advertisements I had read in the *Youth's Companion* and to whom I had written requesting them to send me their circulars. These circulars described remarkable bargains in magicians' card outfits, stamps and coins, pocket-knives, trick spiders, and imitation fried eggs, and they seemed interesting and valuable to me when I got them. The trouble was that Father usually got them and at once tore them up. I then had to write for such circulars again, and if Father got the second one, too, he would sometimes explode with annoyance. He became particularly indignant one year, I remember, when he was repeatedly urged to take advantage of a special bargain sale of false whiskers. He said that he couldn't understand why these offerings kept pouring in. I knew why, in this case, but at other times I was often surprised myself at the number he got, not realizing that as a result of my postcard request my or our name had been automatically put on several large general mailing lists.

During this period I got more of my mail out of Father's wastebasket than I did from the postman.

At the age of twelve or thirteen, I stopped writing for these childish things and turned to a new field. Father and I, whichever of us got at the mail first, then began to receive not merely circulars but personal letters beginning:

> DEAR FRIEND DAY:
> In reply to your valued request for one of our Mammoth Agents' Outfits, kindly forward post-office order for $1.49 to cover cost of postage and packing, and we will put you in a position to earn a large income in your spare time with absolutely no labour on your part, by taking subscriptions for *The Secret Handbook of Mesmerism*, and our *Tales of Blood* series.

And one spring, I remember, as the result of what I had intended to be a secret application on my part, Father was assigned "the exclusive rights for Staten Island and Hoboken of selling the Gem Home Popper for Pop Corn. Housewives buy it at sight."

After Father had stormily endured these afflictions for a while, he and I began to get letters from girls. Fortunately for our feelings, these were rare, but they were ordeals for both of us. Father had forgotten, if he ever knew, how silly young girls can sound, and I got my first lesson in how unsystematic they were. No matter how private and playful they meant their letters to be, they forgot to put "Jr." on the envelope every once in so often. When Father opened these letters, he read them all the way through, sometimes twice, muttering to himself over and over: "This is very peculiar. I don't understand this at all. Here's a letter to me from some person I never heard of. I can't see what it's about." By the time it had occurred to him that possibly the letter might be for me, I was red and embarrassed and even angrier at the girl than at Father. And on days when he had read some of the phrases aloud to the family, it nearly killed me to claim it.

Lots of fellows whom I knew had been named after their fathers without having such troubles. But although Father couldn't have been kinder-hearted or had any better intentions, when he saw his name on a package or envelope it never dawned on him that it might not be for him. He was too active in his habits to wait until I had a chance to get at it. And as he was also single-minded and prompt to attend to unfinished business, he opened everything automatically and then did his best to dispose of it.

This went on even after I grew up, until I had a home of my own. Father was always perfectly decent about it, but he never changed. When he saw I felt sulky, he was genuinely sorry and said so, but he couldn't see why all this should annoy me, and he was surprised and amused that it did. I used to get angry once in a while when something came for me which I particularly hadn't wished him to see and which I would find lying, opened, on the hall table marked "For Jr.?" when I came in; but nobody could stay angry with Father—he was too utterly guiltless of having meant to offend.

He often got angry himself, but it was mostly at things, not at persons, and he didn't mind a bit (as a rule) when persons got angry at him. He even declared, when I got back from college, feeling dignified, and told him that I wished he'd be more careful, that he suffered from these mistakes more than I did. It wasn't his fault, he pointed out, if my stupid correspondents couldn't remember my name, and it wasn't any pleasure to him to be upset at his breakfast by finding that a damned lunatic company in Battle Creek had sent him a box of dry bread-crumbs, with a letter asserting that this rubbish would be good for his stomach. "I admit I threw it into the fireplace, Clarence, but what else could I do? If you valued this preposterous concoction, my dear boy, I'm sorry. I'll buy another box for you today if you'll tell me where I can get it. Don't feel badly! I'll buy you a barrel. Only I hope you won't eat it."

In the days when Mrs. Pankhurst and her friends were chaining themselves to lamp-posts in London, in their campaign for the vote, a letter came from Frances Hand trustfully asking "Dear Clarence" to do something to help Women's Suffrage—speak at a meeting, I think. Father got red in the face. "Speak at one of their meetings!" he roared at Mother. "I'd like nothing better! You can tell Mrs. Hand that it would give me great pleasure to inform all those crackpots in petticoats exactly what I think of their antics."

"Now, Clare," Mother said, "you mustn't talk that way. I like that nice Mrs. Hand, and anyhow this letter must be for Clarence."

Onetime I asked Father for his opinion of a low-priced stock I'd been watching. His opinion was that it was not worth a damn. I thought this over, but I still wished to buy it, so I placed a scale order with another firm instead of with Father's office, and said nothing about it.

At the end of the month this other firm sent me a statement, setting forth each of my little transactions in full, and of course they forgot to put the "Jr." at the end of my name. When Father opened the envelope, he thought at first in his excitement that this firm had actually opened an account for him without being asked. I found him telling Mother that he'd like to wring their damned necks.

"That must be for me, Father," I said, when I took in what had happened.

We looked at each other.

"You bought this stuff?" he said incredulously. "After all I said about it?"

"Yes, Father."

He handed over the statement and walked out of the room.

Both he and I felt offended and angry. We stayed so for several days, too, but we then made it up.

Once in a while when I got a letter that I had no time to answer I used to address an envelope to the sender and then put anything in it that happened to be lying around on my desk—a circular about books, a piece of newspaper, an old laundry bill—anything at all, just to be amiable, and yet at the same time to save myself the trouble of writing. I happened to tell several people about this private habit of mine at a dinner one night—a dinner at which Alice Duer Miller and one or two other writers were present. A little later she wrote me a criticism of Henry James and ended by saying that I needn't send her any of my old laundry bills because she wouldn't stand it. And she forgot to put on the "Jr."

"In the name of God," Father said bleakly, "this is the worst yet. Here's a woman who says I'd better not read *The Golden Bowl*, which I have no intention whatever of doing, and she also warns me for some unknown reason not to send her my laundry bills."

The good part of all these experiences, as I realize now, was that in the end they drew Father and me closer together. My brothers had only chance battles with him. I had a war. Neither he nor I relished its clashes, but they made us surprisingly intimate.

Coventry Patmore

THE TOYS

My little Son, who look'd from thoughtful eyes
And moved and spoke in quiet grown-up wise,
Having my law the seventh time disobey'd,
I struck him, and dismiss'd
With hard words and unkiss'd,
— His Mother, who was patient, being dead.
Then, fearing lest his grief should hinder sleep,
I visited his bed,
But found him slumbering deep,
With darken'd eyelids, and their lashes yet
From his late sobbing wet.
And I, with moan,
Kissing away his tears, left others of my own;
For, on a table drawn beside his head,
He had put, within his reach,
A box of counters and a red-vein'd stone,
A piece of glass abraded by the beach,
And six or seven shells,
A bottle with bluebells,
And two French copper coins, ranged there with careful art,
To comfort his sad heart.
So when that night I pray'd
To God, I wept, and said:
Ah, when at last we lie with tranced breath,
Not vexing Thee in death,
And Thou rememberest of what toys
We made our joys,
How weakly understood
Thy great commanded good,
Then, fatherly not less
Than I whom Thou hast moulded from the clay,

Thou'lt leave Thy wrath, and say,
"I will be sorry for their childishness."

Traditional Folk Song:

THE YOUNG SERVANT MAN

It's of a damsel both fair and handsome;
These lines are true, as I have been told.
Near the banks of Shannon in a lofty mansion
Her parents lived, and had stores of gold.
Her hair was black as a raven's feather;
Her form and features, describe who can.
But still its folly belongs to nature;
She fell in love with a servant man.

Sweet Mary Ann with her love was walking;
Her father heard them, and nearer drew;
And as those true lovers were fondly talking,
In anger home her father drew.
To build a dungeon was his intention,
To part true love he contrived a plan;
He swore an oath that's too vile to mention
He'd part that fair one from her servant man.

He built a dungeon with brick and mortar
With a flight of steps, for 'twas underground;
The food he gave her was bread and water,
The only cheer that for her was found.
Three times a day he did cruelly beat her;
Unto her father she thus began:
"If I've transgressed now, my own dear father,
I'll live and die for my servant man."

Young Edwin found out her habitation,
'Twas well secured by an iron door;
He vowed in spite of all this nation
To gain her freedom, or rest no more.
'Twas at his leisure, he toiled with pleasure
To gain releasement for poor Mary Ann.
He gained his object and found his treasure;
She cried: "My faithful servant man."

A suit of clothing he bought his lover,
'Twas man's apparel, her to disguise;
Saying: "For your sake I'll face your father.
To see me here it will him surprise."
When her cruel father brought bread and
    water,
To call his daughter he then began.
Said Edwin: "Enter. I've cleared your
    daughter,
And I will suffer, your servant man."

Her father found 'twas his daughter vanished,
Then like a lion he did roar.
He said: "From Ireland you shall be banished,
Or with my broadsword I'll spill your gore."
"Agreed," said Edwin, "so at your leisure,
Since her I've freed, now do all you can.
Forgive your daughter. I'll die with pleasure.
The one in fault is your servant man."

When he found him so tender-hearted,
Then down he fell on the dungeon floor.
He said: "True lovers should not be parted,
Since love can enter an iron door."
Then soon they joined, to be parted never;
To roll in riches, this young couple can.
This fair young lady, amidst rural pleasures,
Lives blest forever with her servant man.

Robert Lenzer

J. PAUL GETTY, JR.

Paul junior—"Pabby," as he was nicknamed by his family and friends —grew up in Santa Monica and then later San Francisco, where he lived with his mother and his brother, Gordon. He was "the handsomest boy that ever lived," says his mother. He was rebellious at school but a voracious reader. He seldom saw his father. He recalls that once when he was in high school he wrote Paul senior a letter that was returned with all the grammar and spelling errors corrected but with no personal comment. "I never got over that," he says now. "I wanted to be judged as a human being and I could never get that from him."

Paul Theroux

THE MOSQUITO COAST

At twilight, the air was sooty with insects, and swampwater diseased the dark spaces under the trees. The sky grew clearer as dusk fell. Shadows straightened up and stiffened. Then a dirtying of the sky, and it was night, nothing to see, the black so black you could feel its fur against your face. Without the hot sun to burn it away, the smell from the trees was like the hum of green meat. The full river snuffled like a pack of hogs, and birds lollopped into the branches near us and made loud cranking cries. We felt sick at this still, leftover time of day. We tied up and sat among the smudgepots of our wooden floating hut, and ate whatever we had managed to gather from the drowned villages.

"This is the future," Father said. "The fatal mistake everyone made was in thinking that the future had something to do with high technology. I used to think it myself! But that was before I had this experience. Oh, Gaw, it was all going to be rocket ships."

"Monorails," I said.

Clover said, "Space capsules."

"Smellovision," Father said. "Video-cassettes instead of school. Everything streamlined. Meals were going to be pills—green ones for breakfast, blue ones for lunch, purple ones for dessert. You popped them into your mouth—all the nutrition you needed."

April said, "And space suits."

"Right," Father said. "Stupefied people with pointy ears and names like *Grok* wearing helmets and living in chrome-plated houses. Moving sidewalks, glass domes over cities, and no work except playing with computers and sniffing the smellovision. 'Get into the rocket-ship, kids, and let's go have a picnic on the moon'—that kind of thing."

Mother said, "It might happen."

"Never. It's all bull."

Clover said, "I think Dad's right."

"Science fiction gave people more false hope than two thousand years of Bibles," Father said. "It was all lies! The space programme—is that what you're saying? It was a hollow, vaunting waste of taxpayers' money. There is no future in space! I love the word—space! That's what they were all discovering—empty space!"

April said, "I think Dad's right, too."

"This is the future," he said. "A little motor in a little boat, on a muddy river. When the motor busts, or we run out of gas, we paddle. No spacemen! No fuel, no rocket-ships, no glass domes. Just work! Man of the future is going to be a cart-horse. There's nothing on the moon but ruts and pimples, and those of us who have inherited this senile exhausted earth will have nothing but wooden wheels, push-carts, levers and pullies—the crudest high school physics, that they stopped teaching when everyone flunked it and started reading science fiction. No, it's grow your own or die. No green pills, but plenty of roughage. Hard back-breaking work—simple but not easy. Get it? No laser beams, no electricity, nothing but muscle-power. What we're doing now! We're the people of the future, using the technology of the future. We cracked it!"

He wanted us to feel, in our creaking hut-boat, like the most modern people on earth. We held the secret of existence in our smoky cabin. Now, he never talked about changing the world with geothermal energy, or ice. He promised us dirt and work. That was glory, he said.

But after these short nights, he started the outboard and set the front of the hut against the current, and Jerry whispered to me, "He's killing us."

We stuck to the river's edge, creeping around the reaches and studying the flow of the current before we moved forward. We made five or six miles a day, and still had plenty of spare gas. And what did it matter if we used it all? We had the rest of our lives to get upriver.

I thought everyone except Jerry was convinced. But one day, as we furrowed along, the outboard went mad. It quacked, its noise climbed higher, became more frantic and animal, and soon it was shrieking. Birds exploded out of the trees. Then something snapped, and after a quack or two, the engine went dead. But its echo continued to quiver in the jungle. The boat hesitated and became light and directionless. It tipped, it rolled back.

We were going downstream sideways on the river's tongue in silence under the dropping ants.

"Anchor!" Father vaulted towards the bow. "Get out the lines!"

Our anchor was beautiful—we had found it on the beach near Mocobila—a cluster-fountain of curving barbs on a thick shaft. But it was also very heavy. It took Father's help to get it over the rail, and by then we were moving so fast that it did not seem to take hold. Father jumped overboard and swam to the bank with a line. He secured us, the anchor caught.

We were in a curve of the river—the current swung us out on the line and held us gushing in the middle of the stream. Water plumed from either side and the whole hut-boat tottered as we helped Father aboard. We had lost the shearpin, he said. It wasn't much—only a cotterpin—but it meant the propeller had flown off and spun to the bottom of the river.

"Can't you make a new prop?" Mother asked.

"Sure, I can. Pass me that lathe, the calipers, the machining tools, the set of lugs and files. What's that? You mean, we only have spit and a screwdriver? Then I guess we'll have to dive for that old prop."

We looked upstream at the dark horns of waterflow pumping out of the river.

"Don't worry," Father said. "We have the rest of our lives to find it." He was smiling, biting his beard. He turned to Jerry and said, "What are you smirking at?"

"The rest of our lives. It sounds daffy when you say it like that."

"We'll see how daffy. You're going to dive for it."

"What about the alligators?" I said.

"You're not afraid of alligators," Father said. "You go after Jerry."

Mother said, "No—I won't let those boys go in there."

"Listen to me," Father said. "It's not a question of what you want. It's what I want. I'm captain of this ship, and those are my orders. Anyone who disobeys them, goes ashore. Your lives are in my hands. I'll maroon you—all of you!"

His large scarred hands were still dripping river water. His voice was a weapon—he was threatening to abandon us unless we jumped in—but what I feared most was being slung ashore in his raw fingers. His life here had made his hands terrible.

"Put on this harness," he said to Jerry, and gave him a line to tie around his waist. Jerry, with sick defiant eyes, kicked off his sandals and went to the side.

"It's somewhere in this dogleg," Father said. "We lost it near those trees. Probably hit a rock. The current can't take a lump of solid brass very far. Swim to the bank first, then go and get it."

Jerry held his nose and went overboard like a basket.

"I've been grooming you for this all along," Father said. "It's all preparation for survival." He pulled out a nail from his pocket. "This will do for a new shearpin. But we need the prop." He held the little nail between his fingers. "It's always something small that keeps you from savagery. Like those plugs. Like the prop. Like this. The shearpin held our whole civilisation together. There's no better example of what a delicate balance there is between"—he looked upriver at Jerry's small white feet—"how's he doing?"

Jerry bobbed up and blew out water, but before he could regain his stroke he came downstream and caught hold of the boat.

"I can't see anything. The water's too muddy."

"Try again."

"He's tired, Allie."

"He can rest after he's found our propeller."

Mother said, "Let me go."

Father said, "What if you drown?"

"What if Jerry drowns?"

She said it in a slow suffocated way.

Father scratched his beard with his knuckles.

He said, "I need you here, Mother."

Jerry tried four times. Each time, the current pulled him back to us empty-handed. At last, he was so tired he could not raise his arms, and Father had to tug the harness-line to keep him from being taken down-river.

It was my turn. I swam to shore, then dived to the bottom at the place Father had indicated. I stuck my hands into the mud and raked it. The mud ran through my fingers. The churning river was like vegetable soup, with sunlight knifing into it and showing me long shadows I imagined to be alligators. As my breath gave out, I broke the surface of the river and saw that I had travelled almost to the boat.

"You're not serious," Father said. He made me swim back.

The sludge and weeds at the river bottom disgusted me. The dark current sucked at my legs. Mud floated into my face. But, worse, being on Father's rope was like being a dog on a leash. Staying on it, I was in his power. But if I cut myself free of the rope, I would be swept down-stream to drown.

It was a dog's life. I was glad Jerry had said the things he had. Why hadn't I told Father what I thought of him? A dog's life — because we didn't count, because he was always right, always the explainer, and most of all because he ordered us to do these difficult things. He didn't want to see us succeed, he wanted to laugh at our failure. And not even a gundog could find a small propeller at the bottom of this river.

I told him I had swallowed water and felt sick and could not go down again.

He chuckled — I knew he would — and said, "Children are no use at all in a crisis. Which is ironic, because children are the cause of most crises. I mean, I can look after myself! I don't need food, I don't need sleep — I don't suffer. I'm happy!"

April said, "Dad, is this a crisis?"

"Some people might say so. We've got an engine we can't use. We've got a boat that won't move forward. We've got two cripples who can't find the prop. If the anchor or that line cuts loose we'll be wallowing down the drain. And it's getting dark. And this is the jungle. Muffin," he said, "some people might call that critical."

Mother said, "I want to try, Allie."

But Father was putting the harness around his waist. He tied the free end to the rail. He said the only thing he trusted to hold his lifeline was one of his own knots.

He went over the side with a heavy splash. We watched him take a dive, expecting him to find the propeller on the first try. He came up — he did not raise his hands. He dived again. He was a strong enough swimmer to hold his own against the current, but when he dived a third time, he did not come up.

We waited. We watched the water ribbing over that spot.

Clover said, "Where is he?"

"Maybe he sees it," Mother said.

A whining net of mosquitos came and went.

April said, "He's been down a long time."

"It's dark down there," Jerry said.

We stopped holding our breath.

More minutes passed. I could not say how many. Time did not pass precisely here. The day was light, the night dark — time was lumpish. Every hot hour was the same, silent and blind. He might have been under an hour.

Mother went to the rail and plucked at the line. She lifted it easily and dragged it on board, coiling it, until she had its whole length out of the water. The end was kinked like a mongrel's tail, where the knot had been.

"He's gone!" Clover screamed. She became rigid. And she cried so hard, she gagged, then cried more because she was gagging.

Jerry said, "I don't see him."

But Jerry had stopped looking. He was staring at me. His face was relaxed — very white and hopeful, like someone sitting up in bed in the morning.

Mother shook her head. She gazed at the torrent of water slooshing downstream. She did not speak.

I felt suddenly strong. A moment ago, night was falling, but now everything was brighter. The sky was clear. Tiny insects fussed above the river. A quietness descended, like that sifting of gnats, and silvered the water and streaked it like a new tomb. This stillness sealed it.

"He's somewhere! He's somewhere!" But April's voice did not disturb the river or the trees. She clawed her hair. She held Clover and they gagged together on their sobs.

"We can drift," Jerry said. "We'll tie up tonight and go down the river tomorrow. It'll be easy."

I said, "What if Dad was right?"

"Don't be frightened," Mother said.

Jerry said, "We're not frightened!"

Mother said, "I can't think." Her listening face was lovely. It did not register a single sound. It did not hear April saying we were going to die, or Clover calling out to Father, or Jerry describing our easy trip down to the coast.

Little Jerry, set free, was scampering around the deck.

"Listen," Mother said.

The water trickling silver, the slouching jungle—it was an insect kingdom of small whistles, a world of crickyjeens.

A Zambu went by in a cayuka. That was like time passing, the duration of his coming and going. It was the only time here—a man's movement. This Zambu was alive.

"We won't die," I said.

Mother did not hear me, but I meant it. Our boat was small, and it hung precariously on a line in the middle of the river—on air, it seemed. But I had never felt safer. Father was gone. How quiet it was here. Doubt, death, grief—they had passed like the shadow of a bird's wing brushing us. Now—after how long?—we had forgotten that shadow. We were free.

"In a couple of days we'll be on the coast," Jerry said.

"We'll die there!" Clover said.

It was what Father had always said. I thought I believed it. But he had gone and taken fear with him. I heard myself saying, "We can get rid of this outboard. We'll build a rudder. The current will take us."

Jerry tried to make the twins stop crying. He was saying, "Don't you want to go home?"

Was it that forbidden word that did it?

There was a splash—explosive in this whistling world. There was Father's wet streaming head, his beard brushing the rail, the chunk of the brass propeller hitting the boards, and his howl, "Traitors!" Then all the light was gone.

A. C. Benson

Little boys are odd, tiresome creatures in many ways, with savage instincts; and I suppose many fathers feel that, if they are to maintain their authority, they must be a little distant and inscrutable. A boy goes for sympathy and companionship to his mother and sisters, not often to his father.

Elizabeth Cady Stanton

I passed through a terrible scourging when last at my father's. I cannot tell you how deep the iron entered my soul. I never felt more deeply the degradation of my sex. To think that all in me of which my father would have felt a proper pride had I been a man, is deeply mortifying to him because I am a woman.

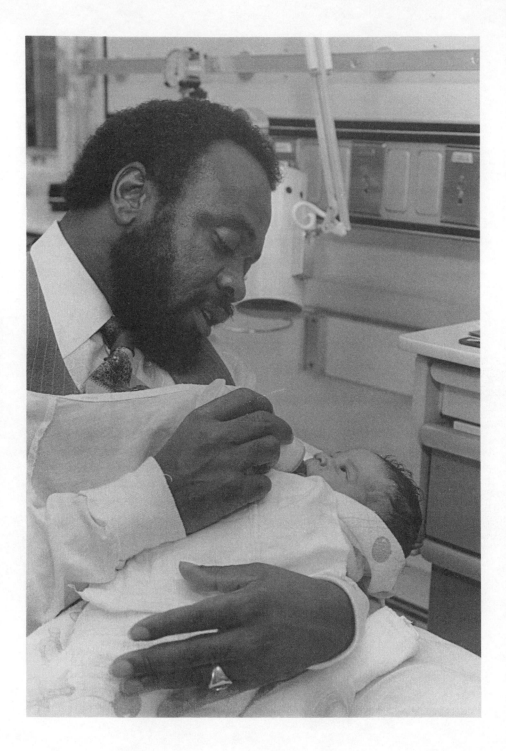

FIRST MEETINGS

No man can possibly know what life means, what the world means, what anything means, until he has a child and loves it, And then the whole universe changes and nothing will ever again seem exactly as it seemed before.

—LAFCADIO HEARN

E. B. White

LETTERS

Joe has a cup made from old silver coins—quite a beautiful thing and a genuine antique, but I don't know how good it would be to drink from. I can now mix his formula—no harder than mixing a good Martini— and am in complete charge of his life and character; he has plenty of both. He weighs, at this writing, eleven pounds no ounces. Much of the time he spends in Washington Square, with the rest of the unemployed. When, after a cry, he stares at me with a critical and resentful gaze, just slightly out of focus, I feel the mixed pride and the oppression of fatherhood in the very base of my spine. This small man, so challengingly complete and so devastatingly remote! But you know about that. In fact I think it was you who told me about it.

Laurie Lee

THE FIRSTBORN

I

She was born in the autumn and was a late fall in my life, and lay purple and dented like a little bruised plum, as though she'd been lightly trodden in the grass and forgotten.

Then the nurse lifted her up and she came suddenly alive, her bent legs kicking crabwise, and her first living gesture was a thin wringing of the hands accompanied by a far-out Hebridean lament.

This moment of meeting seemed to be a birthtime for both of us; her first and my second life. Nothing, I knew, would be the same again, and I think I was reasonably shaken. I peered intently at her, looking for familiar signs, but she was convulsed as an Aztec idol. Was this really my daughter, this purple concentration of anguish, this blind and protesting dwarf?

Then they handed her to me, stiff and howling, and I held her for the first time and kissed her, and she went still and quiet as though by instinctive guile, and I was instantly enslaved by her flattery of my powers.

Only a few brief weeks have passed since that day, but already I've felt all the obvious astonishments. New-born, of course, she looked already a centenarian, tottering on the brink of an old crone's grave, exhausted, shrunken, bald as Voltaire, mopping, mowing and twisting wrinkled claws in speechless spasms of querulous doom.

But with each day of survival she has grown younger and fatter, her face filling, drawing on life, every breath of real air healing the birth-death stain she had worn so witheringly at the beginning.

Now this girl, my child, this parcel of will and warmth, fills the cottage with her obsessive purpose. The rhythmic tides of her sleeping and feeding spaciously measure the days and nights. Her frail self-absorption is a commanding presence, her helplessness strong as a rock, so that I find myself listening even to her silences as though some great engine was purring upstairs.

When awake, not feeding, she snorts and gobbles, dryly, like a ruminative jackdaw, or strains and groans and waves her hands about as though casting invisible nets.

When I watch her at this I see her hauling in life, groping fiercely with every limb and muscle, working blind at a task no one can properly share, in a darkness where she is still alone.

She is of course just an ordinary miracle, but is also the particular late wonder of my life. So each night I take her to bed like a book and lie close and study her. Her dark blue eyes stare straight into mine, but off-centre, not seeing me.

Such moments could be the best we shall ever know — those midnights of mutual blindness. Already, I suppose, I should be afraid for her future, but I am more concerned with mine.

I am fearing perhaps her first acute recognition, her first questions, the first man she makes of me. But for the moment I'm safe: she stares idly through me, at the pillow, at the light on the wall, and each is a shadow of purely nominal value and she prefers neither one to the other.

Meanwhile as I study her I find her early strangeness insidiously claiming a family face.

Here she is then, my daughter, here, alive, the one I must possess and guard. A year ago this space was empty, not even a hope of her was in it. Now she's here, brand new, with our name upon her; and no one will call in the night to reclaim her.

She is here for good, her life stretching before us, twenty odd years wrapped up in that bundle; she will grow, learn to totter, to run in the garden, run back, and call this place home. Or will she?

Looking at those weaving hands and complicated ears, the fit of the skin round that delicate body, I can't indulge in the neurosis of imagining all this to be merely a receptacle for Strontium 90. The forces within her seem much too powerful to submit to a blanket death of that kind.

But she could, even so, be a victim of chance; all those quick lively tendrils seem so vulnerable to their own recklessness — surely she'll fall on the fire, or roll down some crevice, or kick herself out of the window?

I realise I'm succumbing to the occupational disease, the father-jitters or new-parenthood-shakes, expressed in: "Hark the child's screaming, she must be dying." Or, "She's so quiet, she must be dead."

As it is, my daughter is so new to me still that I can't yet leave her alone. I have to keep on digging her out of her sleep to make sure that she's really alive.

She is a time-killing lump, her face a sheaf of masks which she shuffles through aimlessly. One by one she reveals them, while I watch eerie rehearsals of those emotions she will one day need, random, out-of-sequence but already exact, automatic but strangely knowing — a quick pucker of fury, a puff of ho-hum boredom, a beaming after-dinner smile, perplexity, slyness, a sudden wrinkling of grief, pop-eyed interest, and fat-lipped love.

It is little more than a month since I was handed this living heap of expectations, and I can feel nothing but simple awe.

What have I got exactly? And what am I going to do with her? And what for that matter will she do with me?

I have got a daughter, whose life is already separate from mine, whose will already follows its own directions, and who has quickly corrected my woolly preconceptions of her by being something re-morselessly different. She is the child of herself and will be what she is. I am merely the keeper of her temporary helplessness.

Even so, with luck, she can alter me; indeed, is doing so now. At this stage in my life she will give me more than she gets, and may even later become *my* keeper.

But if I could teach her anything at all — by unloading upon her some of the ill-tied parcels of my years — I'd like it to be acceptance and a holy relish for life. To accept with gladness the fact of being a woman — when she'll find all nature to be on her side.

If pretty, to thank God and enjoy her luck and not start beefing about being loved for her mind. To be willing to give pleasure without feeling loss of face, to prefer charm to the vanity of aggression, and not to deliver her powers and mysteries into the opposite camp by wishing to compete with men.

In the way, I believe — though some of her sisters may disapprove — she might know some happiness and also spread some around.

And as a brief tenant of this precious and irreplaceable world, I'd ask her to preserve life both in herself and others. To prefer always Societies for Propagation and Promotion rather than those for the Abolition or Prevention of.

Never to persecute others for the sins hidden in herself, nor to seek justice in terms of vengeance; to avoid like a plague all acts of mob-righteousness; to take cover whenever flags start flying; and to accept her frustrations and faults as her own personal burden, and not to blame them too often, if she can possibly help it, on young or old, whites or coloureds, East, West, Jews, Gentiles, Television, Bingo, Trades Unions, the City, school-milk or the British Railways.

For the rest, may she be my own salvation, for any man's child is his second chance. In this role I see her leading me back to my beginnings, reopening rooms I'd locked and forgotten, stirring the dust in my mind by re-asking the big questions — as any child can do.

But in my case, perhaps, just not too late; she persuades me there may yet be time, that with her, my tardy but bright-eyed pathfinder, I may return to that wood which long ago I fled from, but which together we may now enter and know.

II

She is now only a few months old and at the beginning of it all, rolling her eyes for the first time at the world. A dangerous temptation for any father, new to the charms and vanities of parenthood, to use her as a glass in which to adore his own image, to act miracles and be a god again.

Inert, receptive, captive and goggle-eyed, she offers everything for self-indulgence; her readiness, for instance, to restore one's powers to astonish, and to be shown the whole world new. She laughs easily already, demanding no effort of wit, gulping chuckles at my corniest gestures — a built-in appreciation so quick and uncritical it seems to promise a life-long romance.

But I am late to parenthood and I know I must beware; my daughter and I stand in mutual danger; so easy for either of us to turn the other's head, or for me to ruin her with too much cherishing. A late only child is particularly vulnerable, of course — a target for attentions she might be happier without, or liable to be cast into roles that have little to do with her nature in order to act out some parental fantasy.

Nevertheless, here she is, just a few months old, clear clay to work wonders with. No doubt, if I could, I'd mould her into something wispy and adoring, but fortunately she'll have none of that. Like any other child, she is a unique reality, already something I cannot touch, with a programme of her own packed away inside her to which she will grow without help from me.

Even so, there is much I want to show and give her; and also much I would protect her from. I would spare her the burden of too many ambitions, and too many expectations, such as the assumption that simply because she is mine she must therefore be both beautiful and clever. I'll try not to improve her too much, or use her in games of one-uppance, or send her climbing too many competitive beanstalks; and I'd like to protect her from the need to go one better than her parents in order to improve their status by proxy. One can't help sympathising with the dad who says: "I never had a chance myself, but my kid's going to have the best." But the result very often is a stranger in the house, a teen-age aristocrat served by parent serfs, forced to talk and dress a cut above the old folks and to feel little save guilt and embarrassment.

At the same time I'd best protect her from the opposite kind of freakishness — that of using her as a sociological guinea-pig. For next to circus-trained animals, few creatures look so fundamentally awkward as children who have been forced into experimental postures of behaviour in order to indulge some theoretical fidget of their parents. One feels that children should be left to enjoy their conservative birthright, and not be conscripted as second-hand revolutionaries. A child can, and should, when the time is ripe, initiate its own revolutions.

What I want for my child is an important beginning, a background where she can most naturally grow. My own childhood was rough, but it was a good time too, and I want her to have one like it. I was lucky to be raised in a country district, rich with unpackaged and unpriced rewards; and although we were materially poor (and I don't wish that she should be poor) I believe there are worse things than that kind of poverty. There is, for instance, the burden of abundance, often as stultifying as want, when too many non-stop treats and ready-made diversions can mount almost to infanticide, can glut a child's appetites, ravish it of wonder, and leave it no space or silence for dreams. So I would like to give my child chances to be surprised, periods of waiting to sharpen her longings, then some treat or treasure that was worth looking forward to, and an interval to enjoy and remember it.

I was brought up in a village when childhood and the countryside were simply their own rewards, when electricity had not obliterated the old ghosts in the corners, and songs were not changed once a week. That time and condition can't come again, but I'd like my daughter to know what is left of it. For it still contains people undazed by street lamps, who know darkness and the movements of stars, and who can talk about mysteries the townsman has forgotten, and who are not entirely cut off from the soil's live skin by insulations of cement and asphalt.

I want to take my daughter to this surviving world—not as a visitor, but to be a native in it. So that she may accept it simply as part of creation, and take its light into her eyes and bones. To know the natural intimacy of living close to the seasons, where they are still the gods in possession; to feel the quick earth stir when she treads upon it, to take the smokeless wind in her mouth, to watch the green year turn, lambs drop and stagger, birds hatch, grass grow and seed. To have for her horizons the banks of woods rather than the rented air of office blocks, and to be accompanied on her walks by the coloured squares of fields rather than raddled posters for fags and petrol. Not later, but as soon as she can use her eyes, I'd like her to have this world to live in, so that she can know it and regard it as a place to belong to, and not just a piece of prettiness to be gawped at from a motor car.

I suppose the country can only properly be given to a child—as from birth it was given to me. And as it was given to me, so I'd like to show it to her, and see it again through her eyes—the veils of blue rain wandering up from Wales, streaking the sky before they hit the ground; copper clouds of thunder towering over the Severn, mist wiping great holes in the hillside, the beech-tops breaking into a storm of rooks, the light on the cows in the evening . . . And there will be the naming of plants (if I can remember them), explaining the differences between daws and ravens, collecting woodlice, earwigs, frogs and grasshoppers; and the attempts to tame a fox. I must also refind the valley's traditional playground—the caves and holes in the quarries, Roman snails on the walls and fossilled fish in the stones, the bridge of willows across the stream, pools and springs and water voles, hooked burrs and thistle-seeds, the sharp free food of crab and damson, and the first mushrooms of a September morning. Best of all, at full moon, to be able to take her from her bed, and carry her down through the warm bright wood, to the lake where the heron stands like a spear of silver and the blue pike nibble the reeds . . .

Children can often be grubs, even in a pastoral paradise, and I believe that I was one by nature. Relaxed and drowsy, content to sit in corners, I had to be taught to use my eyes. My mother, sisters and brothers taught me, though I wasn't aware of it at the time. But what they showed me then, I never forgot, and I hope my daughter will find it the same. Yet for all the milk-fed charms of country life, I want her to see it whole, to acknowledge the occasional savageries as well as the soft green days, the dark as well as the light. Unlike the secretive city, the country is naked, and displays most of the truths about us; but even the worst of these truths, being part of a primitive harmony, are seldom exploited and never morbid. So it is against this background, which neither conceals nor excuses, that I think my child can best balance her life, can look on birth and death in their proper relation—not taking them soiled or second-hand from the Press—and and can accept the valley as real, not only in fat-cheeked summer, but also under the dead necessary face of winter.

Given this world to be in, where she can grow reasonably wild, she will also expect the comfort of some authority. To load any child with absolute freedom is to force it to inhabit a wasteland, where it must push its will to find the limits allowed it and grow frantic unless it does. Let her have the assurance, then, of a proper authority, and of a not too inflexible routine, within whose restraints she may take occasional refuge—otherwise I hope she'll be free. I want her to be free from fear to enquire and get answers, free to imagine and tell tall tales, free to be curious and to show enthusiasm, and free at times to invade my silences.

I hope she'll sing when she wants to, and be flattered when she needs it, and not get attention according to timetable. May our house not be so tidy that it inhibits her gusto, nor so squalid that she resigns her pride. She shall love God if she wishes, and have a place for saints and angels, or even dress shrines for the more unfashionable spirits. She shall not be condemned to grey flannel, nor kept for ever in jeans, nor treated as sexless or a pretended boy, but be given nice clothes early, and occasions to wear them, and be encouraged to value her mysteries. She will not be suppressed too much, nor yet spoiled I hope, but taught politeness, good manners and charm — not as affected graces but as ordinary gifts designed to make other people happy. She will not be the first in the family, nor yet the last, but a respected member of it; and when good things occur I'd like her to stay up and share them — and sleep late through the next dull day. As for the arts, I hope she'll want some of these, but not too self-consciously. May she paint herself blue, and the walls and ceilings, but not as part of some art-school posture. And may she dance and spin for the pleasure her young limbs give her, but not with Dame Margot always in mind. She shall have music, too, not wherever she goes, but as an important embellishment of her life. A house without music is like a house without lights, but no light should burn night and day. Today's non-stop music, piped from shuddering plastic boxes, debauches the senses of one of its sacred pleasures. Music should be a voluptuous treat, like a deep hot bath, not a continuous shriek in the plumbing. I'd like my child to have music for consolation, excitement, and occasional exaltation, to think of it as an event and an extravagance of the senses and not just a background for chatter and peanuts. If it's good, I don't mind whether it's jazz or the classics, though I hope she'll feel free to like both. Best of all, may she succeed in playing some instrument herself, which is one of the most intense of musical pleasures. We are all listeners today, passive or otherwise, and for some it can be a genuine enrichment; but to play any instrument, no matter how badly, is worth a thousand hours of listening.

There remains the question of education, usually a subject for snobs or fanatics (I've still time to develop into either). But I would like to give her the sort that matches her curiosity and needs, and not one to make her life a misery. I'll not send her away if I can help it; she's bound to leave soon enough. I hope she'll stay at home, inky fingers and all, and be around where I can watch her grow. It is the privilege of the poor — and the very rich — to keep their children at home; I'm neither, but I'm too jealous of my daugher's childhood to wish to give it away to the pattern-makers. I've no mind to pack her off to some boarding-school, to lose sight of her for months at a time, only to get her back, stiff as a hockey post, and sicklied o'er with the pale thought of caste.

. . . No, I hope she'll be content to get her conformity at a day school and to unravel it back home each night.

She may have other ideas; to be a blue-stocking, for instance, in which case I must give her the chance. But I'd rather she was less clever, and wholly a woman, than a brilliant scholar later frustrated by marriage. Meanwhile, I'll give her a house full of books, with none of them closed to her, but not expect her to prefer Proust to *Pam's Schooldays*. If she's a success I'll be pleased, but I'll not care if she isn't nor measure my approval in terms of her O Levels. May spontaneity and warmth be her main achievements, not grading in academic abstractions. May she feel confident, wanted, take pleasure and give it, be artful (but not want to act), laugh easily, covet no one, forget herself sometimes, never be bored or feel the need to kill time, avoid painting-by-numbers, processed food, processed language, have an antenna for the responses of others, and learn that though animals are often much easier to love than men (and both worth it) loving man needs more talent . . .

These are hopes, of course, rather than exact intentions. For who knows what my girl will be? She's only a few months old, and a surprise already — and I imagine I've got a lot more surprises coming. But in the end, I suppose, I just want to give her love and the assurance of a home on earth. This child was not born merely to extend my ego, nor even to give me unbroken pleasure, nor to provide me with a plaything to be fussed over, neglected, shown off and then put away. She was born that I might give her a first foot in this world and might help her to want to live in it. She is here through me, and I am responsible for her — and I'm not looking for any escape-clauses there. Having a child alters the rights of every man, and I don't expect to live as I did without her. I am hers to be with, and hope to be what she needs, and know of no reason why I should ever desert her.

Rabindranath Tagore

I do not love him because he is good, but because he is my little child.

Alan Coren

SON

Dear Giles—

I'd like you to know that it isn't every kid that gets the chance to have a justifiable grudge against his father so early on in life. Here you are, six hours old, and about to be converted into twelve hundred words-worth of rent and rates. Instant material. Psychiatrists yet unborn may some day use this imperishable tract as the lynchpin of your diagnosis, and if you ever come up before the beak, make sure you have a copy to hand: no jury could remain unswayed at this irrefutable evidence of your old man's selfless devotion to self.

Actually, it's not that way at all. You merely made the mistake of entering the Vale of Tears via that rickety gate reserved for the sons of writers; and like any other father, I am merely addressing the situation in my own way. Had you been born a Bunting, your paterfamilias would currently be out pumping slugs at innocent rabbits in order to provide you with vest and pants, and of the two occupations, I think mine's the cleaner. Just. *Chacun à son metier*, which is French and therefore italicised to show its inferiority to English, a distinction you may not as yet be able to appreciate, since the last time I saw you you were concentrating on mastering the burp. First things first. I dropped that line in, by the way, to show that I work for a magazine of *ton* with a multilingual audience, and not for some second-rate tabloid rag. I tried the second-rate tabloid rags, because that's where the loot is, but they didn't have a vacancy, so if anyone asks you in years to come why it is your feet stick out of the ends of your boots, tell them it's because your old man is an artist.

Or was. This game being the thing of shreds and patches it is, by the time you read this I may well be flogging polythene bags from suitcase premises in Regent Street. I wouldn't have worried as much about this yesterday, when there were just two of us; but now your mother's given birth to a Responsibility, and for the first time in my life I'm telephoning insurance agents, instead of the other way round. Or, rather, *vice-versa*:

at the speed with which Latin is disappearing from the sentences of the world, I'd like to drop something in that you may not understand in five years' time, just so's you'll have a little respect for your father. God knows, it'll be hard enough to come by, with your homework consisting of such items as astro-physics and cybernetics and similar goodies calculated to leave an old Eng. Lit. artificer of the fifties quavering at the post. Still, I'll say this for me, no one ever translated a shapelier rune; dons talk of it yet, and weep for vanished generations.

You were born on a bizarre day, in climatic circumstances not unlike those with which novels about the Old South tend to be fraught: at the end of the hottest spell for two hundred years there was a thunderstorm which, when it departed, left the world more crowded by at least one. All extremely portentous, if a shade hammy. And don't worry about that two-hundred-years bit, and never seeing its like again; one of the things you'll discover about England is that we have the hottest (or coldest) summer for two centuries every three years, or so. Don't ask me why. Meteorology is a subject I have but skirted.

I hope you'll forgive, by the way, all this familiarity from a total stranger; but I wanted to start talking to you immediately because, oddly enough, you and I are probably closer now than we'll ever be from here on in. As of now, we shall be gradually getting to misunderstand one another; I wouldn't fret over this, since, with normal luck, we shall continue to like one another, it's simply that we'll be able to communicate less and less as you learn to communicate more and more. It's to do with generations, and fathomlessly complicated as well as being totally incurable, so there's an end. Within six months, the only response I'll glean from opening a conversation with you will be a faceful of strained apricot, in ten years I shall be failing utterly to explain sex, and in twenty you'll be chucking rocks at the American Embassy, if there's anything left of it, and telling your mates that the old man has never understood you and why doesn't someone just wheel him out into the fading sunlight and let him dribble down his bib? So let me emphasise it: don't get hung up on the understanding bag (that's contemporary argot, incidentally, or at any rate was at the time of going to press)—some of my best friends are complete mysteries to me, and if I have any sense, I'll leave it that way . . .

You're not, probably, in much of a position to guess what Lord Chesterfield, Al Jolson, and William Rees-Mogg have in common, and who could blame you? It's a question that would baffle someone twice your age. What marks out those three gents is their pre-dilection for dinning into their offspring various observations concerning the world into which they have been delivered; and a decent crust they all made out of it, too. I, with few ambitions involving the *Oxford Dictionary of Quotations* or Cinema-Scope, don't intend to chance my arm. Personally, I think we can lay down the requisite codes of behaviour as we go along, pragmatism being nearer to Godliness than abstract morality in my book, which is clearly not the Authorised Version. Neither do I care to foist any potted description of the world upon you, since my view of it is essentially idiosyncratic, and I do mean essentially. No other way to look at it, and if it confuses you more and more with each unfolding orbit of the Earth, at least it'll be your own confusion, and not anyone else's. With a modicum of luck, you and I may get to swop our private confusions (which is called discussion) and gain something from the exchange (which is called laughter).

I've just glanced at my watch, to find that you're twice as old as you were when I started. Since there'll be so many better things to fritter your life on, I'll get out now and leave you to lead it. It occurs to me that I may not have mentioned how deliriously happy I am right now; but, for once in my career, that's something that goes without saying.

Bob Harvey

THE JOY OF FATHERHOOD

When the baby is in the womb it's got a real presence, not only in its movements, its kicking, but it also has a definite personality. You know instinctively that it's listening. It knows, with the wisdom of the ages, what's going on outside. You try and keep the family rows to a minimum.

I felt that my last daughter knew all the family long before she arrived. She probably knew the house layout, the labrador's bark, the doors opening and closing, music playing, the flushing toilet.

Once I read in *Time* that animals bond their young by breathing at the moment of birth on their offspring, a kind of quick snorting through the nose, giving them the smell.

On December 24, 1982 at 5 p.m. I carried out this experiment within seconds of my daughter being born. While nurses checked the baby's well-being, and Barbara checked its sex, I quickly, rather secretively, but determinedly, breathed my life on the baby. I do not practice favouritism with my children, but I know that my bonding with this child is absolute. I've been able to calm her when all else fails; she will sleep in my arms without panic or throwing about as babies are prone to do. The rewards and closeness seem to have justified the act.

Amy McLaren

THE BONNIE EARL

After dinner Sandy took his cigarette out of doors, and wandered about the grounds by himself. He wished to be alone. Myrtle was asleep, and the day had been so full of incidents that he welcomed the peace of that quiet hour when the shades of evening begin to fall.

As he sauntered down the flagged pathway that led to the water-lily pond, an odd feeling came over him that he was not alone. A hot little hand seemed to be dragging at his and an imperious voice commanding shrilly: "Come on, daddy."

He had been that child; history would repeat itself! The water-lily pond had always possessed a seductive lure; and many a time had he been rescued from its brink.

He walked round it, and then stood looking out beyond, to where the ground fell away in grassy terraces to the edge of the sea wall, which girdled the lower ramparts of the castle. The spot commanded a view on every side, and he took it all in, slowly and reflectively. The sea was like glass. Far in the distance, across its tranquil surface, the jagged line of Arran's peaks loomed blue-black against the western glow. Inland were the woods and rich fertile country, the well-timbered park, and the castle itself, set like a jewel in the midst of it all. A noble inheritance, and its future lay in his hands; and yet not altogether so. That newborn life had claims. It was bound up in his.

"She was right," he murmured. "It was fitting that he should be born here. I suppose it is the call of the blood; but that little chap's coming has made me feel it in a way I never did before."

He took a last look round. It was not the look of a man with lingering regrets weighted by sentiment. To hold and to keep that inheritance would mean hard work and more or less an exile's life for a time. Involuntarily he squared his shoulders. His tread took a firmer grip, and his step rang sharply as he retraced his way along the flagged pathway. He had a set purpose in view and the will of a resolute man to carry it out.

Pierre Berton

THE DIONNE YEARS:
A THIRTIES MELODRAMA

The doctor gave her an injection of pituitary to raise her blood pressure and another of ergot to prevent post-natal haemorrhage. At last she was told that she had given birth to five babies. "Holy Mary!" she gasped.

The various narratives of the birth are vague about the whereabouts of Oliva Dionne at this moment. Most agree on two points: he had fled from the room, and he was in a state of nervous collapse that was heightened by the information that in the space of two hours his family had increased from seven to twelve. "My God!" he was reported as saying, "what am I going to do with five babies? It was bad enough to look after one; but how are we going to manage to look after five?"

Theodor Reik

Couvade is the custom observed among many races that the father of a new-born child lies in a bed for a certain period, eating only prescribed foods, abstaining from severe work and from the chase, etc., while his wife who has just given birth to a child carries on her usual occupation . . . the idea of a lying-in on the part of the man.

PARTINGS

You have to dig deep to bury your Daddy.

—GYPSY PROVERB

Penny Junor

MARGARET THATCHER—
WIFE, MOTHER, POLITICIAN

Margaret went straight up to Grantham, where Alf was cremated and his ashes buried in the garden of remembrance. Margaret missed her father enormously. She refers to him as "Pa" nowadays, not "Daddy," and still mentions him quite frequently. It is a great regret in her life that he never lived to see her become a Cabinet Minister, or indeed Prime Minister. But the day she first stepped into Number Ten as premier nine years later, she paid tribute to him.

"He brought me up to believe all the things I do believe, and they're the values on which I fought the election," she said. "It's passionately interesting to me that the things I learned in a small town, in a very modest home, are just the things that I believe have won the election . . . I owe almost everything to my father."

Diane Johnson

THE LIFE OF DASHIELL HAMMETT

A telegram came for Hammett, and he threw it on his desk unopened and did not look at it as the days passed. Mary [his elder daughter] could not help seeing it and thinking about it; there was something ominous and frightening about Hammett's unconcern, as if he knew what it would say. She would never touch things on his desk, but she finally decided that he should open the telegram, and when he would not, she opened it herself. It was from Aunt Reba: Papa's father was dead. It told about the funeral and about his end. Mary wondered, was Papa going to the funeral? "No. I'm paying for it, let somebody else do the crying." Hammett made this remark because he was drinking. Mary understood. Hammett did not go to the funeral, though, or speak of it later. He said he had not loved his father.

A. E. Hotchner

SOPHIA—LIVING AND LOVING

Sophia's sister, Maria
As he lay dying, my father took my hand and carried it to his lips and kissed it. Then he said, "I love you." It was the only time he ever said anything affectionate to me. *"Amore,"* as he lay dying.

I was on a sound stage in Rome making *A Special Day* when my sister unexpectedly came to tell me that our father was in serious condition in the hospital. I immediately left with her. My father was in a room with three other patients. He looked gaunt and wasted, and at first I feared that we had come too late.

"We are here, Papa," Maria said, "Sophia and me."

On hearing our voices, he opened his eyes and managed a slight smile. *"Sono felice,"* he said, which means, I am happy. He closed his eyes. He was heavily drugged for his pain, and after a short while I left. I would have stayed longer, but the other patients in the room had visitors who had recognized me and I felt awkward. I just wanted to be an ordinary person visiting her sick father, not a movie star being set upon by everyone in the room and a few nurses and interns to boot. It was certainly not the time and place for it. But before I left, I managed to have a talk with the woman whom my father had lived with for the past ten years, a very nice German woman named Carol, who had been quietly sitting in the corner. She was taking my father's condition very hard. She had been completely devoted to him and he was the only life she had.

That evening, my thoughts would not leave my father. In a way, strange to say, he was the most important man in my life. I had spent my life seeking surrogates for him—in Carlo, the husband who fathers me, in de Sica, who fathered me as a director, and so forth. Despite all the grandiose gifts I had received in my life, that little blue auto my father gave me with my name on it retained a special place in my memory.

My sister, who has a much more forgiving heart than I, had seen him often, and it was she who told me about his illness and about how, when he felt well enough to leave his flat, he would go to movie houses that were showing my films and sit for endless hours watching me. I wondered what went through his mind as he sat alone in the dark observing me on the screen. Whether he ever recalled the early days of our existence when he had not only turned his back on us but in a curious way tried to punish us. That he refused to give Maria his name in that Pozzuoli courtroom; that he made me pay my first million lire for it, and then, a year later, tried to repudiate the agreement—in order to get another payment out of me, I presume. That he even made it difficult for me to collect the three thousand lire a month ($4.60) which, for a few months of my life, he was obligated to pay for my support. And did he recall condemning us to the police in an attempt to run us out of Rome, back to Pozzuoli? Did he have any memory of, or guilt about, all the times my mother asked for his help when we were starving?

I did not expect him to understand the pain of a young girl branded as illegitimate, nor even the raw shame of his wife screaming at me in front of all those *Quo Vadis* people, "You're not a Scicolone! I am! I'm the only Scicolone here!" But surely some guilt that he sued his own daughter for libeling his reputation when he himself had branded her reputation with the stigma of illegitimacy. That lawsuit had roused anger in me, and for a time I hated my father for what he had done. But as I got older and learned more about people, I came to realize that hate is an acid that eats away—not the person hated but the one who hates.

I had also faced reality about my father: he was what he was, and festering criminations about him was pointless. As my viewpoint about him changed, so did my emotions. I no longer had any hate or scorn for him—only pity. I felt sad for him because, as I said at the start, he could have had a rewarding and fruitful life, and instead he spurned it, spurned the people who wanted to love him, who cared about him, and he seemed always to be living against himself. A self-defeatist. Destructive. Needlessly creating problems that nurtured his bitterness and hostility. I thank God I inherited none of that from him. I don't want to destroy myself or anyone else. My nature is to give and be involved, without a thought to receiving anything for myself. This wellspring of generous giving probably contributes much to my acting, for what is true acting except the ability of the actor to give his emotions and feelings to his audience?

So I pitied my father who couldn't give affection and love to his women and the children whom he brought into his life. Perhaps toward the end he had a glimmer of this. Not long before he went to the hospital, at his request my sister arranged for me to visit him in his apartment in Rome. I had not seen him for many years, and I had never been to a place he lived in. I found him much older than his years. I believe he was suffering from cancer. He was very pleased to see me and took me all around the flat showing me his possessions and mementos.

We did not have much to talk about, but it mattered a great deal to him that I see everything in his home. When it was time to leave, and we stood in the doorway saying good-bye, he took one of my hands in his and said, "Lella, I am very proud of you."

That was the only affectionate thing he ever said to me.

A short time after my first visit to the hospital, Maria again came to fetch me. "Come quickly," she said, "Papa is dying. Quickly!"

My father had been moved to a private room. Several of his relatives stood in a cluster at the far side of the room. And to my amazement, my mother was present. She has a terrible fear of death. She never goes to hospitals or funerals. She had not seen my father for years, but the fatal fascination he had for her had held true even to his death. She had borne him two daughters and he had been the only man she had ever lived with. However she may condemn him, he was the one and only love of her life. And now she had defied her obsessive death-fear to be present at his demise.

Also present was the Carol woman. But my father's first wife, Nella Rivolta, the mother of his two sons, was not there. Nor did she come to his funeral.

My father had an oxygen mask on his face, and an attendant stood beside the bed, monitoring the breathing apparatus. Seated on one side of the bed was a handsome young man, thirty years or so of age, who was holding one of my father's hands in both of his. The young man looked familiar, like someone I had known well a long time ago. Carol led me to the bed and introduced us. Giuseppe was his name, the younger of my father's two sons. He shyly acknowledged the introduction. I felt strange, meeting my brother for the first time at my father's deathbed.

I sat down on the opposite side of the bed and took my father's other hand. I looked across at Giuseppe, joined as we were by my father's hands. There was a soft, gentle quality to his face. I had an illusion that we were old friends. There was a shyness about him with which I identified.

I turned my attention to my father's anguished breathing. Giuseppe had shifted around to look at the monitor beside the bed. It was going erratically. My father's hand felt cold and inert in mine. Life was running out of him.

My mother never took her eyes off my father. Carol sat in the corner, her face covered with her hands. My sister stood beside my mother, watching the breathing machine.

And then the attendant turned off the oxygen and my father was dead. I had never seen anyone die before. The attendant took the mask off my father's face, and placing both his hands on my father's chest, he gave a mighty shove, pushing the last of the oxygen from my father's body.

Carol started to weep. Giuseppe released my father's hand and walked over to the window. I looked at my father's face, now free of the oxygen mask, and I felt compelled to touch his cheek with my fingertips.

"Ciao, papa," I said, and welcome into my heart forever.

My mother had started to cry, not covering her face, letting the tears run freely. My sister, too, was weeping, but she had turned her back to the bed and was weeping against the wall.

I went over to the window where Giuseppe was standing, looking up at the sky. He was striving to hold back his tears. And so was I. Unlike me, as a child Giuseppe had lived with my father, so I guess he felt his loss more keenly. He turned and looked at me; it was a look of distress, of need. I reached out to him and he collapsed against me, releasing his tears. As did I. I put my arms around him and comforted him and felt very much his sister.

United in our sorrow, embraced, shedding common tears, I felt a surge of love for this new brother of mine who wept in my arms. How ironic that at his death, my father, who had given me so little in life, had left me a priceless legacy — a brother. I felt an eerie exultation, as if this young man had risen from the corpse of my father, his flesh and blood, to bring to me the kind of kinship that I had never had with my father.

So there in his death room, I both grieved for my father's demise and experienced the throb of encountering new life. It was a moment of great meaning for me, which will endure for the rest of my life.

Henri Troyat

TOLSTOY

And yet, on November 9, 1873 a tragedy occurred that almost made him forget literature for a while. His youngest son, Petya, the pink and blond baby, was carried off in two days by the croup. Grief-stricken, Sonya wrote in her diary: "He died peacefully. I nursed him fourteen and one-half months. He lived from June 13, 1872 to November 9, 1873. A gay, healthy child. The darling, I loved him too much! They buried him yesterday. What an emptiness now. I cannot reconcile the images of Petya living and Petya dead. They are both precious to me, but what is there in common between that being full of life, light and affection, and this other, motionless, solemn and cold. He was very attached to me. Did it hurt him to leave me?"

Tolstoy managed to restrain his emotions; he had said that Petya was too young to interest him. After the burial, while his wife was wandering tearfully about the silent house, he wrote to his brother Sergey:

"Petya is dead and has just been buried . . . This is something new for us, and very painful, particularly for Sonya. I have just received a letter from the typesetters, telling me that the edition [of my works] will come out on the twelfth of this month. The Dyakovs arrived today. Dyakov is going to Moscow and will leave Masha [his daughter] and Sofya [her governess] with us. I think I ought to go to Moscow too; Sonya would not be completely alone in the house. If you can manage it, let us go the day after tomorrow, the twelfth. Will that be all right? Let me know."

Two lines on the death of his son, the rest on the publication of his books and a forthcoming trip. To be sure, the death of a child was a common occurrence in those days and it was natural for a mother to be more deeply afflicted by the sight of an empty cradle than a father. But how is one to explain the fact that this model head-of-family, this vast compassionate heart, open to all the sufferings of mankind, had only one thought after the funeral: to get away from the house, out of earshot of his wife's lamentations?

Svetlana Aliluyeva (Stalin)

TWENTY LETTERS TO A FRIEND

When someone finally told me that my father had had a stroke in the night and was unconscious I even felt a little relieved. I had thought he was dead already . . .

My father was lying there unconscious. The stroke had been severe. He'd lost his speech and the right side was paralysed. He opened his eyes several times, but his gaze was clouded and no one knew whether he recognised anybody or not. Whenever he opened his eyes they leaned over him, straining to catch a word or even read a wish in his eyes. I was sitting at his side holding his hand and he looked at me, though I'm sure he couldn't see me. I kissed his face and his hand. There was no longer anything more for me to do.

It's a strange thing, but during those days of illness when he was nothing but a body out of which the soul had flown and later, during the days of leave-taking in the Hall of Columns, I loved my father more tenderly than I ever had before. He'd been very remote from me, from us, his children, and all his relatives. During the past few years enormous blown-up photographs of children, a little boy on skis, a boy in a blossoming cherry tree, had appeared in his rooms at the dacha, but he hadn't once found time to see five of his eight grandchildren. Yet even the grandchildren who never saw him loved him and love him still. During those days, when he found peace at last on his deathbed and his face became beautiful and serene, I felt my heart breaking from grief and love.

Neither before nor since have I felt such a powerful welling up of strong, contradictory emotions. As I stood in the Hall of Columns day after day, frozen and unable to speak (I literally stood, for try as they would to make me sit down, and even though they shoved a chair under me, I was unable to sit or do anything but stand in the presence of what was occurring), I realised that a deliverance of some kind was under way. I had no idea what kind of deliverance it was or what form it was going to take, but I saw that it was a release for me and everyone else from a burden that had been weighing on the minds and hearts of us all. They were playing an old Georgian folk tune with a melody that was sorrowful and full of feeling. I looked at that beautiful face in its sadness and repose and listened to the funeral music and felt torn apart by grief. I thought what a bad daughter I was, that I'd been more like a stranger than a daughter to him and had never been a help to this lonely spirit, this sick old man when he was left all alone on his Olympus. Yet he was, after all, my father, a father who had done his best to love me and to whom I owed good things as well as bad — more good than bad, in fact. All those days I couldn't cry and I didn't eat. Grief and a sort of calm had turned me to stone.

My father died a difficult and terrible death. It was the first and so far the only time I have seen somebody die. God grants an easy death only to the just . . .

The death agony was terrible. He literally choked to death as we watched. At what seemed like the very last moment he suddenly opened his eyes and cast a glance over everyone in the room. It was a terrible glance, insane or perhaps angry and full of fear of death and the unfamiliar faces of the doctors bent over him. The glance swept over everyone in a second. Then something incomprehensible and terrible happened that to this day I can't forget and don't understand. He suddenly lifted his left hand as though he were pointing to something up above and bringing down a curse on us all. The gesture was incomprehensible and full of menace, and no one could say to whom or what it might be directed. The next moment, after a final effort, the spirit wrenched itself free of the flesh . . .

Late that night or, rather, when it was nearly daybreak, they came to take the body for the autopsy. I started shaking all over with a nervous tremble of some kind. I couldn't cry. I just trembled all over. The body was laid on a stretcher. It was the first time I had seen my father naked. It was a beautiful body. It didn't look old or as if he'd been sick at all. With a pang like the thrust of a knife in the heart I felt what it meant to be "flesh of the flesh." I realised that the body that had given me life no longer had life or breath in it, yet I would go on living.

You can never understand what this means until you've witnessed the death of a parent with your own eyes. To understand death you have to see it with your own eyes. You have to watch as the "spirit departs the flesh," leaving only the mortal remains. It wasn't so much that I understood this at the time, but I sensed it. The knowledge of it passed across my heart and left a mark.

James Baldwin

NOTES OF A NATIVE SON

I had not known my father very well. We had got on badly, partly because we shared, in our different fashions, the vice of stubborn pride. When he was dead I realized that I had hardly ever spoken to him. When he had been dead a long time I began to wish I had. It seems to be typical of life in America, where opportunities, real and fancied, are thicker than anywhere else on the globe, that the second generation has no time to talk to the first.

Arthur Ransome

AUTOBIOGRAPHY

My next and last attempt to win a scholarship was at Rugby, where there were particular reasons why I wished to do well. My father's old schoolfellow, Robert Whitelaw, was a housemaster there and, partly on his advice, my father had resigned from his chair at Leeds so as to be nearer London and free for political work. He was only forty-six, was making a considerable income from his history-books which were used in schools all over the world, was writing political articles, was to have been temporarily a sixth-form tutor at Rugby and was eagerly looking forward to a political career. He refused to recognise that even the amputation of his leg had failed to save him. He had already moved to Rugby when his illness suddenly grew much worse and when I came there to sit for the scholarship he was lying in bed desperately ill. I went into his room to see him and knew how much he hoped that I would win it.

There were a hundred and two competitors for the nine or ten scholarships and we sat for the examination in New Big School . . .

Next day a list of the first hundred competitors was pinned up on the door of the school, the scholarship winners at the top of the list.

Having a modest (and rightly so) estimate of my learning and having learnt by this time that no matter how well I might know a subject I always did badly under examination, I began reading that list at the bottom, where I expected to see my name. It was not there. By the time I had come half way up the list and had not found it, an incredulous hope began to dawn. Could I, after all have done better than I feared? I read on, higher and higher, name after name, until, in growing excitement, I had reached those names beside which were printed the scholarships that had been awarded to their owners.

Hardly able to breathe I read on until I came to the very top of the list and knew the dreadful truth. I had not won a scholarship. I was not even in the first hundred but was either No.101 or No.102, one of the pair protected by a merciful anonymity from knowing who was last of all.

I went miserably back to Windermere and there, a few weeks later, the headmaster's wife came to me in the dormitory over the gateway in the old square tower that used to rock in high winds. She sat down on my bed and told me that I should not see my father again. He was dead and I lay and wept with my head under the bedclothes. I have been learning ever since how much I lost in him. He had been disappointed in me, but I have often thought what friends we could have been had he not died so young. There were years after his death during which I took no interest in sport of any kind and indeed had not a day to spare from reading and writing and the walking that served both, but later my ancestors began to have their way with me, and by the time I was thirty fishing had become what it has remained, one of the passions of my life. It has been a delight to me to fish the waters he fished, because he fished them.

William Wharton

DAD

When we turn up the Hill's walk, Rita's standing at the door. She has a telegram in her hand . . . My temptation is to run; run up and take the telegram or turn and run away.

I stop. Billy, who's close behind, almost bumps into me. I continue slowly, walking.

"This arrived just after you left, it's from California."

I don't know why I open it there on the steps. Rita moves back inside the door; Billy stands beside me. It's easy to read; yellow, not blue. A. T. & T. printout, not handwriting.

JULY 7

DAD DIED TODAY STOP FUNERAL FRIDAY STOP WIRE FLIGHT STOP

LOVE JOAN

I hand the telegram to Billy.

"Your grandfather died, Bill. We have to go back."

It's as much as I can get out.

I walk past Rita, through the Hill's house, out the backdoor and into their yard. I cry. I don't think I've ever cried so hard in my life. Men don't usually cry well and I'm as bad or worse than most. I'm crying without thinking. I stand in the back of their yard against the wall and cry till I vomit.

I'm crying for many reasons, mostly various forms of self pity. I'm crying the way the boy in that Hemingway story *Bimmi* cried. His big fish got away after he came so close. My Dad got away. I didn't have the guts, the courage, the persistence, the generosity to make those last few hard tugs and pull him in.

I'm crying, too, because I'm going to miss him personally, not be able to hear his voice, see his distinctive moves, smell him, touch him again. He's gone.

I'm crying because I'm scared. I'm scared of death. I'm afraid to be alone; in the logical sequence of time and events, I'm the next one to die.

These are some of the things I know I'm crying about; there are others; they're not all so selfish. I'm crying for Mom, Joan, for Jacky, who will never know him, will remember him only as a name, not as a person. I'm crying for Vron, who loved Dad deeply. But more than anything else, I'm crying because a big part of me, my identity, will be gone.

I hear a sound and Rita's behind me. I turn and we go into each others arms. She's so tiny, smaller than Joan, smaller than Mom, but strong, so strong she holds me harder than I hold her. I'm going catatonic. I don't want to leave this haven, this vaguely sexual source of strength and comfort. It's a reverse union, her vital forces flowing into me, a dying tree gaining sustenance from mistletoe.

At last, I cry myself out. Rita leads me to the house, into the kitchen. We sit, embarrassed, exhausted. Pat's still at school. Billy's upstairs. But I can't talk to her. When I try, I cry. She asks if she should make reservations for Los Angeles. I nod. It makes our car trip seem so futile.

The plane leaves at seven. Rita says she'll drive us to the airport. She also wires Joan our flight number. Billy and I pack; we're not talking much. He knows I'm not up to it and he seems withdrawn. He's my nearest male relative now and I can't touch him.

Rita gets us to the TWA terminal with half an hour to spare. The parking's impossible, so she leaves us there. Billy and I hurriedly unload, wave and turn into the airport. I'm feeling detached, unhooked, moving without thinking much.

We're in line at the ticket counter before I realise Billy is distinctly dragging, is very upset about something. I pull myself together enough to ask what's the trouble. He shakes his head, says it's nothing. But as the line moves forward, he gets more restless. Finally he blurts it out.

"What do you think, Dad? Debby's expecting me to meet her in Paris three days from now. Should I wait till we're in California and send a telegram to American Express or call her parents from here; they might have an address. I was supposed to meet her on the point of the *Ile de la Cite*, where the weeping willow tree is. I hate to think of her waiting and me not coming."

There are three people in front of us now.

"Do you really want to go to this funeral, Bill?"

He looks me in the eye, the first time since the telegram.

"Gosh, Dad! He's your father; of course I'm coming! Nobody'd ever understand if I didn't go to the funeral of my own grandfather."

"I'd understand, Bill; so would your mother. My dad's funeral is not your problem. I can cover for you in California."

We're down to two people.

"I'd hate letting you down like that, Dad."

"That's not the point. I wouldn't want to go if I were in your place; I'd want to meet my girl under that tree. We're next in line; make up your mind."

"You're sure about this?" I nod. He smiles and puts out his hand. We shake. It's the first time we've ever shaken hands. His hands are so much like mine, it's like shaking hands with myself. I turn to the woman behind the desk and buy one ticket. There's no trouble cancelling Bill's reservation. The plane is boarding in fifteen minutes; we go over to check in my baggage.

"Look, Bill, here's four hundred bucks. It would cost that much flying you to California and back. See if you can find a charter cancellation or standby; I'll bet you'll land something for under a hundred bucks if you look around, especially as a student; that way you'll have some money."

I give him the four one-hundred-dollar bills we got from the lady at the whorehouse. Bill sees me to the flight gate and we shake again. We're both hurrying things, trying to get apart before it hits too hard.

I walk through miles of red-carpeted narrow halls with low ceilings. I feel better inside. For once, I've let go in time.

Bill's childhood is finished. Maybe, as a privileged spectator, I can project forward into the life he'll lead. My time with Dad is over; our relationship is made, inside, wrapped up for good.

Machiavelli

"A son can bear with composure the death of his father, but the loss of his inheritance might drive him to despair."

Russell Baker

GROWING UP

Supper was almost ready when we arrived that night at Uncle Miller's. In the few minutes before we sat down Uncle Miller asked my father to come out to the pigpen for a look at the porkers to be slaughtered in the morning. I heard them outside talking and laughing and knew they were having a drink in the darkness. In Morrisonville you learned the symptoms young. There was a certain change in the level of the voice, a laughter slightly more enthusiastic than laughter usually sounded. But they were only outside a few minutes, not long enough to overdo it, and when they returned and we all sat at the table, they looked fine.

We started with fried oysters. Presently my father put his fork down, rose from the table, and went into the yard; we all sat there not saying a word, listening to him outside vomiting. Uncle Miller and my mother went outside then, and after a while my mother returned and took Doris and me off to the bedroom where Audrey was already asleep.

The house was unnaturally quiet next morning. The butchering festival I'd expected was not in progress, and my father was not in the bedroom with us. My mother said he was in Uncle Miller's bedroom because a doctor was coming to see him.

I wandered around the backyard until the sun burned off the frost. After a while my mother came out.

"The doctor's here," she said. "He's going to take Daddy to the hospital in Frederick so he can get better. Come and kiss him good-bye."

To my surprise my father was fully dressed and seated in the doctor's small roadster at the front of the house. He was wearing his blue serge suit, white shirt, and necktie, and looked all right to me. I walked across the lawn to the car, and he leaned out the window on the passenger's side and smiled, but he didn't have much to say to me. Just, "Daddy'll be home in a day or two. Be a good boy till I get back."

My mother held me up, and he gave me a kiss.

"We'd better get going," the doctor said.

My mother set me down and leaned into the car and kissed him. She and I watched the roadster together until it passed over the brow of the hill headed for the Maryland side of the Potomac.

By afternoon we were back in Morrisonville. Next day before sunup she rose to visit the hospital. Uncle Irvey would drive her.

"Is Daddy coming home today?"

"Maybe we'll bring him back with us," she said.

It was a gentle Indian summer morning, and my grandmother told me to go out and play while she minded Doris and Audrey. I set off on one of my daily wandering expeditions, taking the road down toward the creek.

I was down there by myself. You could always find something entertaining to do around Morrisonville. Climb a fence. Take a stick and scratch pictures in the dirt. There were always cows around, or a horse. Throw pebbles at a locust tree. I was busy at this sort of thing when I saw my cousins, Kenneth and Ruth Lee, coming down the road.

Besides Doris, Audrey, and me, they were the only other children living in Morrisonville. Kenneth, two years older than I, was our leader. He was coming down the road with Ruth Lee following as usual. I was happy to see them. We usually played in the fields and around the barns and straw ricks together. Sometimes we ripped open a burlap grain sack to build a tepee in the apple orchard, or picked through the junk pile behind Liz Virts's house to collect enough tin cans and broken dishes to play store. I was glad now to have company.

When Kenneth walked right up to me, though, he stared at me with such a stare as I'd never seen.

"Your father's dead," he said.

It was like an accusation that my father had done something criminal, and I came to my father's defence."

"He is not," I said.

But of course they didn't know the situation. I started to explain. He was sick. In the hospital. My mother was bringing him home right now . . .

"He's dead," Kenneth said.

His assurance slid an icicle into my heart.

"He is not either!" I shouted.

"He is too," Ruth Lee said. "They want you to come home right away."

I started running up the road screaming. "He is not!"

It was a weak argument. They had the evidence and gave it to me as I hurried home crying, "He is not . . . He is not . . . He is not . . ."

I was almost certain before I got there that he was.

And I was right. Arriving at the hospital that morning, my mother was told he had died at four a.m. in "acute diabetic coma." He was thirty-three years old.

When I came running home, my mother was still not back from Frederick, but the women had descended on our house, as women there did in such times, and were already busy with the housecleaning and cooking that were Morrisonville's ritual response to death. With a thousand tasks to do, they had no time to handle a howling five-year-old. I was sent to the opposite end of town, to Bessie Scott's house.

Poor Bessie Scott. All afternoon she listened patiently as a saint while I sat in her kitchen and cried myself out. For the first time I thought seriously about God. Between sobs I told Bessie that if God could do things like this to people, then God was hateful and I had no more use for Him.

Bessie told me about the peace of Heaven and the joy of being among the angels and the happiness of my father who was already there. This argument failed to quiet my rage.

"God loves us all just like His own children," Bessie said.

"If God loves me, why did He make my father die?"

Bessie said I would understand someday, but she was only partly right. That afternoon, though I couldn't have phrased it this way then, I decided that God was a lot less interested in people than anybody in Morrisonville was willing to admit. That day I decided that God was not entirely to be trusted.

After that I never cried again with any real conviction, nor expected much of anyone's God except indifference, nor loved deeply without fear that it would cost me dearly in pain. At the age of five I had become a skeptic and began to sense that any happiness that came my way might be the prelude to some grim cosmic joke.

While I came to grips with death in Bessie's kitchen, its rites were being performed by other Morrisonville women in my father's house. Our floors were being scrubbed, windows washed, furniture dusted, beds made. Visitors would be arriving by the dozen. It was a violation of the code to show them anything but a spotless house.

Prodigies of cooking were already under way in surrounding houses. Precious hams were being removed from smokehouses, eggs and butter were being beaten in cake bowls, pie crusts were being rolled, canning jars of pickles and preserved fruits were being lifted from pantry shelves. Death was also a time for feasting.

It was growing dark when, pretty well cried out and beginning to respond to the holiday excitement in the air, I left Bessie Scott's and walked back down the road to home. The place sparkled with cleanliness, and the women sat clustered in the kitchen, exhausted, I suppose. The men had just begun to arrive, looking uncomfortable in their good dark suits, their shirts and neckties and low shoes. I went outside and stood around with the men in the road. So late in November, the dusk came early. The men seemed unusually quiet. I did not know many of them. They stood in little groups talking quietly, almost in whispers, probably not saying anything very interesting, just feeling self-conscious in their Sunday suits with nothing to do but stand. The men standing and waiting and talking quietly with nothing to do in their good dark suits was part of the ritual too. It was important to have a powerful turnout of humanity. That showed the dead man had been well liked in the community, and it was therefore considered an important source of comfort to the widow.

It was fully dark when someone told me to move around and wait in the backyard, which I did. After a while Annie Grigsby came out and hugged me and said it was all right to come into the kitchen. "They've brought your daddy home," she said.

My mother was in the kitchen, but most of the other women had left now. It was the first time I had seen her since she left for the hospital that morning. She was sitting on a chair looking very tired. Annie took a chair beside her. It was terribly quiet. I wondered where my father was. Annie finally broke the silence.

"Maybe he'd like to see his father."

"Do you want to see your father?" my mother asked.

"I guess so," I said.

The undertaker had come and gone while I was in the backyard, and now that most of the bustle was over and most of the people had gone home for supper, the house felt empty and still. My mother did not seem up to showing me the undertaker's handiwork.

"I'll take him in," Annie said, rising in her weary fashion, taking my hand.

She led me into the adjoining living room. The blinds were drawn. A couple of kerosene lamps were burning. Annie lifted me in her arms so I could look down. For some reason there was an American flag.

"There's your daddy, child," Annie said. "Doesn't he look nice?"

He was wearing his blue serge suit and a white shirt and necktie.

"Yes. He looks nice," I told Annie, knowing that was what I was supposed to say. But it wasn't the niceness of the way he was dressed and the way his hair was so carefully combed that impressed me. It was his stillness. I gazed at the motionless hand laid across his chest, thinking no one can lie so still for so long without moving a finger. I waited for the closed eyelids to flutter, for his chest to move in a slight sigh to capture a fresh breath of air. Nothing. His motionlessness was majestic and terrifying. I wanted to be away from that room and never see him like that again.

"Do you want to kiss your daddy?" Annie asked.

"Not now," I said.

Then I went back to the warmth of the kitchen with Annie, born in slavery, and sat there until bedtime with my mother and Doris while the neighbors came back and stood whispering in the living room.

Mary Webb

PRECIOUS BANE

Father said—
  "What was the text?"
  "Burning and fuel of fire."
  "What was the sermon about?"
  Poor Gideon made out a tale of all the things Tivvy had said. You never heard such a tale! Father sat quite quiet, and Mother was smiling very painful, standing by the fire, cooking a rasher.
  Suddenly Father shouted out—
  "Liar! Liar! Parson called but now, to say was there sickness, there being nobody at church. You've not only taken dog's leave and lied, but you've made game of *me*."
  His face went from red to purple, and all veined, like raw meat. It was awful to see. Then he reached for the horsewhip and said—
  "I'll give you the best hiding ever you had, my boy!"
  He came across the kitchen towards Gideon.
  But suddenly Gideon ran at him and bunted into him, and taking him by surprise he knocked him clean over.
  Now whether it was that Father had eaten a very hearty supper, after a big day's work with the bees, or whether it was him being in such a rage, and then the surprise of the fall, we never knew. However it was, he was taken with a fit. He never stirred, but lay on his back on the red quarries, breathing so loud and strong that it filled the house, like somebody snoring in the night. Mother undid his Sunday neckcloth, and lifted him up, and put cold water on his face, but it was no manner of use.
  The awful snoring went on, and seemed to eat up all other sounds. They went out like rushlights in the wind. There was no more ticking from the clock, nor purring from the cat, nor sizzling from the rasher, nor buzzing from the bee in the window. It seemed to eat up the light, too, and the smell of the white bush-roses outside, and the feeling in my

body, and the thoughts I had afore. We'd all come to be just a part of a dark snoring.

"Sarn, Sarn!" cried Mother. "Oh, Sarn, poor soul, come to thyself!"

She tried to put some Hollands between his lips, but they were set. Then the snore changed to a rattle, very awful to hear, and in a little while it stopped, and there was a dreadful silence, as if all the earth had gone dumb. All the while, Gideon stood like stone, remembering the horsewhip Father meant to beat him with, so he said after. And though he'd never seen anyone die afore, when Father went quiet, and the place dumb, he said in an everyday voice, only with a bit of a tremble—

"He's dead, Mother. I'll go and tell the bees, or we met lose 'em."

John Osborne

A BETTER CLASS OF PERSON

As my mother bit her nails to purplish stumps, my father grew weaker, and I was able to spend more time with him in his bedroom as she huddled over the kitchen grate. We read aloud from the papers to each other and, while his strength lasted, long adventure yarns from his old copies of *Boys' Own Paper, 1908-12*. When he grew tired I would read to him. November came and I began to become excited at the prospect of Christmas. I don't know why, because there seemed little to become exercised about, just the three of us together. However I was sure that lovely Isabel would ask me over, possibly on Boxing Day as I knew my mother wouldn't allow me out of the house on Christmas Day. She would say that I was leaving my father and her all on their own. It was, of course, only half a mile down the road. I think she also suspected that my feelings for Isabel were not just those of childish friendship, Anyway, she was disapproving of the Sells family, thinking that if they ran an hotel they must be rich and privileged, which they clearly were not. She soon developed an overweening jealousy of the family, Isabel in particular, and was always discouraging my visits. "You're not to go down there and worry Mrs. Sells. She's got quite enough to do looking after that hotel. I'm sure that they don't want you round the place—kid like you." As much as I protested that they *liked* me being there, she wouldn't believe it. Well, Boxing Day would at least be free of Grandma Osborne's annual Christmas message.

Round about the end of November, an ambulance, an ordinary white one this time, took my father on a stretcher to the sanatorium between Ventnor and Shanklin. My mother and I accompanied him, helping him out into his wheelchair when we arrived there. It was a huge Edwardian affair, like a Continental hotel, with grand verandahs facing out to the sea, where patients coughed in their beds overlooking the black mist. I waited in a corridor while my mother and father went up to see a doctor. They were not away very long and we returned home in silence. While the ambulance men carried him back up the stairs, my mother said, "Well, your father's only got six weeks. Six weeks to *live*, do you understand?" Would he be alive at Christmas? "I don't know, do I? Don't ask bloody silly questions."

I didn't quite believe my mother. She was not to be trusted. I was determined to give him a nice present, something to keep him going, even alive. I scarcely bothered to think of what I might get for her. One evening I asked him what he would like for Christmas. He told me that there was a new series of books called Penguin Books that could be bought at W. H. Smith's and he said, "I'll give you a list. They're only sixpence." He gave me a selection, which included *Ariel* by André Maurois, a Pelican book in fact, and I think the first. The other two were *Death of a Hero* by Richard Aldington and *A Safety Match* by Ian Hay. I had saved some money from Ewell days, there being little to spend it on anyway on the island and went out and bought the three of them immediately.

Mon Abri, it turned out, was to be a very poor refuge from death and Christmas Day, when it arrived, was a morose affair. Money seemed to be shorter here than it had been in the suburbs and my pillowcase was limp, barely a quarter full. I never had the customary stocking. My mother did not have the thrifty middle-class imagination to attempt filling an inexpensive stocking with makeshift surprise delights. But there was a splendid model yacht, which I stupidly tried to convert into a three-master schooner, making it top-heavy and impossible to sail, a few odds and ends, comics and, best of all, *Boys' Own Annual* and the *Greyfriars Annual*. I gave my father the three books from his list. "But I didn't mean you to get all three of them, Skipper. I only meant you to get me one." But he seemed pleased with them.

Christmas dinner was fretful. My father put his dressing gown on and came down the few stairs into the sitting-room, where he hardly ate anything at all except his favourite bread sauce, saying that he would prefer to have the bird cold. He left nearly all of it while my mother scowled with heavy-breathing and pique. We listened to the King's Speech and toasted him sitting down. My father said this was a traditional custom in the Navy. The King himself was obliged to give up the Christmas 1939 forecast and said: "We cannot tell what it [the New Year] will be. If it brings peace how happy we shall be." Eating my own dinner eagerly, I was suddenly overcome with a panic sense of loneliness that I felt had descended on me for good. Sitting between my father and mother I burst into tears as he struggled to fan the tiny blue flame on Grandma Osborne's Christmas pudding. "What's he grizzling on about?" said my mother. "Leave him alone," my father replied. "The boy's upset. It's not surprising is it?" Or something like it. I left the remains of my dinner while my mother cluttered our plates noisily back into the kitchen. As I went up the stairs to my room I could hear her muttering about all the trouble she had gone to and nobody bothering, not so much as a bloody thank-you, at least she wouldn't have to spend another dead and alive Christmas in *Mon* bloody *Abri*. The following day she allowed me to go down to the Carfax and I almost forgot the sense of inescapable desertion I'd felt the previous day, consoling myself with kissing Isabel underneath the mistletoe, albeit egged on by laughing Raymond. I longed to enfold her passionately.

January 1940 came and I managed to keep away from school more than ever, although the attendance officer was a constant visitor. He was surprisingly friendly but kept pointing out with uncommon official tact that school could not be put off for ever. It was at least a temporary reprieve. However, I was legitimately unwell for a while with a bad cough and often feverish, which prompted my mother to tell the attendance officer convincingly that I was going to be just like my father.

I was sitting in the kitchen reading about two weeks after Christmas, when I heard my mother scream from the foot of the uncarpeted staircase. I ran to see what was happening and stared up to the landing where my father was standing. He was completely naked with his silver hair and grey, black and red beard. He looked like a naked Christ. "Look at him!" she screamed. "Oh, my God, he's gone blind." He stood quite still for a moment and then fell headlong down the stairs on top of us. Between us we carried him upstairs. She was right. He had gone blind.

A day or two later my grandfather arrived. The old man's presence seemed to restrain even my mother, although she still contrived to treat him as a begging tramp at the door, overfeeding him as if he were some wandering supplicant. My father seemed to recover and brighten up in his own father's presence and they spent some time talking to each other. I was curious to know what it was about but never ventured in when they were alone together. Grandfather was rather shyly apologetic about Grandma Osborne's absence, saying that she was, *of course*, not strong enough to make the journey. Besides, it was far too cold for her. Together we went for a few long walks up on the cliff. He said very little to me except to murmur about how I should have to Manage On My Own in future, putting ponderous emphasis on this fact. He was obviously thinking of my mother, who was already making no secret of her relief that it would all be over soon, when she could get out of this dead-and-alive hole and back to London or, at least, to the blacked-out lights of Ewell.

My father's condition soon deteriorated. When I saw him he croaked incoherently and the doctor suggested that it would be a good idea if I were to spend the next few days down at the Carfax with Mrs. Sells and pay a short daily visit to my father. I found myself occupying a bedroom next to Isabel, full of dread for the time when I should soon have to leave it. The day my father died my mother came down to the Carfax and told Mrs. Sells. She tried to insist on my immediate return but she was gently coaxed back. I threw myself into the arms of Isabel for the comfort I felt I would never receive again. The following day I was reluctantly sent back up to *Mon Abri*. My mother would need looking after. She was waiting excitedly for me and at once insisted that I go into my father's bedroom to look at him in his coffin. The smell in the room was strong and strange and, in his shroud, he was unrecognizable. As I looked down at him, she said, "Of course, this room's got to be fumigated, you know that, don't you? Fumigated." Frumigated was how she pronounced it. With my father's body lying in the bedroom across the landing, I had been obliged to share my briefing room with my mother, who spent hour upon hour reading last Sunday's *News of the World*, the bright light overhead, rustling the pages in my ear and sighing heavily. For the first time I felt the fatality of hatred.

A few days later, after hysterical hours of packing up and my grandfather being abused for his meticulous slowness, we left the house taking my father in yet another Daimler ambulance. The journey back to South-ampton was unlike the journey out. I was going back to Ewell but nothing could be the same. Mickey Wall had won a scholarship to Tiffins Boys' Grammar School. Joan Buffen was lost for ever. The funeral in the crematorium in Southampton was unremarkably eerie. From the faded pages of a pencilled diary I can read: "January 31st. Father's funeral today." And then a description of the coffin rattling on its rails, disap-pearing behind the purple curtains. "I met the clergyman who is one of the nicest individuals I have ever met." Who could I have been addressing so self-consciously?

David Storey

SAVILLE

"Have you ever seen this?" his father said. He held out a square-shaped book of greyish, tinted paper. Inside were a number of chalk drawings, some of fruit, some of flowers, their bright colours imprinted on the sheets of protective tissue. The drawings themselves were done with an adult assurance, seemingly effortless and uncorrected.

"Whose are they?" he said, gazing in particular at a drawing of three apples, their redness veering into greenness, lying in a bowl.

"They're by your brother." His father laughed. "Andrew." He turned to the front. The name of the village school and his brother's unfamiliar name, "Andrew Saville," were written on the cover. "He was only seven."

"How did he die?" he said, suddenly reminded.

"He died within a few hours. Of pneumonia," his father said. "He was here one minute, and gone the next. Shortly before that he had an operation. It was that that weakened him, I thought. I'd give ought to have that lad alive."

"How give ought?" he said.

"Well." His father hesitated then turned aside.

On one occasion, some years previously, he'd gone with his father to put some flowers on his brother's grave: it lay in a small plot of ground at the side of the road leading to the colliery, the whole area invisible, behind high hedges, from the road itself. The grave was marked by a small round-headed stone on which were painted his father's initials, H.R.S., and a number. They cleared brambles from the spot, weeded the oblong bed, set a jam-jar in the ground and in the jam-jar set the flowers. "We ought to come each week and keep it tidy," his father had said, yet as far as Colin was aware neither he nor his mother had been again. Now, looking at the coloured drawings in the book, his father said, "We ought to go and have a look. See how that grave is. We haven't been for some time, you know."

"How did it affect my mother?" he said.

"Well." His father, uncertain, gazed at the book steadily now, his eyes intense. "I think that's been half the trouble."

"What trouble?"

"Nay, Andrew dying," his father said.

The house was silent. His mother had gone off that afternoon to visit her sister, taking, after much complaining from his brothers, Steven and Richard with her.

"Why thy's so silent and morose at times."

"Am I silent and morose?" "Nay, thy should know," his father said.

"Well, I don't."

"Nay, I can't be the first to mention it." His father flushed.

"I didn't think I was morose," he said.

"Nay, not all the time," he added. "It's just been lately, I suppose." He gazed at the drawings.

A cup stood on a saucer: looking at the picture Colin, with a peculiar sensation, as if someone had touched him, saw how clear and confident the ellipses were, perfectly drawn by his seven-year-old brother, with scarcely an inflection that broke the line, or a faltering in the shading of their blue-painted pattern.

"Your mother was three months gone, tha knows. It must have had an effect, I reckon. She was very down." His father, almost idly, closed the book. "She was very down, I can tell you that." He added nothing further for a while, "It all seemed very strange at the time."

"Strange in what way?"

"It was as if he wa' gone." His father looked up. "And then, you see, came back again."

There was a freshness in his father's face, as if, briefly, he'd gone back to that moment when he was young himself. He gazed up at Colin directly.

"I'm not Andrew, though," he said.

"No."

His gaze drifted back towards the book: only in the writing of the name was there any uncertainty, he thought; as if his brother weren't quite sure, despite the confidence of the drawings, of who he was.

His father too glanced down at the book: it lay between them like a testament, or a tribulation, a strange denial, he couldn't be sure.

Samuel Johnson

"If the man who turnips
        cries,
Cry not when his father dies,
'Tis a proof that he had rather
Have a turnip than his
        father."

ACKNOWLEDGEMENTS

The Publishers gratefully acknowledge the contributions of the originators of the works and sayings quoted in the book. Every effort has been made to trace the ownership of copyright in the extracts included in this anthology. Any omission is purely inadvertent and will be corrected in subsequent editions, provided written notification is given to the book's creators: The Watermark Press, 29a King Street, Sydney, NSW, 2000.

Works are listed in the order in which they first appear in the book. Extracts from the following are reprinted by kind permission of:

A Fan's Notes by Frederick Exley, Alfred A. Knopf, Inc.
Men & Women How Different Are They? by John Nicholson © John Nicholson 1984, Oxford University Press
Adventures and Letters of Richard Harding Davies ed. Charles Belmont Davis © 1945 Hope Harding Davis Kehrig, Charles Scribner's Sons
The Mayor of Casterbridge by Thomas Hardy, Penguin Books
Bully for Who? by Alan Brien, *Punch*
The Life of Dashiell Hammett by Diane Johnson, Chatto & Windus
The Soul Book by Ian Hoare and others
King George VI, His Life and Reign by John Wheeler-Bennett, Macmillan and Company
Dad by William Wharton, Alfred A. Knopf, Inc.
Fair Play for Fathers by P. G. Wodehouse, *Punch*
Fatherhood Postponed by Carey Winfrey, *The New York Times*
Lettres de Claude Debussy a Sa Femme Emma ed. Pasteur Vallery Radot, Flammarion
Father's Day by Richard Yallop, "The Age"
Twenty Letters to a Friend by Svetlana Aliluyeva (Stalin), Avon, New York
Robert J. Hawke by Blanche d'Alpuget, Lansdowne—Rigby and Blanche d'Alpuget
The French by Theodore Zeldin, Collins, London
Speak Roughly to Your Little Boy or Try Ignoring Him by Stanley Reynolds, *Punch*
Verses from 1929 On, Ogden Nash
Leaves of Grass by Walt Whitman, The New American Library
George Orwell A Life by Bernard Crick, Secker & Warburg Ltd.
Dance of the Happy Shades from "Images" by Alice Munro, McGraw Hill Ryerson Limited, Toronto

The Rules of the Game by Nicholas Mosley published by Martin Secker and Warburg, and reprinted by permission of A. D. Peters and Co. Ltd.

Robert Morley — Responsible Gentleman by Robert Morley and Sewell Stokes, William Heinemann Limited

Nostalgia Isn't What It Used to Be by Simone Signoret, Harper & Row

Noah's Ark by Barbara Trapido, Victor Gollancz Ltd. and Literistic Ltd.

Early to Rise — A Sussex Boyhood by Bob Copper, William Heinemann Limited

My Father Moved Through Dooms of Love by e e cummings reprinted from The New Oxford Book of American Verse ed. Richard Ellmann by permission of Harcourt Brace Jovanovich Inc.

Cocteau by Francis Steegmuller, Macmillan, London and Basingstoke and Francis Steegmuller

I Never Saw My Father Nude by Don Coleman, Arthur Baker Limited

My Papa's Waltz by Theodore Roethke reprinted from The New Oxford Book of American Verse ed. Richard Ellmann

Baby Driver by Jan Kerouac, St. Martins Press, New York

Home Sweet Home by Mordecai Richler, extracts used by permission of the Canadian publishers, McClelland and Stewart Limited, Toronto

The Manageress and the Mirage from "The Bodysurfers" by Robert Drew, James Fraser

Twenty-One Years by Randolph S. Churchill, Houghton Mifflin

Nancy Mitford — A Memoir by Harold Acton, Macmillan, London and Basingstoke

The Secret Diary of Adrian Mole Aged 13¾ by Sue Townsend, Methuen, London

How to Be Topp from "The Compleet Molesworth" by Geoffrey Willans and Ronald Searle published by Pavilion Books by kind permission of the Tessa Sayle Agency

The Autobiography of Malcolm X by Alex Haley, Huchinson and Co. Limited

Queen of the Head-Hunters The Autobiography of The Rt. Hon. Sylvia Lady Brooke, Ranee of Sarawak, Sidgwick and Jackson Limited, London

My Father from "Meet My Folks" by Ted Hughes, Faber and Faber Limited

Bullet Park by John Cheever, Jonathan Cape Limited and Estate of John Cheever

A Traveller's Life by Eric Newby, William Collins Sons and Co. Limited, London

Brideshead Revisited by Evelyn Waugh, Methuen Ltd.

A Better Class of Person by John Osborne, Faber and Faber Limited

Tell Me Daddy, about the Bees and the Fleas by Ralph Schoenstein, *Punch*

Passages by Gail Sheehy, E. P. Dutton and Co. Inc.

I'll Never Forget What My Father Told Me by Paul Mann reprinted from the Australian Men's Journal Quarterly, by permission of Paul Mann

Father's Footsteps by Damon Runyan Jr. extract quoted in "The Father" ed., Evan Jones, André Deutch Ltd.

Selected Letters of William Carlos Williams ed. John C. Thirlwall, MacDowell Obolensky Inc.

My Life and My Films by Jean Renoir, William Collins Publishers, London

Portrait of a Marriage by Nigel Nicholson, Weidenfeld and Nicolson, London

Laughter in the Next Room by Osbert Sitwell, Macmillan and David Higham Associates Ltd.

Letters to My Son by Eric Nichol, Macmillan, Toronto, and Eric Nichol

My Father and Myself by J. R. Ackerley, Penguin and David Higham Associates Ltd.

The Bodley Head Scott Fitzgerald Volume 2, Bodley Head

The Promise and the Performance by Lewis J. Paper © 1975 by Lewis J. Paper used by permission of Crown Publishers Inc.

Melodies and Memories by Dame Nellie Melba, Thomas Nelson Australia and Liberty Library Corporation

The Enchanted Places by Christopher Milne, Eyre Methuen and Curtis Brown

Clinging to the Wreckage by John Mortimer, Weidenfeld and Nicolson Limited

Philby — The Spy Who Betrayed a Generation by Bruce Page, André Deutsch

The Boy I Left Behind Me by Stephen Leacock, Doubleday Canada Ltd.

Daddy by Sylvia Plath from The New Oxford Book of American Verse ed. Richard Ellmann

The Stone Angel by Margaret Laurence, McClelland and Stewart, Toronto

The Stern Parent and *L'Enfant Glacé* from "Ruthless Rhymes for Heartless Homes" by Harry Graham, Edward Arnold (Publishers) Limited

Marvin Gaye 1939–1984 by Ben Fong-Torres and Kurt Loder reprinted from *Rolling Stone*

The Life of Katherine Mansfield by Antony Alpers, Jonathan Cape Limited

The Life of D. H. Lawrence by Keith Sagar, Eyre Methuen Ltd.

Life with Father by Clarence Day, Alfred A. Knopf Inc.

The Young Servant Man from the Vaughan Williams Collection of Folk Songs, The Madden Collection, the Syndics of Cambridge University Library

Getty: The Richest Man in the World by Robert Lenzer, Hutchinson Ltd. and John Farquarson Ltd. and John Ware Literacy Agency

The Mosquito Coast by Paul Theroux, Hamish Hamilton Limited

The Letters of E. B. White, Harper & Row

The Firstborn from "I Can't Stay Long" by Laurie Lee, André Deutch

Son by Alan Coren, *Punch*

The Joy of Fatherhood by Bob Harvey, first published in the Auckland Metro

The Dionne Years — A Thirties Melodrama by Pierre Berton, McClelland and Stewart, Toronto

Margaret Thatcher, Wife, Mother, Politician by Penny Junor, Sidgwick and Jackson Ltd. London

Precious Bane by Mary Webb, Jonathan Cape and the Executors of the Mary Webb Estate

Sophia — Living and Loving by A. E. Hotchner, Michael Joseph Ltd.

Tolstoy by Henri Troyat, Doubleday and Company Inc.

Notes of a Native Son by James Baldwin, Dial Press, New York

The Autobiography of Arthur Ransome ed. Rupert Hart-Davis, Jonathan Cape Ltd., and the Arthur Ransome Estate

Growing Up by Russell Baker, Congdon & Weed Inc.

Saville by David Storey, Jonathan Cape Ltd.

The editor gratefully acknowledges the work of the compilers and publishers of the following books, which frequently provoked recall and proved to be invaluable sources of reference.

Palgrave's Golden Treasury of Songs and Lyrics Ed. J. H. Fowler, Macmillan, London and Basingstoke

The Faber Book of Aphorisms, Faber and Faber

The Macmillan Book of Relevant Quotations, Macmillan

The International Thesaurus of Quotations, Penguin Reference Books

The editor would also like to thank the following for their invaluable help: Elizabeth Blackall, Don Chapman, Martin Hendry, Dr. Emma Letley, Peter Letley, Leigh Missen and Judy Zavos. Special thanks to Claude Parsons and James Somerled for access to their extensive libraries.

PICTURE CREDITS

INDEX